D1355906

AMORUM LIBRI

The Lyric Poems of Matteo Maria Boiardo

♦

MEDIEVAL & RENAISSANCE TEXTS & STUDIES

Volume 101

AMORUM LIBRI

The Lyric Poems of Matteo Maria Boiardo

♦

Translated with Introduction and Notes

by

Andrea di Tommaso

Medieval & Renaissance texts & studies
& Dovehouse Editions Inc.
1993

We are pleased to acknowledge assistance towards publication costs generously provided by Wayne State University and by the Ministero degli Affari Esteri, Direzione Generale Relazioni Culturali, through the Embassy of Italy, Ottawa.

For distribution write to:

Medieval & Renaissance Texts & Studies
State University of New York
Binghamton, New York 13902-6000

ISBN 0-86698-117-9 (cloth)

Dovehouse Editions Inc.
1890 Fairmeadow Cres.
Ottawa, Canada K1H 7B9

ISBN 1-895537-10-X

Library of Congress Cataloging-in-Publication Data

Boiardo, Matteo Maria, 1440 or 41-1494.
[Amorum libri. English & Italian]
Amorum libri : the lyric poems of Matteo Maria Boiardo / translated with an introduction and notes by Andrea di Tommaso.
p. cm. – (Medieval & Renaissance texts & studies ; v. 101)
English and Italian.
Includes the text of the Italian edition edited by Pier Vincenzo Mengaldo (Bari: Laterza, 1964).
Includes bibliographical references and index.
ISBN 0-86698-117-9 (cloth)
1. Boiardo, Matteo Maria, 1440 or 41-1494—Translations into English. I. di Tommaso, Andrea. II. Mengaldo, Pier Vincenzo. III. Title. IV. Series.
PQ4612.A9B6513 1992
851'.2–dc20 92-21719
CIP

This book is made to last.
It is set in Bembo, smythe-sewn,
and printed on acid-free paper
to library specifications

Printed in the United States of America

Contents

Preface

"... cum ea que dicimus cuncta ... canamus...." "... since all that we put in verse ... we sing...," explains Dante in the *De Vulgari Eloquentia* as he begins a discussion of the appropriate lengths of stanzas and verses in vernacular poetry. I was confronted by this thought as I pondered my task as the first English translator of Matteo Maria Boiardo's *Amorum Libri*. How would I preserve the lyrical quality of his poetry and still keep it close enough in style, structure, and meaning to the original to have the translation be considered of scholarly value? I turned to Petrarch for advice or reassurance, at least, that my choices (soon to be explained) were valid ones. Petrarch, after all, had done nearly as much for music as he had for poetry. As Robert Durling says, throughout Europe "Petrarch's influence ... meant a new conception of the music possible in verse" (1976, vii). In a letter to Boccaccio dated 18 August 1360, Petrarch takes up the subject of translation and observes:

> You say that prose should be translated word for word. On this subject hearken to Saint Jerome, in his preface to the *De temporibus* of Eusebius of Caesarea, which he translated into Latin. I set down the exact words of that great man, so skilled in the two languages and in many others, and so famous as a translator. He says: "If anyone thinks that the charm of a language is not lost in translation, let him put Homer literally into Latin. I shall go farther; let him render Homer word for word in the prose of his own language. He will see that the word order is ridiculous, and that he has reduced the most eloquent poets to a gabble."
>
> I have quoted this in order to warn you, while there is time, not to waste an immense amount of labor. I want the job to be done in whatever way. So sharp is my hunger for great literature that like a starving man who needs no fancy cooking I shall welcome eagerly any sort of food for the spirit (Bishop, 215–16).

Having read that letter to Boccaccio, I could not help thinking that any translator would be fortunate to have Petrarch as a reader, not because Petrarch is tolerant of shoddy translation, but because he can see through the translation to the original text. All that any translator of poetry can hope for is that the translation will be accepted as a guide to the original. Dorothy Sayers, disagreeing with Mathew Arnold, believed that it was impossible for a translator to produce "upon the best scholars the same effect which the original produces upon them. . . . [The scholar] is inoculated against it, because he knows too much" ("The Translation of Verse," 1963, 129–30). Furthermore, whether the translator of poetry *ultimately* chooses to render the original in prose, or blank verse, or rhymed verse, or in some hybrid form, there is inevitably a feeling, a certainty, that something has been missed. The best defence against that certainty is, of course, for the translator and the reader to have a theory of translation with which to parry the inevitable thrusts of absence. Yes, some will be disappointed by the constant lack of rhyme in a blank verse translation, others will be irritated by the free-wheeling style of a rhymed translation, and still others will be dismayed by the drone of a prose translation, even assuming that, by the guidelines of our theory, each of the aforementioned types could be termed "excellent." Furthermore, and more legitimately, the inevitable infelicities of translation that result from a lack of correspondence between two languages in such elements as gender differentiation, vowel frequency, assonance and dissonance, and the like would work to prove that the most poetic texts are, indeed, the most untranslatable.

Through what torturous tests did I decide to put Boiardo's text? It was hardest of all to discount the literal approach to translation, what Cicero called *verbum pro verbo*, the "scholarly" approach of Boccaccio. Yet I cannot say that *any* prose translation of the *Aeneid* or the *Divine Comedy* has inspired me to read more than a paragraph at a time, even if the literal accuracy of the translation exceeded that of verse alternatives. My recommendation to readers of Petrarch's lyrics in translation is to read Thomas Bergin's verse and Robert Durling's prose simultaneously. It is a recommendation which rests on the unhappy conviction that the literary and lyric complexities of Petrarch's verse cannot be captured in translation by one form alone.

The easiest alternative to reject in translating Boiardo's lyrics was that of a rhymed translation, which would surely have wandered far and wide on the pathways of signification in search of ingenuity as meaning was forced to surrender to sound. Even in the best rhymed translations we face the nagging question: Is it Jefferson Butler Fletcher or Thomas Bergin or is it Petrarch? If we answer that it is not Petrarch, are we then to conclude that the translator is a fine poet in his own right? In some cases we know the answer is affirmative. Among translators of prose, if we say that Scott-Montcrieff is not Proust, do we conclude that Scott-Montcrieff is an outstanding English novelist? Clearly, he is not. I have chosen to avoid such questions.

I have ostensibly chosen to do a blank verse translation (an occasional Renaissance solution) of Boiardo, but not quite. It is rather a hybrid form, at least to some degree. My premise is that I am not trying to recreate the original but to create a translation. The restrictions imposed on a translator need not be those imposed on a poet. I have therefore stretched the rules of blank verse composition in iambic pentameter. In addition to the standard allowable deviations in meter, I have also allowed myself use of the anapest and dactyl, and liberal use of feminine endings. In fact, a number of verses read like hendecasyllables, with hyper-syllabic endings, rather than like pentameters. Many verses will scan only if more than one deviation is accounted for in each.

My fidelity to the notion of fidelity is inconstant. I have attempted to be faithful to meaning and metaphor, syntax and diction, mood and tone, imagery and color, music and message, as the occasion has allowed. My goal has been to be faithful to each poem and to the work as a whole (as represented by the interaction of syntax, rhetoric, mood, and sentiment) rather than to component parts, while still retaining as much of the syntax and rhetoric of the original as possible. Thus, in the opening sonnet, for "nel dolce tempo de mia età fiorita," I finally rejected what I thought was an inspired translation offered by one reader: "back in the easy days when I was young." That version of the second verse lives in some of the more than a dozen variations on the first sonnet that I have produced. The suggestion of another reader convinced me that it was important to preserve the idea of "mia età fiorita," ("my flowered age") and sustain the metaphorical image that culminates in verse twelve with "nel fior de' soi primi anni" ("in the flower of his first years")—which led to "back in my easy days of youthful bloom," and "he whose flowering youth."

Certain structural features of the text, such as the acrostics and the recurring end-words of the sestina, seemed essential, however artificial the resulting verses may have sounded. At times the translation achieves an effect which was not intended in the original, but which seems appropriate and worth retaining. The last stanza of the fourth sonnet, for example, begins and ends "with her," thus embodying in its form the inherent Petrarchan platonism of the poem and the idea of the cyclical return of the Golden Age which the poet identifies with the Lady's appearance on Earth. In the course of juggling such elements, I have invoked Accuracy (in reproducing the combined effect of the original poetry's tone and meaning) and Readability (by the standard of a speaker of English accustomed to reading lyric poetry) as my muses. Between the Scylla of the prosaic and the Charybdis of the original, I hope to have steered a moderately safe course.

Without a doubt this project would not have been completed without the kindness and generosity of a number of institutions, colleagues, and friends. I am especially grateful to the Research Division of the National Endowment for the Humanities for a translation grant which launched the project, and to Wayne State University for a Faculty Research Award and additional encouragement along the way. It is my pleasure also to thank for their patience and kindness the Directors and staff of the Biblioteca Nazionale Marciana and the Museo Correr of Venice, the Biblioteca Nazionale of Florence, the Biblioteca Communale of Ferrara, and the Biblioteca Estense of Modena. The staff of the latter two libraries showed exceptional tolerance in allowing me to set up and use my own photographic equipment without an advance request.

I thank the anonymous reviewers of my NEH proposal and subsequent manuscript for a host of constructive comments, especially when those comments compromised their anonymity. While I would hope that the work presented here would be judged on its own merits and not by the *coterie* affiliations of its author and readers, some public acknowledgement of gratitude is in order. Let me therefore thank Julia Conaway Bondanella for her kind encouragement, Charles Ross for unknowingly being a source of inspiration, and Mauda Bregoli-Russo and Antonella Cortese for help in obtaining materials. I am indebted to the friends and colleagues who read and commented upon various portions of the manuscript, and especially to Robert Durling, who saved me from several errors in the selections he so kindly read. I thank my graduate student Amelia Tundo for reading the entire text and for her many insightful comments and suggestions. It is a pleasure also to thank the staff at MRTS, and in particular Catherine Di Cesare for her careful and thoughtful review of the manuscript. I thank my sons Matteo and Dante for convincing me that the brooding "courtly" spirit does exist (even today), and my daughters Ivana and Mia Rose for helping me to believe that the Petrarchan ideal may also be a reality. At last I am pleased to say that I am most grateful to Janet Langlois, reader, colleague, friend, and spouse, without whose constant encouragement, patience, and optimism this project would have been far less satisfying.

AMORUM LIBRI

The Lyric Poems of Matteo Maria Boiardo

♦

INTRODUCTION

The Poet

The Boiardo family, whose roots are lost in the eleventh century, was destined to become one of the most important and influential families attached to the Este courts in Renaissance Italy. In 1362, Selvatico and Feltrino Boiardi, who had performed military service against the Gonzagas of Mantua under the banner of the duke of Milan, entered into the service of the pope and the marquis Niccolò II d'Este, lord of Ferrara. In addition to a monthly stipend, the marquis immediately granted them feudal rights to certain lands, including Rubiera, a town midway between Reggio nell' Emilia and Modena on the ancient Via Aemilia. When, in 1432, Feltrino's son, Feltrino, Jr., returned Rubiera to Niccolò III, the new marquis bestowed upon him all feudal rights to various other estates, including the picturesque town of Scandiano, which lies at the foothills of the Apennines a few miles southeast of Reggio. (Niccolò had taken possession of Scandiano in 1409, when, abandoned by the duke of Milan, it had been informally conceded to Este control.) Feltrino Boiardo petitioned the duke of Milan, Filippo Maria Visconti, to grant Scandiano the status of County, and to declare its independence from the authority of Reggio. In a declaration dated 13 December 1432, Visconti did just that, naming Feltrino first count of Scandiano and his male descendants as legitimate heirs to the title. With the extinction of the Visconti male line in 1452 and the conferral by the emperor Frederick III of the title of duke of Modena and Reggio to Borso d'Este in May of that year, Reggio itself and the House of Este attained full independence from the Duchy of Milan.

At some time under the sign of Gemini in the year 1441 (or, less likely, 1440), Matteo Maria Boiardo was born in the family castle at Scandiano. Matteo Maria was the grandson of Feltrino, Jr., and the son of Giovanni Boiardo and of Lucia Strozzi, the sister of the illustrious humanist poet

Tito Vespasiano Strozzi. Giovanni's duties brought him to the spectacular court of Ferrara, where Matteo Maria spent most of the first ten years of his life. It was an auspicious time for a young child to be in Ferrara, which, at the time, possessed one of the finest schools in Italy, established in 1429 by the renowned humanist educator Guarino da Verona. Guarino had gone to Ferrara in 1429 specifically to tutor Leonello d'Este and the other children of the court.

In the same year that Matteo Maria was born, Niccolò d'Este died and was succeeded by the erudite Leonello, who became known as "the progenitor of Ferrarese culture, *pater civilitatis*."[1] Ferrarese culture, including Guarino's school, flourished under Leonello, and Matteo Maria received his early education in the company of the children of the Este family and entourage.

When Matteo Maria's father died in 1451 in Ferrara, his mother returned with her child to Scandiano, where he came under the careful tutelage of his grandfather. Feltrino was an educated man, a friend of Guarino, of Leonello, and of other noted humanists like Angelo Decembrio, Poggio Bracciolini, and Leonardo Bruni.[2] Matteo Maria's youthful translations from Latin and Latin compositions confirm that, while other young men of his social class elsewhere may have dedicated themselves to tournaments and hunting, as Antonia Benvenuti suggests (1972, 293–94), he continued to receive a serious humanistic education from his grandfather.

Feltrino Boiardo died in 1456. In February 1460, not yet twenty years old, Matteo became the head of the family following the death of his uncle, Giulio Ascanio. The very first letter conserved in the correspondence of Matteo Maria Boiardo is dated 8 February 1460. In that letter, a grief-stricken Matteo Maria informs a friend in Reggio of the death of his uncle, whom he refers to affectionately as "mio bon padre messer Julio,"[3] and he asks his friend, the count Silvio di San Bonifacio, to help fill that paternal role. However brief, the letter unmistakably reveals the already well-refined, courtly manner of a man who would feel quite at home in the Este court, and would come to be considered "a perfect gentleman in every respect."[4] His family's hospitality and courtesy were even then

---

[1] Werner L. Gundersheimer, *Ferrara: The Style of a Renaissance Despotism* (Princeton: Princeton Univ. Press, 1972), 92.

[2] Antonia Tissoni Benvenuti, "Matteo Maria Boiardo," *La Letteratura Italiana: Storia e Testi*, 10 vols. (Bari: Laterza, 1972), vol. 3, tome 2, *Il Quattrocento: L'Età dell'Umanesimo*, 293–363.

[3] Matteo Maria Boiardo, *Opere Volgari: Amorum Libri-Pastorale-Lettere*, ed. Pier Vincenzo Mengaldo (Bari: Laterza, 1962), 175. Cited hereafter as *OV*.

[4] Umberto Renda, *Matteo Maria Boiardo* (Turin: Paravia, 1941), cited in Domenico

legendary, and according to Angelandrea Zottoli, a common invocation in Scandiano was "Iddio ti mandi a casa Boiardi"—"may God send you to the house of the Boiardi."[5]

While he was fond of the quiet life of Scandiano, he spent most of the winter of 1461–1462 in Ferrara and subsequently became a frequent participant in the life at the court of Sigismondo d'Este at Reggio. (In December of 1462 Sigismondo had been named governor of Reggio and his brother Ercole had been named governor of Modena.) Thereafter, he participated in all of the major celebrations and solemn occasions of the Este lords of Ferrara, Reggio, and Modena. Most notably, he attended the grand reception for the emperor Frederick III in January 1469 on the occasion of the emperor's week-long stay in Ferrara; he journeyed to Rome in 1471 with his close friend Borso d'Este when Borso was to be crowned duke of Ferrara by Pope Paul II; he travelled to Naples in 1473 as a member of an entourage of five hundred courtiers who were sent to accompany back to Ferrara Eleanora (Leonora) of Aragon, the fiancée of Borso's successor, Ercole I.

When on 22 January 1476 Ercole d'Este published the official registry of his family and that of his wife, Matteo Maria's name figured at the top of the list of his "compagni," his most intimate companions (Zottoli, 9). Matteo Maria entered into the service of the duke, residing in the ducal palace at Ferrara, and remained there for the next two years. As intimate a friend as he may have been, however, there is never any doubt that he was the duke's servant. In 1474, Marco de' Pii di Carpi conspired with Matteo Maria's aunt Taddea (Marco's sister) and Taddea's son Giovanni to poison Boiardo in an assassination attempt resulting from a water rights and property dispute. Ercole reacted with seeming indifference. The many letters written to the duke by Boiardo as captain of Modena and, later, of Reggio are the record of the existence of a humble servant trivialized by the most mundane matters of bureaucratic administration.

In September 1478, Ercole was made captain general of the league of Florence, Venice, and Milan against Pope Sixtus IV and the king of Naples; Matteo Boiardo immediately retired with the duke's permission to Scandiano in order to work on the *Orlando Innamorato*, which was anxiously awaited by its courtly audiences. (Isabella d'Este would write from the court at Mantua, eagerly imploring the poet to send more cantos.) He continued to receive his stipend as an official of the court. Soon after, in

---

Medici, "La Critica Boiardesca dal 1800 al 1976: Bibliografia Ragionata," *Bollettino Storico Reggiano* 10, no. 34 (July, 1977): 79.

[5] Angelandrea Zottoli, introduction to *Tutte le Opere di Matteo M. Boiardo*, ed. Angelandrea Zottoli, 2 vols. (Milan: Mondadori, 1936–37) 1:x. Hereafter cited as Zottoli.

February of 1479, Matteo Maria married Taddea dei Gonzaga di Novellara. In 1480, Ercole made Matteo Maria captain (governor) of Modena, an office he held until his resignation in the final days of 1482. Three months later Boiardo published the first edition of the *Orlando Innamorato*, which at that point consisted of the first two books. In 1487, Ercole named Boiardo captain of Reggio Emilia, an office he held until his death in Reggio, on Friday, 19 December 1494. Undoubtedly in accord with Matteo Maria Boiardo's own wishes, he was buried in the place he loved best, the town of Scandiano.

The year 1477 saw the appearance of the definitive manuscript version of the *Amorum Libri*, now the British Museum's Codex Egerton 1999. Judging by the date *die quarto Ianuarii MCCCCLXXVII* which is penned at the end of the manuscript, the final touches were put to the *Amorum Libri* during Boiardo's residence at the ducal palace in Ferrara. Two irreconcilable elements of the history of this text are its established definition as the best work of the courtly lyricists of the quattrocento, and its failure to be incorporated into the official canon of Italian literature over the centuries. To understand the nature of this work, its relationship to its antecedents, its socio-literary function in the Este social world, and its uniqueness, we need to take a closer look at the socio-literary scene and Boiardo's place in it.

That Matteo Maria was at home in aristocratic circles is revealed not only by the fact that by 1476 he had become one of the closest friends of Ercole d'Este and the second highest paid of Ercole's "*compagni*,"[6] but also by his personal manner. Giovanni Ponte notes, for example, that the young Boiardo uses the intimate *tu* form of address in his dedication to Ercole d'Este of his early translation of Cornelius Nepos' *De Viris Illustribus*. Ercole was a military man unversed in Greek and Latin, and the stories of the "lives of illustrious captains" of antiquity were well suited to his tastes. That Boiardo addressed him with the *tu* form rather than with the more formal *Vostra Eccellenza* or *Vostra Celsitudine*, as he will in his later letters, is an indication that the future duke of Ferrara and the young courtier had established an intimate relationship (Ponte, 11). Ercole, at the time, was recovering from war wounds which would leave him with a permanent limp, and Matteo was entertaining him with his translation to ease his recovery. The relationship between the two must have been particularly close, for, most of the time, Boiardo was not one to ignore

---

[6] Giulio Reichenbach, *M. M. Boiardo* (Bologna: Zanichelli, 1929), 102. Cf. Giulio Bertoni, *La Biblioteca Estense e la Cultura Ferrarese ai Tempi di Ercole I (1471–1505)* (Turin: Loescher, 1903), 138, and Giovanni Ponte, *La Personalità e L'opera del Boiardo* (Genoa: Tilgher, 1972), 13.

protocol and formality. One sees, for example, that in his correspondence he always uses his title, *Comes Scandiani Casalgrandisque etc.*, except when, addressing one of the Este lords, he uses the humble *Servitor.* In contrast, his illustrious successor, Ludovico Ariosto, likewise a *Comes*, never used his title. Ariosto's complaints in his *Satires* that the Este treated him like a mere functionary and did not appreciate him as a man of letters further suggest (blatantly, actually) that he and his literary predecessor in the court of Ferrara had far different relations with their aristocratic employers.

Another of Boiardo's letters is curiously revealing.[7] In 1494 (the year of his death), Boiardo writes to Ercole on 26 August and describes a certain Don Giuliano, a French captain of the bowmen in the army of Charles VIII who is passing through Reggio. Boiardo describes the Frenchman as elegantly dressed and wearing many jewels—all of which are false. The same benevolent Matteo Maria Boiardo who had forgiven his aunt and cousin when they attempted to poison him is less merciful to the foreign captain. Not only his jewels are false, he goes on to say, but his drinking cups and everything about him are adulterated and false, including his mode of discourse [*ragionamenti*] (*OV*, 297). The argument is, of course, that of arms and letters which appears in the *Orlando Innamorato* and many other Renaissance texts.

The French, in this case, are the uneducated fighting men from the north, and the Italians are both knights and prototypical Renaissance gentlemen who trace their tradition back, at least, to circa 1460 and the *De Politia litteraria*, a symposiac dialogue written by Angelo Decembrio, a disciple of Guarino da Verona. The dialogue, modeled on the classical *Symposia* of Xenophon and Plato, is of the type that "flourished in the Italian courts, where erudite dialogues paid tribute to the cultivation of the ruler and his adherents."[8] Decembrio's dialogue "celebrates the erudition of Leonello d'Este and his mentor Guarino Veronese at the court of Ferrara (Marsh, 6)." More importantly, perhaps, it defines the elements that are lacking in a man like the French captain Don Giuliano—*politia* and *urbana conversatione*, social grace, elegant refinement, and eloquent speech. It is, as such, an early precursor of the courtesy books that followed in the tradition of Baldassar Castiglione's *Book of the Courtier* and Stefano Guazzo's *Civil Conversation* in establishing the ideal of the Renaissance gentleman.

Many among the gentlemen of the Este courts were not only well-bred gentlemen, but poets as well. The *Amorum Libri* show not only the influ-

---

[7] The letter is given a very full analysis by Eduardo Saccone in *Il "Soggetto" del* Furioso *e Altri Saggi tra Quattro e Cinquecento* (Naples: Liguori, 1974), 74ff.

[8] David Marsh, *The Quattrocento Dialogue: Classical Tradition and Humanist Innovation* (Cambridge, Mass.: Harvard Univ. Press, 1980), 6.

ence of Ovid, Provençal poetry, Dante and the *stilnovisti*, and Petrarch, but also that of orthodox but less gifted court poets like Giusto de' Conti. While Giusto was not attached to the Este courts but rather to that of Sigismondo Malatesta, lord of Rimini, his work was well known to Matteo Boiardo and is used as a metrical and thematic model in the *Amorum Libri*.

In the mid-fourteenth-century courts of the Emilia region, court poets, many of them rigid Petrarchists, were displacing the local vernacular with the literate Florentine language of Dante, Petrarch, Boccaccio, and their literary descendants. Gianotto Calogrosso's *Nicolosa Bella* (1447–1459), as Raffaele Spongano says, clearly shows that the Tuscanized literary language of writers in Emilia in mid-century, and even of a southerner like Calogrosso, is far less removed from standard, literate, Florentine Italian than other evidence may suggest.[9] Pier Vincenzo Mengaldo has shown precisely the nature of Boiardo's lyric language in the *Amorum Libri* and the interplay of latinisms, the regional *koinè* and standard (Florentine) Italian in this most "Tuscanized" of Boiardo's vernacular works.[10] Nevertheless, because these writers, Boiardo included, remained attached to the Este courts, and did not consciously or deliberately embrace Florentine literary hegemony to improve their fortunes, their work did not enter the official canon of Italian Renaissance literature. Other non-Tuscan Renaissance writers like Jacopo Sannazaro and Ludovico Ariosto fared much better and achieved national status by adapting to the Florentine literary standard.

The success of systematic Tuscanizers like Sannazaro and Ariosto is due, as Mengaldo says, to a slow and patient effort of revision and refinement of the linguistic surface of the text, and not to an instantaneous acquisition of Tuscan literary competence (*LBL*, 42). The great *Questione della Lingua* that has, across the centuries, tormented Tuscan writers (who had to choose between contemporary Florentine Italian or "classical" Italian as exemplified by Dante, Petrarch, and Boccaccio), but most especially non-Tuscan writers (Ariosto, Tasso, Manzoni, and Svevo, to name a few) is one that has yet to be resolved for Italian writers with a strong regional linguistic grounding.

The great indignity suffered by Matteo Maria as a poet was that his enormously popular *Orlando Innamorato* was faulted for its hybrid language and defective style, and was rewritten by Francesco Berni and again by Lodovico Domenichi. It survived as a Renaissance text *only* through sani-

---

[9] Raffaele Spongano, *Gianotto Calogrosso: Nicolosa Bella: Prose e Versi del Secolo XV* (Bologna: Commissione per i Testi di Lingua, 1959).

[10] Pier Vincenzo Mengaldo, *La Lingua del Boiardo Lirico* (Florence: Leo S. Olschki, 1963). Cited hereafter as *LBL*.

tized Florentine versions like those of Berni and Domenichi. These Florentine *rifacimenti*, which sought to improve the poem by replacing Boiardo's "coarse" Emilian language with Tuscan elegance, received numerous editions and little opposition. After the early editions, Boiardo's original was not reprinted again until 1830, when it was rediscovered by Antonio Panizzi, an Italian political exile living in London who published a combined edition of the *Innamorato* and Ariosto's *Furioso*. The *Amorum Libri*, which are written in a language much more like that of Florence than is the recidivous language of the *Orlando*, nonetheless suffered the same critical fall into oblivion. After the initial posthumous editions of 1499 (Reggio) and 1501 (Venezia), the *Amorum Libri* had no complete edition until Antonio Panizzi's of 1835 (reprinted in Milan in 1845 by the Società Tipografica dei Classici Italiani), one "selected" incomplete edition in 1820 (Modena), and limited inclusion, never more than a dozen or so poems, in occasional anthologies between 1565 and 1850 (*OV*, 333–35).

As well as knowing its resident poet Boiardo, Ferrara knew its share of poet-ambassadors like Pietro Jacopo de Jennaro from Naples and other accomplished poets like Niccolò da Correggio, whose mother, Beatrice, was the illegitimate daughter of Niccolò III d'Este, father of Borso and Ercole. In 1471 Niccolò da Correggio, like Matteo Boiardo, was a member of the entourage which accompanied Borso d'Este to Rome on the occasion of his being proclaimed duke of Ferrara by Pope Paul II,[11] and he remained in Ferrara at the Este court at least until 1490. The very prolific poet Antonio Tebaldeo was born in Ferrara on 4 November 1463. At age twenty-three he was at the Este court as a composer of occasional verse and as an actor in the classical theatrical productions which were a frequent courtly entertainment (Pernicone, 521). The number of Este court poets in Boiardo's epoch includes several others, the Veronese humanist Felice Feliciano, Ludovico Sandeo, and Niccolò Cosmico among them.[12] The cultural legacy of Guarino, who died in 1460, and of Leonello d'Este was well preserved in Ferrara throughout Boiardo's lifetime. Yet, their passing diminished considerably the humanistic emphasis that both had placed on Latin, and allowed for greater use of the vernacular in the eras of Borso and Ercole.

---

[11] *Antologia della Letteratura Italiana*, ed. Vincenzo Pernicone (Milan: Rizzoli, 1966), 2:515. Hereafter cited as Pernicone.

[12] Antonia Tissoni-Benvenuti, "Rimatori Estensi di Epoca Boiardesca," in *Il Boiardo e la Critica Contemporania: Atti del Convegno di Studi su Matteo Maria Boiardo, Scandiano-Reggio Emilia 25–27 Aprile 1969* (Florence: Leo S. Olschki, 1970), 503–10.

The name ANTONIA CAPRARA is emblazoned across the text of the opening book of the *Amorum Libri* like the name of Venus on the frontal of a temple (as one reader has suggested).[13] The initial letters of the first fourteen sonnets of the first book combine to form an acrostic which spells her name. Conveniently, her name is composed of fourteen letters, so that the initial letters of each of the verses of the fourteenth sonnet again combine to repeat the name of this "celestial beauty" (2.2) who will be seen to have power over Nature itself as well as over the heart and mind of the poet. That she may be a *Venus Bifrons* is not apparent to the poet until the second book, where, in a sonnet dedicated to his friend Guido Scaiola (84), the poet may be suggesting that he and Guido are both in love with the same person (or is it merely the same Petrarchan type?), as, to his dismay, Guido picks roses in a garden while he picks thorns in a desert.

The reader of the *Amorum Libri* has most often seen the love experience recorded there as personal and intimate, and not like the mystical and spiritual key to Dante's place in salvation history or Petrarch's Provençalizing, temporary detour on the road to spiritual reintegration and reconciliation with his Creator. Indeed, in terms of nomenclature, the name of Antonia Caprara does not lend itself to manipulation under the medieval exegetical formula which decrees that *nomina sunt consequentia rerum*, that names are a reflection of the substance of things. While Dante[14] can say that his "new life" began with the mystical moment (after which, events in his life were no longer fortuitous) when he first encountered Beatrice, whom everyone immediately recognized as a *beatrice* (one who blesses) without knowing her name, Antonia Caprara plays no such role in Boiardo's life. And while Laura, in luring Petrarch away from eternal sanctity in the illusions of a *breve sogno*, is allowing him to immortalize himself by immortalizing her, there is no trace in the *Amorum Libri* of the Horatian notion of *Le exegi monumentum*, that the poet has erected a monument in veneration of himself that will survive the proverbial ravages of time. There is, however, a deliberate and unmistakable adoption of the Provençal/Petrarchan paradigm of transgression and abjuration, and of recognition that, if any kind of reintegration of the self is possible through

---

[13] Mauda Bregoli-Russo, *Boiardo Lirico* (Potomac, Md.: José Porrúa Turanzas [Studia Humanitatis], 1979), 111.

[14] In such a context, I mean to say Dante's narrator in the *Vita Nova* or Petrarch's narrator in the *Rerum Vulgarium Fragmenta*, and so on. I shall make no attempt to sort out the relationship between the linguistic figurations of a self in the *Amorum Libri* and the "personal," psychological history of the author.

religious conversion, the reintegrated self will still be emphatically unreconciled to the poet's youthful self. The "easy days of youthful bloom" of the prefatory opening poem are transformed, in the final poem of the third book into the "wanton, vain and fragile age of love."

Nevertheless, the name of Antonia Caprara deliberately introduces the reader to the *Amorum Libri*, and the entire work is seemingly dedicated to her. This then is not a book of *loves*, as the already perplexing Ovidian title might suggest, but a recounting of the stages of a single, dominant, and obsessive love founded, as the tradition required, on the impossibility of fulfilment. If a Renaissance reader were, indeed, to imagine the name of Antonia Caprara like that of Venus carved across the frontal of a temple, the suggestion would surely be of a temple in ruin. The reader knows immediately from the prefatory sonnet that his world is a derivative of Petrarch's world, and that his venerations, like Petrarch's, were merely a youthful error and all too brief a dream.

Presumably, the object of the poet's desire was a lady in the court of Sigismondo d'Este in Reggio whom Matteo Maria met in 1469 when he was twenty-eight years old. The love affair, assuming it even existed, is said to have ended in 1471. The only concrete evidence of the existence of Antonia seems to be the parish record of an "Antonia del reggiano Benedetto Caprari" having been baptized in Reggio on 13 October 1451.[15] The poet's interest in the literary dynamics of such a love continued, however, for years after; the *Amorum Libri*, the story of that brief interlude, appeared in integrated manscript form, as we know, in 1477.

The Social Instrument

In a lecture presented in 1969 at the *Collège de France* with the title "What is an Author?," Michel Foucault makes a distinction between texts that are endowed with an author function and those that function anonymously without "authority." Foucault also notes that texts which we regard as "literary" (narratives, stories, epics, tragedies, comedies) were at one time received, put into circulation, and valorized without bringing under examination the question of authorship. On the other hand, scientific texts depended entirely on the *auctoritas* of those who had written them: "Hip-

---

[15] 13 October is the date provided by Scaglione and Ulivi in their commentaries. Antonio Panizzi reported in 1830 that an Antonia Caprara was *born* on 31 [*sic*] October 1451. "Life of Boiardo," in *Orlando Innamorato di Bojardo: Orlando Furioso di Ariosto: With an Essay on the Romantic Narrative Poetry of the Italians*. 9 vols. (London: Pickering, 1830), 3:viii.

pocrates says," "Pliny recounts," and, in the case of the greatest secular authority of all, Aristotle, one needed only to say *ipse dixit.* The intent was not to identify the author, but to offer scientific proof. Since the seventeenth and eighteenth centuries, Foucault says, the invocation of the author function has been reversed. Now literary discourse cannot be consecrated if not endowed by an author function. The *ipse dixit* is now the *nihil obstat* for admission into the accepted canon of official literature.[16] Foucault adds that authors are not simply the authors of their own texts, but are responsible for the generation of other texts as well. Thus, an author may not only number his or her own personal writings under the rubric of authorship, but he or she may set the conditions for the production of an entire genre. Foucault's argument, leaving aside the evolutionary aspects, raises interesting questions for lyric, the most ego-reductive of genres, and its use-value within courtly socio-literary circles in the fifteenth century.

If any writer can be said to have "authored" an entire genre, Petrarch would surely have to figure high on the list of those that did. On the other hand, if the imitators turn obediently to the laws of composition laid down by Dante or by Petrarch, like one reading a traffic signal, it may not always be clear whether they do so because *ipse dixit,* or because those rules are now a disinherited text that functions anonymously as law, much like traffic signs. Foucault makes a distinction between literary authors who may inspire the creation of a genre based on similarity and analogy, and "founders of discoursivity," like Marx and Freud, who create the possibility not for similitude and analogy, but for difference. Thus, that Freud is the founder of psychoanalysis does not mean that each of his concepts will be found in all subsequent psychoanalytical writings. If Petrarch, then, is a "founder of discoursivity," we should find in his imitators not only similitude and analogy (among the intransigent) but also some form of redirection (among the creative imitators).

Among such imitators, Boiardo is an inspired handler of traditional models who brings a sense of freshness and experimentation to his writing. Traces of Petrarch's imprint are everywhere in the *Amorum Libri.* From the opening sonnet-as-prologue, through the sweetness of Book One, the bitterness of Book Two, the bittersweetness of Book Three, down to the final moment of conversion, we see how familiar Boiardo is with Petrarch, and yet how very different in temperament and style. Unlike the more rig-

[16] Michel Foucault, *Scritti Letterari,* ed. Cesare Milanesi (Milan: Feltrinelli, 1971), 1–21. The text to which I refer is an Italian translation of the French original. English version in Michel Foucault, *Language, Counter-Memory, Practice: Selected Essays and Interviews* (Ithaca, N.Y.: Cornell Univ. Press, 1977), 113–38.

idly formal and cerebral Petrarch, Boiardo stretches metrical models to their limit and beyond. Unlike Petrarch, his use of classical myth is limited. Where Petrarch tends toward abstraction, Boiardo concretizes. Readers have repeatedly noted the power of his visual imagination and his affinity to the pictorial traditions of northern Italy. He plays with his borrowing, fusing seemingly incongrous elements of the lyric tradition, much as he tinkers with elements of epic and romance in the *Innamorato*, creating isotopes which are charged with a vitality all their own.

A rigidly orthodox reader might find the variety of his rhythmic and metrical solutions exasperating and his rhetoric (such as his persistent use of apostrophe) banal or boring. It may be, as has been suggested, that he is not especially a Petrarchist (the view of Antonia Tissoni-Benvenuti), or that the characteristically Petrarchan moments in his poetry are at times heavy-handed and tedious, as suggested by Aldo Scaglione. Sonnets 123, 124, and 131 in particular are faulted for their antithetical style. From our perspective they might be strained; from the perspective of a Gian Battista Marino, or of the Provençal poets (whose influence on Boiardo has, I think, been underestimated), these sonnets might be judged less harshly.

In his commentary on Ariosto's *Orlando Furioso*, Giulio Bertoni explains that a popular game in the Ferrarese court, called the "gioco delle sorti," the game of chance, consisted of drawing slips of paper from an urn. Each of these "brevi" or "polizze" or "bollettini" addressed to a lady or gentleman of the court bore a verse or maxim drawn usually from Petrarch's *Canzoniere*.[17] We may ask, at this point, what has become of Petrarch as author. Is the selection of texts from the *Canzoniere* made because *ipse dixit* or has the author function been completely subsumed into the texts, which then become their own "authority," like the stories, tragedies, and comedies alluded to by Foucault? Petrarch as courtly social game, whether present as "Petrarch" the text or Petrarch the authorial ego behind the lyric narrative, has literally become the physical embodiment of disintegrated articulations of a divided self alluded to in the title of the *Rerum vulgarium fragmenta*. These fragmented maxims and *bons mots* have become a social fact, and the linguistic and psychological matter of the *Canzoniere* has become a "galateo-vocabolario," a kind of courtesy-book dictionary for the ladies and gentlemen of the court (*LBL*, 19).

In this process of "socialization of the petrarchan experience," as Mengaldo says, the court has a decisive role not only in reducing Petrarchism to a social game, but also of defining the quattrocento Petrarchan lyricist

[17] Giulio Bertoni, *L'*Orlando Innamorato *e la Rinascenza a Ferrara* (Modena: Umberto Orlandini, 1919), 211.

as less an "elitist" than Petrarch, less individualistic and less cosmopolitan (now tied to a specific, regional social context) than Pietro Bembo and the sixteenth-century lyricists, and, eventually, as a courtly virtuoso. The text then becomes not the simple manifestation of the voice of an individual author who presents his own idiosyncratic interpretation of reality, but the vehicle of expression of the entire social construct. As Love dictates to Dante (Love's scribe) his "authoritative" definition of love, so the courtly recipients of courtly lyrics dictate to the socialized courtly poet the definitions of *politia* within their socio-literary microcosm (*LBL*, 19–20).[18]

Boiardo hints throughout the *Orlando Innamorato* at the social function of his grand chivalric composition. The life of the court can be quite leisurely, and in the early afternoon (about the time of the modern "soap opera"), the courtiers would gather to hear the poet declaim his verses of passion and adventure. The *Amorum Libri* are ostensibly more personal and private. Yet, whatever autobiography may be embedded in that text, its role as a social instrument in the public domain cannot have been any less than that of the *Innamorato*. Both texts were intended to be heard and read, and guided to "publication" by the author himself. Both texts were instruments used to mirror the values of an idealized courtly world. The *Amorum Libri* are to the *Orlando Innamorato* what Dante's *Vita Nova* is to the *Divine Comedy*: the microcosmic key to the elaboration of a macrocosmic history. If there is a life story in the *Amorum Libri*, it is as much the life story of a fictional courtly society as it is the personal history of a fictionalized author. It was a listening society that defined itself by its eagerness to accidentally overhear the private thoughts of the distraught lover. The dominant pretense is that the controlled act of composition is an uncontrolled emotional experience (even when the author is Dante, and the pretense is never disavowed by an act of recantation). It is regrettable for readers of lyric that the one brief letter of the author to his wife that remains in his correspondence is not of that mold: "Mia mogliere. Fati che . . . *Consors*, Mattheus Maria." "My wife. See to it that . . . [signed] Your consort, M. M."

[18] It may be coincidental that rhythmic and metrical complexity and virtuosity, the hallmark of Provençal courtly lyric, should be submerged in Dante and Petrarch and the (bourgeois) Florentine Petrarchans of the sixteenth century, but revived by the lyricists of the courtly ambient of the nothern Italian provinces in the quattrocento.

Formalities

The *Amorum Libri* consist of 180 poems divided into three books. Each book contains fifty sonnets and ten compositions of various other metrical forms, mostly *canzoni*, but also including *ballate*, a *madrigale* (and a canzone-like poem which Boiardo labels *mandrialis*), a rondeau, and a single sestina. What is soon apparent to the reader of the *Amorum Libri* who knows Petrarch's *Canzoniere* and the *canzonieri* of the more orthodox Petrarchan lyricists of the fifteenth and sixteenth century is the rich variety of "rhythmical solutions" and metrical variations that it contains.[19] More importantly, one finds a smaller percentage of doctrinaire literate forms, a greater percentage of popular forms, like ballads and madrigals, and a much freer adaptation of the traditional *canzone* forms (poem 104 is, in the eyes of most commentators, a *canzone*). The meticulous analysis of the language of the *Amorum Libri* by Pier Vincenzo Mengaldo (*LBL*) shows two very clear tendencies in Boiardo's lyrics: one toward the adoption of the precisely defined/refined aristocratic tones of Petrarch, and another which moves more toward an unrestrained and independent freedom of exploration and expression.

The traditional title and the division into three books are clearly reflective of the influence of the *Amores* of Ovid, while the Latin titles given to a number of the poems might be considered a form of homage paid to Propertius, Catullus, and Ovid, as suggested by Giancarlo Mazzacurati (21). There is at the same time an overlay of Dantesque and Petrarchan order to the collection. The adoption of a Latin title may also have been inspired by Dante's *Vita Nova* (from the rubric in Dante's book of memory which says "Incipit vita nova") and Petrarch's *Rerum Vulgarium Fragmenta*. More obviously Petrarchan is the inclusion of a penitential prefatory poem which confesses that the story about to be told is the result of a youthful error, and a final poem in which the author pleads for mercy for a soul oppressed by sin and corruption. As with Petrarch, the literary microcosm and the greater Christian world seem to be irreconcilably at odds. This author, however, argues in his introductory poem that, youthful error or not, he who lives his youthful years without the warmth of love may seem to be alive, but, indeed, lives without a heart (1.13–14).

The first authority of record to turn to for an explanation of the literary nature of the "illustrious vernacular," of Italian versification and metrical formulation is Dante Alighieri. In his *De Vulgaria Eloquentia*, Dante

---

[19] Giancarlo Mazzacurati, *Il Problema del Petrarchismo Italiano (dal Boiardo a Lorenzo)* (Naples: Liguori, 1963), 20.

claims that the literary language he proposes will be based on all fourteen of the Italian dialects (seven east and seven west of the Apennines):

> Having therefore found what was sought, I declare the illustrious, cardinal, courtly, and curial illustrious vernacular language in Italy to be that which belongs to every Italian city but appears to belong to no one of them, by which all the dialects of the Italians are measured, weighed, and compared (*De Vulgari Eloquentia*, I.16.6).

The echo of the scriptural praise of divine Wisdom (Wisdom, 11.21: "but thou hast ordered all things in measure, and number, and weight") in the final phrase would seem to confirm the truth of what Dante says. In effect, however, he makes the Tuscan language his model and opens the door to the eventual Florentine domination of the Italian linguistic and literary landscape. To have them accepted into the offical canon of Italian literature, authors must dress their works in the mantle of the Florentine language.

On the subject of the composition of poetry in Italian, Dante says "we do not have any poets who, computing a verse by syllables, have exceeded eleven syllables or used less than three (*DVE*, II.V.2)." Dante opens the second book of the *De Vulgari Eloquentia* by ackowledging openly that the illustrious vernacular is as useful for prose as for poetry. But, he is quick to add, "the prose writers receive it from those who join it musically to verse." It is therefore appropriate to begin a study of the illustrious vernacular as a model by examining its use in poetry. Somewhat magisterially, *alla dantesca*, he poses the question: Should all who write verse use this vernacular? No, he concludes, for as magnificence is appropriate to the powerful, and royal purple to the noble, the illustrious vernacular seeks out those who excel in wit and learning. Nor is any subject to be treated, for the history of poetry in the vernacular mirrors the tripartite nature of the soul (vegetative, animal, and rational), and shows the only appropriate subjects to be arms, love, and righteousness.

Next he discusses the matter of which metrical forms are suited to the new language. He recalls that some poets writing in the vernacular have adopted the canzone, others the ballata, others the sonnet, and still others exceptional forms that cannot be defined by any precise rule. Naturally, the most worthy subjects, treated in the most worthy language, require the most excellent form. That "most noble form" for Dante is the canzone, for tradition has given it a name which means "song" par excellence. It alone is *per se* a complete form, while the ballata, for example, "is brought to light" only by the intervention of dancers. The canzone confers more honor on its composer; it is better conserved in books; and, finally, it comprehends in itself all the art of poetry. Just as the canzone is superior to the ballata, Dante adds, so too is the ballata superior to the sonnet. Why? Because no one doubts this, he says.

Here then is an evaluation of the dominant metrical forms used by Italian poets, Boiardo among them. Add to these the sestina, the madrigal, and the occasional ill-defined variant and we have all the forms used by Dante, Petrarch, and their successors in the writing of poetry in the vernacular language. There are, of course, other secular poetic forms set to music that were enormously popular in the Renaissance, especially in the courts of northern Italy, such as the *barzelletta*, *strambotto*, *oda*, *capitolo*, *frottola*, and the dances that became the rage in Europe in the sixteenth century (*pavane*, *gagliarde*, *saltarelli*). Some of the forms underwent drastic transformations between the fourteenth and sixteenth century. The madrigal, which originated in northern Italy probably in the 1320s, had already attained its final form by the 1340s.[20]

Dante's definition of the canzone is generic: a unified composition written by one who composes in words with modulation, or a sense of harmony. From this he concludes that canzoni, ballate, sonetti, and all other harmonious metrical compositions may be called canzoni. The one that is supreme among these, however, is the *cantio superexcellentia*, the one that is called the "song par excellence"—the canzone.

Dante's description of the structure of the canzone describes the now traditional Italian canzone or, as it is sometimes called, the *canzone petrarchesca*, which is, as Robert Durling says, "a form in which Petrarch's greatness as a poet reaches its fullest expression."[21] Each stanza of the canzone has a *fronte* and a *coda* or *sirma*, each of which may be the longer of the two division, and composed of verses of varying lengths as pleases the poet. A less common type has, in place of an indivisible *coda* (the Petrarchan type) a secondary division into two *volte* or *versi*. Most often the canzone is composed of seven syllable (*settenario*) and eleven syllable (*endecasillabo*) verses.[22] The *fronte* usually consists of two *piedi* of at least three or four verses each, rhyming in any number of ways: ABC ABC or ABC BAC or ABC BCA; ABBA ACAC or ABBA BABA, and so forth. The *coda* or *sirma* begins with a verse, the *diesi*, which marks the melodic shift from *fronte* to *coda*, and may or may not repeat the rhyme of the final verse of the *fronte*. The stanza often ends with a final consecutively rhymed dis-

---

[20] Stanley Sadie, gen. ed., *The New Grove Dictionary of Music and Musicians*, 20 vols. (London: Macmillan, 1980), 11:461.

[21] Robert M. Durling, ed. and trans., *Petrarch's Lyric Poems: The* Rime Sparse *and Other Lyrics* (Cambridge, Mass.: Harvard Univ. Press, 1976), 14. Cited herafter as *PLP*.

[22] The number of syllables is not strictly held to seven or eleven. More important is that the final stress fall on the sixth and tenth syllables.

tich (*rima baciata*). The canzone itself usually ends with a *volta*, which may be the length of an entire stanza, but most often is not. In the *volta* (sometimes called *tornata* or *ritornello*) the poet may address his "farewell" to the canzone, thus making the *volta* a *commiato* or *congedo* or *licenza*.

Like his predecessors, Boiardo composed stanzas and canzoni of varying length. His longest stanzas are of twenty-two verses and his shortest of seven verses. Poem 50, with stanzas of only seven lines (rhyming abcdEfE; ghijKlK, . . .) and no *congedo*, is modeled on the Provençal *canso*, rather than the Italian canzone. It is also a good example of Boiardo's fascination with metrical variation.[23] The rhyme progesses toward the central stanza, which shifts rhyme and verse lengths (to sTsTsTs), and then reverses the progression to conclude in the seventh stanza with a double reverse image (line length and rhyme) of the first stanza. (EFEDcBa).

The most recurrent type of poem in the *Amorum Libri* is, as would be expected, the sonnet. It is composed of two parts, an octave of two *piedi* (quatrains) and a sestet of two *volte* (tercets). The octave in Boiardo's sonnets is usually written in *rima chiusa* closed rhyme form (ABBA ABBA), and when it is written instead in *rima alternata*, alternating or open rhyme, he calls it *cruciatus*. The sestet may have alternating rhyme (CDC DCD) as in sonnet 3, or some pattern of interlaced rhymes, as in sonnet 1 (CDE CDE) or 31 (CDE DCE). The melody requires a minimum of four musical units; that is, there is no crossover of rhyme from the octave to the sestet as one may find in sixteenth-century types which sometimes rhyme with only three rhymes (ABBA ABBA ABC ABC).

The division into two major units is of obvious importance to the logical structure of the composition. The division into quatrains and tercets is also skillfully exploited by the poet, as the opening sonnet shows clearly. The first quatrain tells what happened in the poet's youth ("A love . . . warmed me in its gentle sun"), and how that experience impinges upon the present ("invites me to reflect . . ."), while the second explains the action that resulted from the experience of youth and the lingering effects of that experience ("So now I've gathered . . ."). The first tercet announces a dramatic change in the poet's life, while the final tercet qualifies the value of that change by re-validating, to a degree, the experience described in the opening quatrain:

> But yet I know that he whose flowering youth
> is passed away without the warmth of love
> may seem to live, but lives without a heart.

---

[23] The reader of the English translation can easily appreciate the original Italian text's formal complexities even with no knowledge of the language.

The ballata is the most frequent type in the *Amorum Libri* after the sonnet. There are at least seven types distinguished in the literature: *Ballata Grande, Ballata Maggiore, Ballata Mezzana, Ballata Minore, Ballata Piccola, Ballata Minima,* and *Ballata Stravagante.* Except for the Ballata Maggiore, they are usually defined by the number of verses and types of verses (all hendecasyllables or hendecasyllables and *settenari*) in the *ripresa* or *ritornello*, which I shall call a reprise (even in the initial position) rather than a refrain since, in Boiardo's ballate, neither the words nor the rhyme are repeated exactly as in the initial statement. As defined by the number and type of verses in the reprise, the ballate types are: Ballàta Grande: four verses (all hendecasyllables or mixed); Mezzana: three verses (all hendecasyllables or mixed); Minore: two verses (two hendecsyllables or one each); Piccola (one hendecasyllable in the initial reprise and one or two hendecasyllables, or mixed in the second reprise); Minima: a reprise of a single verse less than an hendecasyllable; Stravagante: a reprise of more than four verses.

In Boiardo's ballate, except for poem 109, the second reprise picks up at least one of the rhymes of the initial reprise. We find, for example: ABAB . . . BABA in 25; ABaB . . . DBbA in 56; ABbA . . . EFfA in 77; AbA . . . DbA in 20; ABA . . . AGA, and so on. In addition, the second reprise, with three exceptions, begins with the rhyme of the last verse immediately preceding it. Thus, the first ballata (poem 20, a Ballata Mezzana) rhymes in its entirety as follows: AbA CDDC. DCCD. DbA. The exceptions are 139 (ABA CDED. FEEG. AGA) and the two anomalous variations: 89 (AAbB CdC. DEeA) and 109 (ABA CBC. cbc. aba DdeE).

The definition of the Ballata Maggiore is even murkier. I shall define it as having three verses (hendecasyllables or mixed) in the initial reprise and four verses in the second reprise, or vice versa.

All of Boiardo's ballate, except for 139, are basically of the one stanza type, including the lengthy number 56 which rhymes: ABaB CdC. CdC. DcD. DcD. DBba.[24] Ballata 37, of two stanzas, is most like a Petrarchan ballata, even though Petrarch favors the one stanza form. Poem 37 clearly has a reprise and two stanzas with reprises: AbA CDCD. DbA EFEF. FbA

The madrigal is represented in the *Amorum Libri* by two examples: 8 and 104. Since the term has no single, precise meaning, it is difficult to say what distinguishes them as madrigals, except that the author calls the first *mandrialis* (madrigal) and the second *mandrialis cantu* . . . (madrigal in song). From the musical composer's point of view, because it is a "through-com-

[24] Please note, however, that in arranging the Italian text and the translation I have "disjoined" the stanzas into tercets and quatrains in order to remind myself and the reader of the rhyme pattern. Excluding 139, each ballata should be thought of as a *ripresa* or *ritornello* and a single stanza ending with a *ripresa*.

posed" form, it concedes primacy to the text. Whatever the poet writes will be set to music, and it seems that there was a great deal of latitude given to the author of the text. It has been stated with authority that:

> the [fourteenth-century] madrigal attained its final form in the 1340s in northern Italy: two or three-line verses (*stanze*), usually with identical music, and a one- or two-line terminating ritornello, usually with a change of time signature.[25]

Neither of Boiardo's madrigals fit the textual part of the definition, and poem 104 looks "for all the world" like a canzone. Why did Boiardo call it *mandrialis cantu*, a madrigal in song, since all his compositions are *cantu*, that is, meant to be sung? I understand the title to mean "A Madrigal in song with two intersecting meters," and shall leave it at that, with the title "A Madrigal Song in Tercets and Quatrains."

Boiardo's sestina (115) is exemplary; it follows all the rules of form and content, with the least complications, that its inventor, Arnaut Daniel, and its Italian masters, Dante and Petrarch, imposed upon it. The order of the rhyme scheme of the six six-verse stanzas and the three-verse ritornello is standard: ABCDEF FAEBDE CFDABE ECBFAD DEACFB BDFECA ABCDEF. As Robert Durling says, "the sestina is a particularly clear example of a cyclical form expressing the embeddedness of human experience in time (*PLP*, 14)." This movement from form to experience is found in Boiardo's sestina, which is a soliloquy on Antonia's eternal intransigency, unmoved by Pity, and the poet's impending death.

The single rondeau (27) is Boiardo's most hybrid composition. Its metrical form has been closely studied by Scaglione and by Benvenuti, who sees it as a blend of the *rondeau-bergette*, *canto carnescialesco*, *barzelletta*, *ballata*, and the *rondeau*, and confidently brought to perfection by Boiardo via his obsession for "acrobatic metrical symmetries" (555).[26]

---

[25] *The New Grove Dictionary*, 11:462.

[26] Aldo Scaglione, "Contributo alla Questione del Rodundelus del Boiardo," *Giornale Storico della Letteratura Italiana* 128 (1956): 313–16. Antonia Tissoni Benvenuti, "Tradizioni Letterarie e Gusto Tardogotico nel Canzoniere di M. M. Boiardo," *Giornale Storico della Letteratura Italiana* 137 (1960): 533–92. Benvenuti, continuing the argument of Georg Weiss, sees Boiardo's interest in elaborate metrical arrangements as an example of late "International Gothic" style which flourished in Western European art in the early fifteenth century.

The Poetics

If there is a point of disjuncture between writing lyric and reading lyric, or between teaching about poetry and writing about poetry, it is at the level of revelation. How much ought one reveal; how much *can* one reveal? The "socratic" teacher, and the best of lyrics poets, become aphasic just as they are on the verge of being most eloquent. The inexpressibility topos, or some variation, raises their level of verbal impotence to a new level of rhetorical power. As great a scholar as Gianfranco Contini has said that Boiardo's poetry lacks a psychology.[27] Yet there is ample evidence of aphasia (the discourse of impotent or failed discourse), ego-disintegration, jealousy, environmental dissonance, and psychological disorientation in his lyrics. The lyric narrator, Boiardo's included, often struggles with the problem of verbal impotence in the revelation of a failed sexual fantasy. The lyric reader often assumes the narrator's auto-diagnosis is correct, and begins to fill in the gaps. The principal remedial sin of the lyrical reader/physician is to over-medicate. Commentaries and expositions too often belabor the obvious, give a fragmented view of allusions to other texts (perhaps inevitably), and worst of all, do not allow the text to tell its own tale.

With this in mind, an "introduction" to the poetics of an author who is perhaps being read for the first time should orient the reader, but should not anticipate the revelations of the text itself. To be sure, there is much to be said about the poet's veneration of a certain lady, *his* frustration and disappointment, *his* psychological rehabilitation, *his* sense of orientation to the rest of the world, *his* perception of that world (chromatic and otherwise), the hierarchy of moods and sentiments, the progression of moods, style, and tone from book to book, the narrative as a historical record, and so on. But these are all parts of the story that the narrative overtly tells on its own.

The subject of influence and literary antecedents is an important one for the study of any author. Pier Vincenzo Mengaldo's exhaustive study of Boiardo's lyric lexicon, *La Lingua del Boiardo Lirico*, shows that he was a learned reader of modern and classical literature, and was comfortably familiar with the lyric traditions of his predecessors. Virgil and Ovid foremost among the Latin poets, Pliny above all among Latin prose writers, Dante (especially the *Divine Comedy*) and the *stilnovisti*, the Petrarch of the *Rime Sparse* and *Triumphs*, Giusto de' Conti and other court poets (past and contemporary) contributed significantly to shaping the *Amorum Libri*. So did personal experience. He presents the idealized life at court:

[27] "Sostanzialmente, il Boiardo ha solo problemi rappresentativi, non ha psicologia." *Esercizi di Lettura* (Florence: Le Monnier, 1947), 303.

Ocio amoroso e cura giovenile,
gesti legiadri e lieta compagnia,
solazo fuor di noglia e di folia,
alma rimota da ogni pensier vile,

donesco festeggiar, atto virile,
parlar accorto e giunto a cortesia,
sono quelle cose, per sentenzia mia,
che il viver fan più lieto e più zentile. (44.1–8)

Love's idleness, the diligence of youth,
some gracious gestures, cheerful company,
escape from boredom and from folly's grip,
a soul removed from every wicked thought,

the merriment of women, deeds of men
wise conversation joined by courtesy,
these are the very things, in my opinion,
that make our lives much richer and more joyful.

and those activities that Boccaccio described as the men's diversionary privileges:

E' correnti cavalli e i cani arditi,
che mi solean donar tanto diletto,
mi sono in tutto dal pensier fugiti. (110.9–11)

The galloping horses and eager hounds
that gave me so much pleasure in the past
have fled completely from my every thought.

and friendship (and jealousy?):

Tieco fui preso ad un lacio d'or fino,
gentil mio Guido. . . . (84.1–2)

With you, my gentle Guido, I was caught
in a fine gold snare. . . .

As for the psychology of the *Amorum Libri*, one need not look beyond the prefatory opening sonnet to find it. From the beginning, and this is clearly a tautology, the psychic drama is cloaked in rhetorical strategies. One reader has proposed the *adynaton* as a key to the ordering of that drama.[28] Better clues to the dynamics and temper of that psychic drama are

---

[28] Mauda Bregoli-Russo, "Uno Strumento Intepretativo degli *Amores* di Boiardo," *Critica Letteraria* 32 (1981): 519–26.

offered by two other rhetorical figures. One is personification, which Boiardo probably adopted from the spirit-dominated psychology of the poets of the *Dolce Stil Novo*, Dante and Guido Cavalcanti in particular. The stilnovistic passion for personification, Mengaldo notes, was enthusiastically adopted by the poets of northern Italy. He gives an example of a poem (of De' Rossi) in which the heart cries, the lung speaks, the spleen laughs, and the gall bladder and liver are also personified (*LBL*, 310). Another clue is the use of apostrophe, a related trope that Jonathan Culler has called an embarrassment for readers of lyric,[29] and one to which Paul de Man devoted a great deal of attention in his study of "anthropomorphism" and "trope" in Baudelaire.[30]

In the opening sonnet of the *Amorum Libri*, the poet says that Love, which shone warmly upon him in his youth, has invited him once again to consider what, back then, brought him pleasure, and what brought pain. For this reason he has decided to make a collection:

Così raccolto ho ciò che il pensier fole
meco parlava a l'amorosa vita,
quando con voce or leta or sbigotita
formava sospiranto le parole.

So now I've gathered all those musings here
that maddened thought addressed to me in love,
when, with a voice now cheerful, now forlorn,
I formed my words accompanied by sighs.

The stanza is fairly clear in meaning, but difficult to translate. There is no concrete reference to what it is that is collected, just *ciò che* . . . that which mad thought said while speaking *with* me (*meco parlava*) during the amorous life (my amorous life?, our amorous life?), when I/He/It (*formava* may be first or third person singular) fashioned words while/by sighing. In the third stanza we imagine seeing the soul in flight, escaping the clutches of youthful error. Clearly, what constitutes the consciousness of the poet is disjoined. "Il pensier fole" is the mind of the poet projected, in part at least, out of his remaining self. (I have been strongly tempted to capitalize Thought, Soul, Heart, and Will in the translation to underscore the personification when there is a clear sense of agency, but have resisted actually doing so, except in a very few instances.) Since *formava* is both first and

---

[29] "Apostrophe," *The Pursuit of Signs: Semiotics, Literature, Deconstruction* (Ithaca, N.Y.: Cornell Univ. Press, 1981).

[30] "Anthropomorphism and Trope in the Lyric," *The Rhetoric of Romanticism* (New York: Columbia Univ. Press, 1984).

third person singular, it is not clear whose voice forms the words-in-sighs. Does the collection constitute a monologue or a dialogue? The intent of *meco parlava* seems to be dialogic; the disintegration of the "Ego" is unmistakable. And time may have somewhat healed the wound, but the poet is not "single-minded." The soul flees now, but the poet affirms his conviction that the experience of love (in youth) was what defined him as a living human being. Even now he is of "two minds." Because of its Christian and confessional nature, much of the traditional, vernacular lyric poetry of Boiardo's predecessors centers on the transformation that confession makes possible from the old self to the new. Petrarch writes in the first sonnet of the *Rime Sparse*: ". . . when I was in part another man from what I am now." The rhetorical strategy is Augustinian and didactic for Petrarch (see my error; it was all a foolish dream; let me show you what not to do), but not quite so for Boiardo (I see my error, but to what degree was it an error?). How will Matteo Maria's collection end? Will there be an invocation to the Blessed Virgin that echoes Petrarch's, or not? Are the *Amorum Libri* another chapter in salvation history, or has lyric poetry's confessional mode been thoroughly secularized?

The *topos* of the person "beside himself" is an old one. In the *Tusculan Disputations* ("On Grief of Mind"), Cicero says the Greeks were quite clever in calling the state of soul deprived of the light of the mind a "being out of one's mind," "a being beside oneself." Latin, he says, as in most matters, expresses the idea better than does Greek. Nothing expresses the idea better than the usual Latin, which says of those who are "unbridled" (*qui effrenati feruntur*) in lust or in wrath (the lust of vengeance) that they have lost command of themselves: *exisse ex potestate* dicimus eos, qui effrenati feruntur aut libidine aut iracundia.[31]

The medieval lyric tradition abounds in literalized examples of this notion of the divided self. The more the poet is filled with the spirit of the lady, the more he (his spirit) is driven out of himself. Giacomo da Lentini, for example, says ("Molti amador la lor malatia"):

[31] See my "Insania *and* Furor: A Diagnostic Note on Orlando's Malady," *Romance Notes* 14, no. 3 (1973): 583–88. For the use of the *topos* of unbridled self in Renaissance epic see A. Bartlett Giamatti, "Headlong Horses, Headless Horsemen: An Essay on the Chivalric Epics of Pulci, Boiardo and Ariosto," *Italian Literature: Roots and Branches. Essays in Honor of Thomas Goddard Bergin*, eds. Giose Rimanelli and Kenneth John Atchity (New Haven: Yale Univ. Press, 1976), 265–307.

cad io non sono mio né più né tanto
se non quanto madonna è de mi fore
ed uno poco di spirito è 'n meve.

for I am no more and no less mine than to the
degree that my lady is out of me and a little
spirit is in me.

The division of self from self caused by the lady (145.70) leads to disorientation and a crisis of identity for Boiardo's poetic persona:

Sono ora in terra, on sono al ciel levato?
Sono io me stesso, on dal corpo diviso?
Sono dove io veni, on sono in Paradiso,
che tanto son da quel che era mutato? (17.1–4)

Am I on earth, or have I gone to heaven?
Am I myself, or am I just a spirit?
Am I where I once was, or is this paradise,
so different as I am from what I was?

The divided self, like the ancient Greeks who projected their own mental processes onto Nature and discovered an animated force that governed the world, sees the cosmos as fragmented, anthropomorphized, and alienated:

Vaghi augelleti, voi ne giti a volo
perché forsi credeti
che il mio cor senta dolo,
e la zoglia che io sento non sapeti. (8.10–13)

You lovely birds fly off when I am near
because, perhaps, you think
my heart feels only pain,
and so you do not know the joy that's mine.

He is *diviso* against himself by the lady's steady gaze (93.11; 112.4), against pain (82.5), even against his own heart (174.4). Love, Time, and Fortune conspire against him; his world is shattered by cold indifference, just as the *flos fractus* in the *carpe diem* motif of poem 46 is shattered by the season's chill. He apostrophizes his lady (by synecdoche as "heart of stone"), her face and eyes, his own gaze, his heart and thoughts, the age he lives in, colors, flowers, desire, passion, the sky, the stars, the sun, his destiny, his verses, heavenly Justice, eternal witnesses to his torment, the metaphorical key to his heart, a fugitive dream, and so on. The continuity of tradition thus works to erect a monument to the discontinuity of the poet's amorous reverie.

Many have discussed, and could still, the coincidence of rhetoric and imagery which links Boiardo to Petrarch. But, beyond that, one is tempted to wonder what greater bond may hold the fragments together and link the poetics of the one poet to the other. Is there a discernible response in Boiardo's text to the poetic strategy of Petrarch? Certainly, one does not find the kind of "anxiety of influence" here that John Freccero finds in Petrarch's response to Dante.[32] Petrarch presents us with the illusion of history, and Boiardo presents us with the fragmented history of an illusion. In Freccero's reading, Petrarch employs a poetic strategy which is grounded in Augustine's Theology of the Word, wherein the process of unlimited semiosis is interrupted, and signification is made possible by making God the Word "at once the end of all desire and the (ultimate) interpretant of all discourse" (36). By, in effect, short-circuiting the referentiality of his signs, Petrarch literally idolizes Laura by turning her into a reified sign which interrupts what otherwise would be a limitless process of signification. Any interpretant which does not point beyond itself partakes of divinity. A poetics of idolatry is established which not only makes a goddess of Laura, but which also sacralizes the text and makes the Lover/Poet a de-temporalized monument to the author's own scriptural authority.

In the *Amorum Libri*, the poetic strategy is not nearly so complex. Boiardo's "poetics of idolatry" takes the form of an idolatrous pantheism which anthropomorphizes, and, at the same time, reifies the entire cosmos. The lady is a divinity reflected in all the elements of Nature; she is a goddess who is coextensive with every referent within the system (as in poem 43). The entire cosmos thus becomes an idol, that is to say, a metaphor for the lady. To Antonia's ineffable Aphrodite (ever absent and yet everywhere present) the poet plays the injured Hephaestus, whose jealousy bursts forth early in the second book. A theme which was irrelevant in the poetics of Petrarch becomes literally central to the *Amorum Libri*. In poems 91 and 92 the poet first fears that his suffering causes another to rejoice, and then openly admits that he is trapped in a labyrinth of jealousy. In poem 93 he turns in desperation to Divine Justice, hoping to reclaim his due, "my words, my sighs, that laughter that was mine" that are now bestowed upon another.

Any attempt to create the illusion of organic unity in the *Amorum Libri* fails. The poet achieves neither salvation through the mediation of a Beatrice, nor "temporal salvation" through the idolization of a beloved "laurel" Laura. If the acrostics naming Antonia Caprara in the first four-

---

[32] John Freccero, "The Fig-Tree and the Laurel: Petrarch's Poetics," *Diacritics* 5 (Spring, 1975): 35–41.

teen sonnets of Book One are an inscription not unlike that of the Temple of Venus Genetrix in Rome's ancient Forum of Caesar, they are a relic which, from the beginning, remind us of the poet's apparent attempt to idolize the lady, and the failure of that poet to immortalize himself through the strategy of idolatrous veneration. The sacralization of the text as the venerable history of the poet's (self-) love, and an idolization of the text as a monument to its author, is countermanded by the intrusiveness of a multiplicity of personified referents, many of which are fragmented elements of the self. Whereas Petrarch begins with discreet fragments and creates the illusion of continuity, Boiardo begins with the illusion of felicitous unity and deconstructs it into a world of unredeemable fragments. The three books are not a history, but three histories. In the *Amorum Libri* the object of devotion is, in the end, too human to be sanctified or idolized. The poetics of the *Amorum Libri* are grounded in the world of contingency and temporality. The key to the social immediacy of such a poetics is to be found in the expanded social role of lyric authorship in fifteenth-century courtly society. The lyric is no longer the instrument of self-apotheosis, but the mirror of collective adoration.

The Text

The text follows closely the excellent Italian edition of Pier Vincenzo Mengaldo cited in the bibliography. It is reproduced here with the kind permission of the publishers Giuseppe Laterza & Figli, Bari, Italy. Except for the choice *ardore/errore* in 106.3, there are no lexical problems to be resolved in the *Amorum Libri*; the modern editions vary only in orthography and punctuation. I have modified Mengaldo's punctuation somewhat, corrected a few obvious typographical errors, eliminated some orthographic inconsistencies, and made the following changes (given by poem and verse number) for the sake of simplicity, to avoid confusion, or to clarify the meaning:

8.1 vagi > vaghi
8.14 vag[h]i > vaghi
27.15 ragionarni > ragionarne
43.54 campagnia > compagnia
62.7 sonto > sono
93.14 Oh, iustitia > O iustitia
101.11 compagne > campagne
118.12 convertite > convèrtite
125.2 piatade > pietade
161.7 che qualle > ché quale

168.18 dogli<a> > doglia

At times I have used one stanzaic format in Italian and adopted a different format in English. The reader should find the reading and referencing easier in English without losing the option of seeing the Italian in an alternate configuration.

Finally, let me note that the Latin titles to some of the poems, especially those that attempt to define the nature or form of the compositions, have no meaningful English equivalents when translated literally. I have therefore incorporated in each my description of the composition without recourse to a footnote.

Abbreviations for works cited in the notes

Commentaries:

OV *Opere Volgari: Amorum Libri-Pastorale-Lettere.* Ed. Pier Vincenzo Mengaldo. Bari: Laterza, 1962.

S *Le Poesie Volgari e Latine di Matteo Maria Boiardo, Riscontrate sui Codici e sulle Stampe.* Ed. Angelo Solerti. Bologna: Romagnoli-Dall'Acqua, 1894.

SC *Orlando Innamorato, Sonetti e Canzoni di Matteo Maria Boiardo.* Ed. Aldo Scaglione. 2 vols. Turin: UTET, 1951.

ST *Il Canzoniere (Amorum Libri).* Ed. Carlo Steiner. Turin: UTET, 1927.

U *Opere di Matteo Maria Boiardo.* Ed. Ferruccio Ulivi. Milan: Mursia, 1986.

Z *Tutte Le Opere di Matteo M. Boiardo.* Ed. Angelandrea Zottoli. 2 vols. Milan: Mondadori, 1936–37.

References:

CH *The New Century Classical Handbook.* Ed. Catherine B. Avery. New York: Appleton-Century-Crofts, Inc., 1962.

EB *Encyclopaedia Brittanica.* 11th ed. 29 vols. New York: The Encyclopaedia Brittanica Company, 1910.

EPP *Encyclopedia of Poetry and Poetics.* Ed. Alex Preminger. Princeton, N.J.: Princeton Univ. Press, 1965.

LBL Mengaldo, Pier Vincenzo. *La Lingua del Boiardo Lirico.* Florence: Leo S. Olschki, 1963.

OCD *The Oxford Classical Dictionary.* 2d ed., ed. N. G. L. Hammond and H. H. Scullard. Oxford: Clarendon Press, 1970.

MATÆI MARIE BO
IARDI AMORV LIBER
PRIM9 INCIPIT

Biblioteca Nazionale Marciana (Venezia), MS. It. IX,545 (= 10293), f. 1r

Mataei Marie Boiardi Amorum Liber Primus Incipit

1

Amor, che me scaldava al suo bel sole
nel dolce tempo de mia età fiorita,
a ripensar ancor oggi me invita
quel che alora mi piacque, ora mi dole.

Così racolto ho ciò che il pensier fole
meco parlava a l'amorosa vita,
quando con voce or leta or sbigotita
formava sospirando le parole.

Ora de amara fede e dolci inganni
l'alma mia consumata, non che lassa,
fuge sdegnosa il püerile errore.

Ma certo chi nel fior de' soi primi anni
sanza caldo de amore il tempo passa,
se in vista è vivo, vivo è sanza core.

Here Begins
The First Book of Love Lyrics
of Matteo Maria Boiardo

1. Sonnet 1

Amor, who warmed me in his gentle sun
back in my easy days of youthful bloom,
invites me to reflect once more today
on that which pleased me then and now gives pain.

So now I've gathered all those musings here
that maddened thought addressed to me in love
when, with a voice now cheerful, now forlorn,
I formed my words accompanied by sighs.

And now my soul, so wearied and consumed
by disappointed trust and sweet deceits,
flees from my youthful error in disdain.

But yet I know that he whose flowering youth
is passed away without the warmth of love
may seem to live, but lives without a heart.

Like Petrarch's *rime sparse* ("scattered verses"), Boiardo's collection of love poems begins with a sonnet which recalls the poet's youthful error and affirms the transitory nature of romantic love.

The initial letter of this poem ("**A**") combines with the initial letters of the thirteen following poems to create an acrostic which spells the name of Antonia Caprara, the object of the poet's devotion. Boiardo is said to have met a lady of that name in the court of Sigismondo d'Este at Reggio Emilia in 1469, and to have courted her in the years 1469–71. Nothing more is known of her, except that the records show that an Antonia, daughter of Bernardo Caprari, was baptized in Reggio on 13 October 1451 (*U*).

2

Non fia da altrui creduta e non fia intesa
la celeste beltà de che io ragiono,
poiché io, che tutto in lei posto mi sono,
si poca parte ancor n'hagio compresa.

Ma la mia mente che è di voglia accesa
mi fa sentir nel cor sì dolce sono
che il cominciato stil non abandono,
benché sia disequale a tanta empresa.

Così comincio, ma nel cominciare
al cor se agira un timoroso gielo
che l'amoroso ardir da me diparte.

Chi fia che tal beltà venga a ritrare?
on qual inzegno scenderà dal cielo
che la descriva degnamente in carte?

3

Tanto son peregrine al mondo e nove
le dote in che costei qui par non have,
che solo intento al bel guardo süave
a l'alte soe virtù pensier non move.

Ma più non se ralegra el summo Jove
aver fiorito el globo infimo e grave
di vermiglie fogliete e bianche e flave,
quando fresca rogiada el ciel ne piove;

Verse 1: = *Orlando Innamorato*, I.17.3.1.

Verses 1 & 2 repeated in *Pastorale*, Eclogue 5, 25–26 as the only two verses of Menalca that Gorgo remembers. Verse 2: cf. Petrarch 23.

Verse 14: = *Orlando Innamorato*, I.18.46.8. The last tercet is especially reminiscent of Provençal and Sicilian poetry. Cf. Bernard de Ventadorn (*Non es meravelha s'eu chan*), Sordello (*Aitant ses plus vis hom quan viu jauzens*) and Giacomo da Lentini (*Molti amadori la lor malatia*).

2. Sonnet 2

None other will believe or comprehend
the heavenly beauty of which I would here speak,
since even I, who have surrendered all
my thought to it, have grasped but just a part.

Yet does my mind, inflamed by its desire,
evoke such dulcet sounds within my breast,
that I will not give up this poet's art
although my skill's unequal to the task.

So now I shall begin: but once begun
a fearful chill takes hold about my heart
and drives away the warmth of passion's flame.

Who will create the portrait of such beauty?
What wit from Heaven's realm will soon appear
to treat it worthily upon the page?

---

passion's flame: Aristotle determined that "all the soul's modifications do seem to involve the body—anger, meekness, compassion, and joy and love and hate." (*De Anima*, 403a2ff.) Traditionally, physiologists and poets understood love to be a response to the heating of the blood within the heart.

Who will create: a rhetorical variation on the inexpressibility *topos*.

3. Sonnet 3

Those unmatched qualities that are her gift
are here so rare, so alien to this world,
that my own thought, intensely fixed upon
her looks, moves not to note her other charms.

But mighty Jove does not rejoice the more
for having dressed this lowly, weighty globe
with petals painted red and white and gold
when heaven rains its freshening dew on them.

né tanto se ralegra aver adorno
il ciel di stelle, e aver creato il sole
che gira al mondo splendido d'intorno,

quanto creato aver costei, che sòle
scoprir in terra a meza notte un giorno
e ornar di rose il verno e di vïole.

4

Ordito avea Natura il degno effetto
ch'or se dimostra a nostra etade rea,
ne l'amoroso tempo in che volea
donar a li ochi umani alto diletto.

Ragiunti insieme al più felice aspetto
se ritrovarno Jove e Citerea
quando se aperse la celeste Idea
e diette al mondo il suo gentil concetto.

Sieco dal ciel discese Cortesia,
che da le umane gente era fugita,
Purità sieco e sieco Ligiadria.

Con lei ritorna quella antica vita
che con lo effetto il nome de oro avia,
e con lei inseme al ciel tornar ce invita.

5

Novellamente le benegne stelle
escon da l'occeàno al nostro clima,
la terra il duol passato più non stima
e par che il verde manto rinovelle.

Nor does he so rejoice in having filled
the sky with stars, in having made the sun
that circles round the earth in all its splendor,

as he does in having made the one
who turns the midnight darkness into day,
and colors winter rose and violet.

---

lowly, weighty globe: the farthest place from heaven and the center of the Aristotelian-Ptolemaic conception of the created world, it bears all the weight of the universe. Cf. Dante, *Inferno*, 34.

4. Sonnet 4

Ordained by Nature was this gracious being
presented now to our intemperate age
when she first thought, in times inspired by love,
to grant such high delights to human eyes.

Venus and Jupiter had met again,
and found themselves aligned in joyful bond,
just when the heavenly Mind laid bare its thought,
and gave its noble concept to the world.

With her from heaven descended Courtesy,
which from humanity had long since fled;
with her came Purity and Loveliness.

With her returns that ancient life which bore
the name of gold as well as its effect,
and she invites us back to heaven with her.

Venus and Jupiter had met: at conjunction: the planets of the goddess of earthly love and the Roman sky-god were in alignment with the earth along the axis of the sun at the propitious moment of her birth.

5. Sonnet 5

Now once again familiar, friendly stars
rise from the sea to reinvest our clime.
The earth no longer heeds past pains endured,
and, so it seems, its mantle greens anew.

Amor, che le dorate sue quadrelle
più tien forbite, e il suo potere in cima,
questa beltà non mai veduta in prima
vuol dimostrar con l'altre cose belle.

Con bianchi zigli e con vermiglie rose,
coi vaghi fiori e con l'erbetta nova
l'ha dimostrata al parangone Amore.

così Natura e lui fra sé dispose
veder d'ogni beltà l'ultima prova
e dar il pregio a lei come a magiore.

6

Il canto de li augei de fronda in fronda
e lo odorato vento per li fiori
e lo ischiarir de' lucidi liquori
che rendon nostra vista più ioconda,

son perché la Natura e il Ciel seconda
costei, che vuol che 'l mondo se inamori;
così di dolce voce e dolci odori
l'aër, la terra è già ripiena e l'onda.

Dovunque e' passi move on gira il viso
fiamegia un spirto sì vivo d'amore
che avanti a la stagione el caldo mena.

Al suo dolce guardare, al dolce riso
l'erba vien verde e colorito il fiore
e il mar se aqueta e il ciel se raserena.

7

Aventurosa etade in cui se mira
quanto mirar non puote uman pensiero,
tempo beato e degnamente altero
a cui tanto di grazia el Cielo aspira

And Love, who keeps his golden darts well honed,
aware that they have been his source of power,
desires to put her beauty on display
with all the other things of rare design.

Love's shown that she fares well when she's compared
to the lily and the crimson-colored rose,
to lovely blossoms, and to tender grass.

The God of Love and Nature thus conspired
to have all things of beauty show their worth
so that the prize, as finest, would be hers.

---

familiar, friendly stars: the spring constellations (Leo, Virgo, Boötes, et al.), which replace those of winter (Taurus, Orion, Canis Major, et al.).

6. Sonnet 6

If still the birds' songs bound from bough to bough,
and scented breezes blow from bloom to bloom,
and glistening waters fill our eyes with joy
when we admire their sparkling clarity,

it is because both Nature and Heaven support
the one who wants the world to be in love;
so air and land are filled, and sea as well,
with sweet-toned voices and sweet fragrances.

Wherever she walks by or turns her eyes,
a spirit full of love bursts forth like fire
which well before its time brings summer's warmth.

Before her peaceful gaze, her gentle smile,
the grass grows green, the flower takes on its hue,
the sea turns calm, the sky serene above.

7. Sonnet 7

A lucky age are you that can admire
what human thought cannot conceive at all,
a blessed time, and justly proud, are you,
for Heaven's having granted you such grace,

che solo a' zorni toi donar desira
uno effetto celeste, un ben intero,
qual non ha questo on quel altro emispero
né tutto quel che 'l sol volando agira;

quella stagion che fu detta felice
e par che al nome de auro ancor se alumi,
quanto può invidïarti, o nostra etade!

Ché se nectare avea ben nei soi fiumi
e mèle avean le querce e le mirice,
giamai non ebbe lei tanta beltade.

8

Mandrialis

Cantati meco, inamorati augelli,
poiché vosco a cantar Amor me invita;
e voi, bei rivi e snelli,
per la piagia fiorita
teneti a le mie rime el tuon süave.

La beltà de che io canto è sì infinita
che il cor ardir non have
pigliar lo incarco solo,
ché egli è debole e stanco, e il peso è grave.

Vaghi augelleti, voi ne giti a volo
perché forsi credeti
che il mio cor senta dolo,
e la zoglia che io sento non sapeti.

Vaghi augeleti, odeti:
che quanto gira in tondo
il mare e quanto spira zascun vento,
non è piacer nel mondo
che aguagliar se potesse a quel che io sento.

for only to your days does it concede
a true celestial gift, a perfect being,
as can be found in neither hemisphere,
nor even in the circuit of the sun.

That season that was said to be most joyful,
and takes its splendor from the name of gold,
how much it envies you, O present age!

For if indeed its rivers flowed with nectar,
and if its oak and tamarisk gave honey,
yet never was such beauty hers to hold.

---

season: the Golden Age.

8. Madrigal 1

Madrigal

Come sing with me, you little love-struck birds,
since Love invites me now to sing with you;
and you fair, rapid streams,
accompany my verse
with your sweet voice along your flowered banks.

The beauty which I sing is so intense
my heart's not bold enough
to face the task alone,
because it's weak and tired, and the burden weighs.

You lovely birds fly off when I am near
because, perhaps, you think
my heart feels only pain,
and so you do not know the joy that's mine.

Sweet birds, hear what I say:
in all that the sea surrounds,
as far as any wind may blow,
there is in all the world
no pleasure that compares to what I feel.

The titles given to some poems (see the Italian text) appear in the Oxford manuscript

9

Ad Amorem

Alto diletto che ralegri il mondo
e le tempeste e i venti fai restare,
l'erbe fiorite e fai tranquillo il mare,
ed a' mortali il cor lieto e iocondo,

se Jove su nel cielo e giù nel fondo
fecisti il crudo Dite inamorare,
se non se vide ancora contrastare
a le tue forze primo né secondo,

qual fia che or te resista, avendo apreso
foco insüeto e disusato dardo
che dolcemente l'anima disface?

Con questo m'hai, Signor, già tanto inceso
per un süave e mansüeto guardo
che in altra sorte vita non mi piace.

10

Pura mia neve che èi dal ciel discesa,
candida perla dal lito vermiglio,
bianco ligustro, bianchissimo ziglio,
pura biancheza che hai mia vita presa;

and the first edition, and are, by consensus, almost certainly Boiardo's own. They are given, here, below the numbered heading, even at the risk of repetition. See the Introduction for a discussion of the metrical forms used in the *Amorum Libri.* Although poem 104 is termed a madrigal, poem 8 is the only composition herein that fits the common notion of the madrigal as a brief and monostrophic verse form.

9. Sonnet 8

To Love

Ah sweet delight, who spread your joy on earth,
who soothe the winds and put great storms to rest,
who let the flowers bloom and seas grow calm,
and make the hearts of mortals brim with joy,

if first you forced great Jove to fall in love,
and then cruel Dis that dwells in Hell below,
and if no other power yet is seen
which has withstood the force that you exert,

who can resist you now that you've acquired
new instruments of war, rare darts and fire,
that move so sweetly to undo the soul?

With these, My Lord, you so compel me now
to contemplate a gaze so kind and sweet,
that I can want no other life but this.

---

sweet delight: the god Love; reminiscent of Lucretius' invocation of Venus in the *De Rerum Natura* (I.1–9).

forced great Jove to fall in love: the father-god had many loves and fathered many children.

cruel Dis: Hades, god of the dead and lord of the infernal regions, whose love for Persephone led him to abduct her.

My Lord: Love.

10. Sonnet 9

Purest snow of mine from heaven sent,
lustrous and silvery pearl from the Red Sea's shore,
white privet blossom, whitest lily bloom,
pure whiteness that has taken hold of me;

o celeste biancheza, non intesa
da li ochi umani e da lo uman consiglio,
se a le cose terrene te assumiglio
quando fia tua vagheza mai compresa?

Ché nulla piuma del più bianco olore
né avorio né alabastro può aguagliare
il tuo splendente e lucido colore.

Natura tal beltà non può creare,
ma quel tuo gentil lustro vien da Amore,
che sol, che tanto puote, te 'l pò dare.

11

Rosa gentil, che sopra a' verdi dumi
dai tanto onor al tuo fiorito chiostro,
suffusa da Natura di tal ostro
che nel tuo lampegiar il mondo alumi,

tutti li altri color son ombre e fumi
che mostrerà la terra on ha già mostro:
tu sola sei splendor al secol nostro,
che altrui ne la vista ardi, e me consumi.

Rosa gentil, che sotto il giorno extinto
fai l'aria più chiarita e luminosa
e di vermiglia luce il ciel depinto,

quanto tua nobiltade è ancor nascosa!
Ché il sol, che da tua vista in tutto è vinto,
apena te cognosce, o gentil rosa.

12

A la rete d'Amor, che è texta d'oro
e da Vagheza ordita con tanta arte
che Ercule il forte vi fu preso e Marte,
son anche io preso, e dolcemente moro.

O heavenly whiteness, which no human eye
or human mind has ever apprehended,
if I compare you now to earthly things,
how will I ever make your beauty known?

Indeed, no feather from the whitest swan,
nor ivory, nor can alabaster match
the clear and splendid color of your face.

Nature cannot create this kind of beauty;
that gentle glow of yours is born of Love,
for only Love, so powerful, can grant it.

11. Sonnet 10

Rose, noble rose, set high upon green thorns,
you bring such honor to your flowered cloister;
suffused by Nature with so red a glow,
you light the world with your bright radiance.

The many other hues that have appeared
on earth, or will appear, are smoke, are shade;
you, you alone, the splendor of our age,
blaze bright in others' eyes, and me consume.

O noble rose that make the failing light
of dying day seem clear and bright again,
and paint the sky with your vermilion light,

how much is your nobility still hidden!
The sun, entirely subdued by you,
has barely come to know you, noble rose.

The sun . . . has barely come to know you: she must seem very young to her admirer. In 1469 Boiardo would have been twenty-eight years old and Antonia Caprara (most likely) no more than eighteen or nineteen.

12. Sonnet 11

A net was made by Love with strands of gold,
and set by Beauty with such skillful art
that mighty Hercules and Mars were trapped,
and now I too am caught and sweetly die.

Così morendo il mio Signor adoro
che dal lacio zentil non me diparte,
né morir voglio in più felice parte
ca religato in questo bel lavoro.

Non fia mai sciolto da le treze bionde,
crespe, lunghe, legiadre e peregrine
che m'han legato in si süave loco.

E se ben sua adorneza me confonde
e vame consumando a poco a poco,
trovar non posso più beato fine.

13

Ride nel mio pensier la bella luce
che intorno a li ochi di costei sintilla,
e lèvame legier come favilla
e nel salir del ciel se me fa duce.

Là veramente Amor me la riluce
e con sua man nel cor me la sigilla;
ma l'alma de dolceza se distilla
tanto che in forsi la mia vita aduce.

Così, rapto nel ciel fuor di me stesso,
comprendo del zoir di paradiso
quanto mortal aspetto mai ne vide.

E se io tornasse a quel piacer più spesso,
sarebbe il spirto mo' da me diviso,
se il soverchio diletto l'omo occide.

And, dying, I sing praises to my Lord,
who will not free me from the tender trap,
nor do I wish to die less painfully
than bound like this by Love in sweet travail.

May I not be released from those fair bonds,
those long and curly, gaily flowing locks,
that have me tied to this so sweet a place.

And even though she rules me with her looks,
confounding me, consuming me by steps,
I know for me I'll find no end more blessed.

Hercules: the poet may be thinking of Hercules' capture of Iole, which precipitated a series of events that led to his death. It is also the name of his friend and patron, Ercole d'Este, duke of Ferrara.

Mars: the Roman god of war was often remembered in the quattrocento as the prisoner of Venus.

13. Sonnet 12

Radiant laughter racing through my thought
is now that light that glimmers in her eyes,
and like a weightless spark it bears me up
and guides me as I soar up to the stars.

There, high above, Love truly makes it shine,
and with his hand he seals it in my heart;
my soul is so dissolved by such delight
I think it will deprive me of all life.

Transported thus to heaven by ecstasy,
I've come to know the joys of Paradise
that mortal intellects have never shared.

But if I were to taste such joys too often,
my soul and flesh would instantly divide,
if excessive pleasure kills a man.

14

Capitalis

Arte de Amore e forze di Natura
Non fur comprese e viste in mortal velo
Tutte giamai, dapoi che terra e cielo
Ornati fòr di luce e di verdura:
Non da la prima età simplice e pura,
In cui non se sentio caldo né gielo,
A questa nostra, che de l'altrui pelo
Coperto ha il dosso e fatta è iniqua e dura,
Accolte non fòr mai più tutte quante
Prima né poi, se non in questa mia
Rara nel mondo, anci unica fenice.
Ampla beltade e summa ligiadria,
Regal aspetto e piacevol sembiante
Agiunti ha insieme questa alma felice.

15

Cantus Comperativus

1. *Chi troverà parole e voce equale*
che giugnan nel parlare al pensier mio?
Chi darà piume al mio intelletto ed ale
si che volando segua el gran desio?
Se lui per sé non sale,
né giugne mia favella
al loco ove io la invio,
chi canterà giamai de la mia stella?
Lei sopra l'altre cose belle è bella,
né col pensier se ariva a sua belleza,
perché a lo inzegno umano il Ciel la cella
né vuol che se salisca a la sua alteza,

14. Sonnet 13

Acrostic

All Love's old skills and all of Nature's powers
Not ever under human veil were seen
Together bound, since earth and sky were first
Ornately dressed by verdure and by light.
Not since the pure and simple age of gold
In which no heat or freezing chill was felt,
And not in ours, which, clothed in others' skins,
Cruel and iniquitous remains at heart.
All those same gifts were neither then nor now
Placed in a single soul, except in this
Rare phoenix, yea, unique, whom I love so.
Abounding beauty and unbounded grace,
Regal bearing, features, oh, so fair
Are now conjoined in this one blessèd soul.

As the title suggests, each of the fourteen lines of this sonnet begins with a letter of Antonia Caprara's name.

clothed in others' skins: an allusion to the fashion of wearing furs.

rare phoenix: in Egyptian mythology, a bird of great beauty which was the only one of its kind. After living for hundreds of years in the wilderness, it was consumed by flames on a funeral pyre of its own making, only to rise again from the ashes in all its youthful splendor.

15. Canzone 1

A Song of Comparisons

1. Who will discover words and voice so matched
that in their utterance they reach my thought?
Who'll grace my intellect with feathered wings
and let it soar to meet my great desire?
If it fails to rise alone
and my discourse cannot reach
that place to which I send it,
who'll ever sing the praises of my star?
She is more lovely than all lovely things;
Our thoughts, unaided, cannot know such grace,
for Heaven hides it from the human mind
and does not want our wit to rise so high,

se forsi Amor non degna darci aita
acciò che la vagheza
sia del suo regno qui fra noi sentita.

2. *Porgime aita, Amor, se non comprende*
il debol mio pensier la nobiltade
che a questo tempo tanta grazia rende,
che gloriosa ne è la nostra etade.
Sì come più resplende,
alor che il giorno è spento,
intra le stelle rade
la luna di color di puro argento,
quando ha di fiame il bianco viso cento
e le sue corne ha più di lume piene,
solo a sua vista è il nostro guardo intento,
ché da lei sola a nui la luce viene:
così splende qua giù questa lumiera,
e lei sola contiene
valor, beltade e gentileza intiera.

3. *Come in la notte liquida e serena*
vien la stella d'Amore avanti al giorno,
de ragi d'oro e di splendor sì piena
che l'orizonte è di sua luce adorno,
ed ella a tergo mena
l'altre stelle minore
che a lei d'intorno intorno
cedon parte del cielo e fangli onore;
indi rorando splendido liquore
da l'umida sua chioma, onde se bagna
la verde erbetta e il colorito fiore,
fa rogiadosa tutta la campagna:
così costei de l'altre el pregio acquista,
perché Amor la accompagna
e fa sparir ogni altra bella vista.

4. *Chi mai vide al matin nascer l'aurora,*
di rose coronata e de jacinto,
che fuor del mar el dì non esce ancora
e del suo lampegiar è il ciel depinto,
e lei più se incolora
de una luce vermiglia,
da la qual fòra vinto
qual ostro più tra noi se gli asomiglia;

except perhaps when Love decides to aid our flight
so that beauty such as dwells
in his domain is sensed on earth as well.

2. Love, help me if my feeble thought now fails
to comprehend the noble excellence
which fills the day again with so much grace,
and makes our age so much more glorious.
As the silver-colored moon
will shine with purer radiance
as soon as day is spent,
in a field of waning stars,
when its white face is tinged as though with flames,
and both its horns are filled with brighter light,
and our sight intensely fixes on her face
alone, since she alone provides us light:
so does this other light shine here below,
and she alone possesses
true gentility and worth and beauty.

3. Just as the star of Love appears near dawn
amid the still and limpid shades of night,
so rich golden rays and full of splendor
that the horizon is adorned with light,
As she leads the lesser stars
that occupy her path and
yet are quick to cede to her
their little bit of sky, and show respect;
And as she shakes from locks of dampened hair
a glistening liquid which descends to wet
the new, green grass and brightly-colored flower,
and cover all the fields with drops of dew:
So does that Lady take the prize from others,
since Love is always with her,
and makes each rival beauty disappear.

4. Whoever's seen the dawn in early morning,
wearing a crown of hyacinths and roses,
repaint the sky with all its blazing light
before the sun has surfaced from the sea,
acquiring the color
of a deep vermilion light
surpassing every shade
of red that here on earth resembles it,

e il rozo pastorel se maraviglia
del vago rossegiar de lo orïente
che a poco a poco su nel ciel se apiglia,
e con' più mira più se fa lucente:
vedrà così ne lo angelico viso,
se alcun fia che possente
se trovi a riguardarla in vista fiso.

5. *Qual fuor de l'occeàn, di raggi acceso,*
risurge il sole al giorno matutino,
e si come fra l'unde e il ciel suspeso
va tremolando sopra il suol marino;
e poi che il freno ha preso
de' soi corsier focosi,
con le rote d'or fino
ad erto adriza e' corsi luminosi;
vista non è che amirar fermo lo osi,
ché di vermiglio e d'oro ha un color misto
che abaglia gli ochi nostri tenebrosi
e fa l'uman veder più corto e tristo:
tal è amirar questo mirabil volto,
che, da li ochi mei visto,
ogn'altro remirar a lor ha tolto.

Vago pensier, che con Amor tanto alto
volando vai, e del bel viso canti
che ti fa nel pensar il cor di smalto,
membrando di sua forma e dei sembianti,
rimanti da la impresa si soprana,
però che tanto avanti
non va la possa de natura umana.

16

Già tra le folte rame aparir veggio
ambe le torre ove il mio cor aspira;
già l'ochio corporale anche lui mira
la terra che ha l'effetto e 'l nome reggio.

and the humble shepherd is amazed to see
the blushing redness coming from the east
relentlessly inflame the sky above
and grow in brightness as he watches it,
will see no less in that angelic face,
if there be one who thinks
he has the strength to gaze into her eyes.

5. As when from ocean depths with burning rays
the sun arises at the break of day
and moves between the waters and the sky
with trembling steps above the ocean's surface,
taking up the reins
of his fiery, charging steeds,
and charting with his golden wheels
a lighted course upon an upward path,
and finds no eye that dares to stare at him
since he possesses colors, red and gold,
that blind our eyes (more used to shaded light)
and clouds all human sight and cuts it short:
That's how it is for me when I admire
that wondrous face of hers
that keeps my eyes from seeing other sights.

You wandering thoughts, that soar so high with Love
and sing the praises of that countenance
whose beauty glazes hard your heart against
all else, as you recall its form and features,
abstain from such a lofty enterprise;
to reach so high a goal
is not within the power of human nature.

3.1, *the star of Love*: the planet Venus.

16. Sonnet 14

Through dense-leaved branches I already see
the double towers toward which my heart is aimed;
my eye beholds at last that land called Reggio,
which is in name and fact a ruler's place.

Alma cittade, ove Amor tien suo seggio
e te sopravolando sempre agira,
qual nascosta cagion tanto me tira
che altro che esser in te giamai non chieggio?

Deh, che dico io? Ché la cagion è aperta
a le fiere a li augelli ai fiumi ai sassi
e ne l'abisso e in terra e in mare e in celo.

Ormai del mio furor per tutto sciassi,
ché a poco a poco è consumato il gielo
che un tempo ebbe mia fiama in sé coperta.

17

Sono ora in terra, on sono al ciel levato?
Sono io me stesso, on dal corpo diviso?
Son dove io veni, on sono in paradiso,
che tanto son da quel che era mutato?

Oh felice ciascun, ciascun beato
a cui lice amirar questo bel viso
che avanza ogni diletto e zoglia e riso
che possa al core umano esser donato!

Mirate, donne, se mai fu beltate
equal a questa, e se son tal costumi
or ne la nostra, on fur ne l'altra etate!

Dolci, amorosi e mansüeti lumi,
come sconvènne a quel che for mostrate
che per miraryi un cor se arda e consumi.

You city of my soul, where Love holds court
and always hovers in the air above you,
what hidden cause is there that draws me so
that I seek nothing but to be at home in you?

But wait! What do I say? The cause is clear
to all the beasts and birds and streams and stones;
from hell to earth to sea to heaven above

my madness is by now exposed to all,
because the frost that once contained my flame
and kept it hidden is itself consumed.

Reggio: Reggio nell'Emilia, named *Regium Lepidi* in the second consular term of M. Aemilius Lepidus, who constructed the Via Aemilia and founded the cities of Parma and Modena (second century BC). In Boiardo's day it was the seat of the court of Sigismondo d'Este, younger brother of Ercole I. *Regium*, in Latin, means "royal" or "regal."

17. Sonnet 15

Am I on earth, or have I gone to heaven?
Am I myself, or am I just a spirit?
Am I where I once was, or is this paradise,
so different as I am from what I was?

Oh so happy and so truly blessed
are those allowed to gaze upon this face
which offers every pleasure, every joy
and smile that may be granted to the heart.

Look, Ladies, now, and think if ever beauty
were equal unto hers, or if such virtue
in our age, or in the past, were found.

How unbecoming to your outward look,
sweet, gentle, loving eyes, that for admiring
you a heart should burn and be consumed.

18

Ad Guidonem Scaiolam

De avorio e d'oro e de corali è ordita
la navicella che mia vita porta;
vento süave e fresco me conforta,
e il mar tranquillo a navicar me invita.

Vago desir coi remi a gir me aita,
governa el temo Amor, che è la mia scorta,
Speranza tien in man la fune intorta
per porre il ferro adunco a la finita.

Così cantando me ne vo legiero
e non temo de' colpi de Fortuna
come tu che li fugi e non sciai dove.

Crede a me, Guido mio, che io dico il vero:
càngiasse mortal sorte or bianca or bruna,
ma meglio è morte qua che vita altrove.

19

Ad Amorem Interogatio

—Che augello è quello, Amor, che batte l'ale
tieco nel cielo ed ha la piuma d'oro,
mirabil sì che in croce mi lo adoro,
ché al senso mio non par cosa mortale?

Hanne Natura al mondo un altro tale?
Formòlo in terra, on sopra al summo coro?
Fece tra noi più mai altro lavoro
che a questo di beltade fusse equale?—

—Là dove il giorno spunta e' ragi in prima,
nasce questa fenice, al mondo sola,
che di sua morte la vita ripiglia.

Più mai non la vedète il nostro clima:
però, se e' toi pensieri al tutto invola
vista sì rara, non è maraviglia.—

18. Sonnet 16

To Guido Scaiola

The little vessel which transports my life
is richly trimmed with ivory, gold and coral;
A fresh and gentle breeze inspires me,
inviting me to sail a tranquil sea.

A restless longing helps me man the oars
while Love, that is my guide, attends the helm;
Hope holds a twist of rope in hand and waits
to drop the anchor at the journey's end.

And so with a light heart singing I am off,
not fearing what the strokes of Fortune bring,
somewhat like you who flee, not knowing where.

Believe me, Guido, friend, I speak the truth:
Our luck in life can turn from fair to foul,
but death is better here than life elsewhere.

The friend to whom this sonnet is dedicated was of a prominent family of Reggio. See also poem 84.

19. Sonnet 17

Questions Put To Love

"What golden-feathered bird is that, O Love,
which beats its wings with you up in the sky?
so like a miracle, I worship it;
my senses say to me it is not mortal.

Has Nature blessed the world with any other?
Did she form it here, or where the angels dwell?
And did she undertake some other task
on earth that ever equalled this in beauty?"

"There, where day first shows its rays of light,
this phoenix is born, unaided, to the world,
for it regains its life from its own death.

Our world has never seen its like before;
so if so rare a vision robs you now
of every single thought, it is no wonder."

20

Chorus Sinplex

L'alta beltà, dove Amor m'ha legato
con la catena d'oro,
ne la mia servitù me fa beato.

Né più lieto di noglia esce e di stento,
sciolto da' laci, il misero captivo,
quanto io, di poter privo
e posto in forza altrui, lieto me sento.

Quel vago cerchio d'or che me tien vivo
ed hami l'alma e il core intorno avento,
me fa tanto contento,
che de alegreza su nel cielo arivo.

E così quando io penso e quando io scrivo
del mio caro tesoro,
me par sopra le stelle esser levato.

21

Comperativus

Né più dolce a' nostri ochi il ciel sfavilla
de' lumi adorno che la notte inchina,
né il vago tremolar de la marina
al sol nascente lucida e tranquilla,

né quella stella che de su ne stilla
fresca rogiada a l'ora matutina,
né in giazio terso né in candida brina
ragio di sol che sparso resintilla;

né tanto el veder nostro a sé ritira
qual cosa più gentil ed amorosa
su nel ciel splende on qua giù in terra spira,

quanto la dolce vista e grazïosa
de quei begli ochi che Amor volve e gira:
e chi no il crede, de mirar non gli osa.

20. Ballata 1

Ballata Mezzana

That lofty beauty to which I am bound
by Love with golden chains,
does bless me in my state of servitude.

No wretched captive, freed from slavery's bonds,
rejoices more to flee his pain and torment
than I rejoice deprived
of strength and placed in someone else's power.

That lovely, golden ring that holds me fast,
and girds together both my heart and soul,
makes me so happy now,
I'm on my way to heaven borne by joy.

And so it is that, as I think and write
about my precious treasure,
I feel as though I'm raised above the stars.

---

golden chains . . . golden ring: her golden hair; the standard of beauty is, of course, Petrarchan (dark eyes, golden hair, alabaster skin).

21. Sonnet 18

Comparisons

The sky does not more brightly shine for us
when sparkling stars adorn it through the night;
nor do the gentle ripples of the sea
at sunrise when the water's calm and clear;

nor even does that star which from above
rains freshly gathered dew in early morning;
nor does that glittering ray of scattered sunlight
reflected by dense ice or by white frost;

nor do our eyes in searching ever find
a thing more gentle or more full of love
that shines above us, or that breathes on earth

than the sweet and gentle sight of lovely eyes
whose movements are determined by Love's will:
and who denies this dares not look at them.

22

Cruciatus

L'ora del giorno che ad amar ce invita
dentro dal petto il cor mi raserena,
vegendo uscir l'aurora colorita,
e a la dolce ombra cantar Filomena.

La stella matutina è tanto piena
che ogn'altra intorno a lei se è dispartita,
ed essa appo le spalle il sol si mena,
di sua stessa belleza insuperbita.

Ciò che odo e vedo süave ed ornato
a lo amoroso viso rasumiglio,
e convenirse al tutto l'ho trovato.

Più volte già nel rogiadoso prato
ora a la rosa l'hagio ed ora al ziglio,
ora ad entrambi insieme acomperato.

23

Io vado tratto da sì ardente voglia,
che 'l sol tanto non arde ora nel cielo,
benché la neve a l'alpe, a' rivi il gielo,
l'umor a l'erbe, a' fonti l'unda toglia.

that star: not a star, but the brilliant planet Venus that is known as the evening or morning star because of its appearance in the twilight hours.

22. Sonnet 19

Crossed

That hour that invites us all to love
brings back to me a peace that calms my heart,
seeing the colored dawn as it emerges,
and the softly-shadowed Filomena in song.

So full of splendor is the morning star
that every star around it vanishes,
and she, now proudly sensing her own beauty,
in solitude directs the sun to follow.

All I hear and see that is refined
and pleasing, I compare to her dear face,
and find that each comparison is apt.

So often have I on a dewy meadow
compared her to the rose or to the lily,
and then again, at other times, to both.

Crossed: the recurring title *cruciatus* probably refers only to the alternating rhyme scheme; Antonio da Tempo (*S*, p. xxi) suggested that whenever a sonnet has alternating rhyme it has an underlying tone of torment (*cruciatus*) as well; the suggestion does not hold for Boiardo.

That hour: in the early morning, when Venus is visible.

Filomena: Philomela, daughter of Pandion, King of Athens, and sister of Procne. In the Greek tradition, the gods transformed Procne into a nightingale and Philomela into a swallow. The Latin authors reversed the tradition, with Philomela becoming the nightingale. See especially Ovid, *Metamorphoses*, 6.424ff.

23. Sonnet 20

I am possessed by such an ardent passion
that now to me the sun seems not to burn,
even though it melts the alpine snow
and river's ice, and dries both grass and spring.

Quando io penso al piacer che 'l cor me invoglia,
nel qual dal caldo sol me copro e velo,
io non ho sangue in core o in dosso pelo
che non mi tremi de amorosa zoglia.

Spreza lo ardor del sole il foco mio,
qualor più caldo sopra a' Garamanti
on sopra a gli Etïòppi o gli Indi preme.

Chi ha di sofrenza on di virtù desio
il viver forte segua de li amanti,
ché amor né caldo né fatica teme.

24

Qual benigno pianetto o stella pia
in questo gentil loco m'ha drizato?
Qual felice destin, qual dextro fato
tanto ablandisse a la ventura mia?

Canti süavi e dolce melodia
intorno a me risonan d'ogni lato;
null'altro è di me in terra più beato,
né scio se forsi in cielo alcun ne sia.

Quello angelico viso, anci quel Sole,
che tole al core umano el tristo zelo
e del mio petto fuor la notte serra,

e lo accento gentil de le parole
che sopra noi risona insino al celo,
me fan de li altri più felice in terra.

When I think how my heart is seized by pleasure,
which, like a cloak protects me from the sun,
no drop of blood in me, no hair of mine
is there that does not tremble with Love's joy.

My flame disdains the ardor of the sun,
which beats now hotly on the Garamants,
and now oppresses Ethiops or Indians.

Whoever would learn patience and endurance
must go the harder way-of-life of lovers,
for love fears neither heat nor tribulation.

Garamants: *Garamantes* to the Romans, cited by Dante (*Convivio*, III.5.12 & 18) as the people of northern Africa living closest to the equator. See poem 135 and *Orlando Innamorato*, II.1.57.

24. Sonnet

What kind planet or what star of mercy
has guided me to this ennobled place?
What happy destiny, what lucky fate
sustains my venture with its blandishments.

Sweet melodies and soothing songs
reverberate and fill the air around me;
there is no one on earth more blessed than I,
nor do I know if such exists in heaven.

That angelic face, I mean that Sun,
that drives the chill of sadness from men's hearts,
and shuts the nighttime's darkness from my breast,

joins with the gentle way she shapes her words
so that its echo rings as high as heaven,
to make me happiest of men on earth.

---

this ennobled place: where he could see and hear his lady (*ST*).

25

Chorus Unisonus

Deh, non chinar quel gentil guardo a terra,
lume del mondo e spechio de li Dei,
ché fuor di questa corte Amor si serra
e sieco se ne porta i pensier mei.

Perché non posso io star dove io vorei,
eterno in questo gioco,
dove è il mio dolce foco
dal qual tanto di caldo già prendei?

Ma se ancor ben volesse io non potrei
partir quindi il mio core assai o poco,
né altrove troveria pace né loco
e sanza questa vista io morerei.

Deh, vedi se in costei
Pietade e Gentileza ben s'afferra,
come alcia li ochi bei
per donar pace a la mia lunga guerra.

26

In Natali Dominae

Ecco quella che il giorno ce riduce,
che di color rosato il cielo abella;
ecco davanti a lei la chiara stella
che il suo bel nome prese da la luce.

Principio sì giolivo ben conduce
a la annüal giornata, che fu quella
che tolse giù dal ciel questa facella
di cui la gente umana arde e riluce.

Questo è quel giorno in cui Natura piglia
tanta arroganza del suo bel lavoro
che de l'opra sua stessa ha maraviglia.

25. Ballata 2

Ballata Grande with Unified Rhyme

Please! Do not cast down your gentle eyes,
dear earthly light and mirror of the Gods,
for Love refuses to appear beyond
this court, and keeps my thoughts there locked with him.

Why can't I stay here, where I wish to stay,
eternally rejoicing,
with my sweet and gentle flame
from which I have already drawn much warmth?

Indeed, the truth is that I cannot move
my heart from here no matter how I wish it;
nor would I find another resting place
or peace, and I would die without this vision.

Please! Look at her and see
if Pity and Kindness are discerned in her
when she lifts up her eyes
to bring the gift of peace to my long war.

Unified Rhyme: the *-ei* rhyme is maintained.

26. Sonnet 22

On My Lady's Birthday

Behold the one that gives us back the day,
that paints the sky the color of the rose;
behold ahead of her the brilliant star
that took the lovely name it bears from light.

So cheerful a beginning surely leads
to the annually recurring day
that seized from heaven and brought to earth this light
whereby humanity is seen to burn and shine.

This is the very day on which the goddess
Nature takes such pride in her fine skills
that even she can marvel at her work.

Più de l'usato sparge e' ragi d'oro
il sol più bello e l'alba più vermiglia:
oggi nacque colei che in terra adoro.

27

Rodundelus Integer Ad Imitacionem
Ranibaldi Franci

Se alcun de amor sentito
ha l'ultimo valor, sì come io sento,
pensi quanto è contento
uno amoroso cor al ciel salito.

1. *Da terra son levato e al ciel son gito,*
e gli ochi ho nel sol fisi al gran splendore
e il mio veder magiore
fatto è più assai di quel che esser solia.
Qual inzegno potria
mostrar al mio voler e' penser mei?
Perché io stesso vorei
cantar mia zoglia, e non esser odito.
Se alcun de amor sentito.

2. *Io son del mio diletto sì invagito*
che a ragionarne altrui prendo terrore;
né in alcun tempo amore
fu mai né sarà senza zelosia.
Ben fòra gran folia
a scoprir la belleza di costei,
ché ben ne morerei
se io fusse per altrui da lei partito.
Se alcun de amor sentito.

3. *Beato viso che al viso fiorito*
fusti tanto vicin che il dolce odore
ancor me sta nel core,
e starà sempre insin che in vita sia,

Much more than usual do a fairer sun
and redder dawn now scatter golden rays:
the one I love on earth was born this day.

An anniversary poem.
the lovely name: Lucifer, light-bearing, a Latin name for the planet Venus.

27. Rondeau

Complete Rondeau After the Manner of the French Poet Rambaud

If anyone has felt
the power of love in full, as I do feel it,
just think how happy is
the loving heart that's made its way to heaven.

1. I've lifted up from earth and gone to heaven,
I've fixed my eyes upon the Sun's great splendor,
and now my vision is
much stronger than it ever was before.
What ingenuity
could show my thoughts as I would wish them shown?
For I myself would sing
about my joy, and want not to be heard,
If anyone has felt. . . .

2. I am so much in love with my beloved
that I dread to speak of her to others,
for at no time did love
exist, nor will it, without jealousy.
Well would it be a folly
to reveal her beauty to the world,
for I would surely die
if parted from her by another lover.
If anyone has felt. . . .

3. O lucky eyes, that came to be so close
to her beflowered face, that its sweet smell
still lingers in my heart,
and will remain as long as I'm alive;

tu l'alta legiadria
vedesti sì di presso e gli ochi bei;
tu sol beato sei,
se il gentil spechio tuo non t'è rapito.
Se alcun de amor sentito.

4. *Felice guardo mio che tanto ardito*
fusti ne lo amirar quel vivo ardore,
chi te potrà mai tòre
lo amoroso pensier che al ciel te invia?
Ben scio certo che pria
e l'alma e il core e il senso perderei;
ben scio che io sosterei
anzi di cielo e terra esser bandito.
Se alcun de amor sentito.

5. *Ligato sia con meco e sempre unito:*
se meco insieme l'anima non more,
non se trarà mai fore
questo unico mio ben de l'alma mia.
Dolce mia segnoria,
a cui ne' mei primi anni me rendei,
sanza te che sarei?
Inculto rozo misero e stordito,
Se alcun de amor sentito.

6. *Per te, candida rosa, son guarnito*
de spene e zoglia, e vòto de dolore;
per te fugi' lo errore
che in falsa sospizione el cor me apria.
Tu sola sei la via
che me conduce al regno de gli Dei;
tu sola e' pensier rei
tutti hai rivolti, e me di novo ordito.
Se alcun de amor sentito.

7. *Per te sum, rosa mia, del vulgo uscito,*
e forsi fia ancor letto el mio furore,
e forsi alcun calore
de la mia fiamma ancor inceso fia;
e se alcuna armonia
oguagliar se potesse ai pensier mei,
forsi che ancor farei
veder un cor di marmo intenerito.
Se alcun de amor sentito.

you saw such loveliness
with those alluring eyes so near to you;
It's you alone that's blessed,
if that gentle mirror is not snatched from you.
If anyone has felt. . . .

4. My happy eyes, that were so full of ardor
when you gazed upon that glowing flame,
who can ever take
from you the thought of love that leads to heaven?
I am convinced that first
I'd lose my soul and heart and all my senses;
I know that I would rather
face my banishment from heaven and earth.
If anyone has felt. . . .

5. May it always be bound up with me;
and if my soul lives after I have died,
this treasure of my soul
will never be drawn out of me by force.
My sweet domination,
to which I had surrendered in my youth,
what would I be without you?
Uncultured, tactless, wretched, and unfeeling.
If anyone has felt. . . .

6. Because of you, white rose, I am now armed
with hope and joy, and emptied of all pain;
through you I fled the error
that opened up my heart to false suspicion.
You only are the way
that takes me to the kingdom of the Gods.
And you alone have altered
my misguided thought and fashioned me anew.
If anyone has felt. . . .

7. Because of you, my rose, I've left the crowd;
and so perhaps my passion's tale will live;
perhaps the heat my flame
gives off will warm the spirit of another:
and if my verse could match
in harmony the grandeur of my thoughts,
perhaps I might yet see
a marble heart reveal some tenderness.
If anyone has felt. . . .

8. *Cantiamo adunque il viso colorito,*
cantiamo in dolce nòtte il zentil fiore
che dà tanto de onore
a nostra etade che l'antiqua oblia.
Ma l'alta fantasia
ne la qual già pensando me perdei,
nel rimembrar di lei
da me m'ha tolto e sopra al ciel m'ha sito.
Se alcun de amor sentito.

28

Chi tole il canto e péne al vago augello,
le foglie e il color vivo tole al fiore,
e l'erbe la verdura e il primo odore,
e il fiore e l'erbe tole al praticello,

e le ramose corne al cervo isnello,
al cielo e stelle e sole e ogni splendore,
quel puote a un cor gentil togliere amore,
e la speranza al dolce amor novello.

Ché sanza amore è un core sanza spene,
un arbor sanza rame e sanza foglie,
fiume sanza unde, e fonte sanza vene.

Amore ogni tristeza a l'alma toglie,
e quanto la Natura ha in sé di bene
nel core inamorato se racoglie.

8. Let us, therefore, praise that fine complexion.
Let sweet notes praise in song the gentle flower
that now bestows such honor
on our age that it forgets the past.
Indeed, the lofty fantasy
in which I lost myself when I was deep in thought,
remembering my lady,
took my soul and placed it up in heaven.

If anyone has felt
the power of love in full, as I do feel it,
just think how happy is
the loving heart that's made its way to heaven.

More like a Provençal *dansa* than a rondeau (*SC*); a hybrid form that reflects the author's inventive approach to metrical composition. Rambaldus, or Rambaud, has not been identified.

Complete: the entire refrain, rather than just the first verse, is repeated.

7.1, *I've left the crowd*: cf. Dante, *Inferno*, 2.105. In the doctrine of courtly love, the lover rises above the crowd by virtue of his devotion to his lady.

8.5, *the lofty fantasy*: cf. Dante, *Paradiso*, 34.142, where Dante is also transported to Heaven by his *alta fantasia*.

28. Sonnet 23

The one who steals the song and plumes of birds,
and steals the flower's brightly-colored petals,
and the grass's verdure and its early fragrance,
and strips a field of grass and of its flowers,

and the sleek and slender deer of branching horns,
and the sky and stars and sun of all their splendor,
can also rob a gentle heart of love,
a sweet and youthful love of all its hope.

A heart that has no love can have no hope;
it is a tree without its leaves and branches,
a river with no water, a sourceless spring.

Love denies all sadness to the soul;
and all there is in Nature that is good
is gathered up in every heart that loves.

29

Cum In Suburbano Vacaret Ludis Puellaribus

Gentil città, come èi fatta soletta!
come èi del tuo splendor fatta ozi priva!
E un picol fiumicel su la sua riva
di tanto ben felice se diletta.

Io me ne vado dove Amor me aspetta,
che è gito in compagnia de la mia Diva;
Amor che ogn'altra cosa ha vile e sciva
e di lasciar costei sempre sospetta.

Sanza di lei né tu né altro me piace,
né sanza lei tra l'Isole Beate
né in ciel, ch'io creda, sentiria mai pace.

Rimanti adunque tu, gentil citate,
poiché una tua villeta è tanto audace
che ozi te spoglia di tua nobiltate.

30

Qual nei prati de Idalo on de Citero
se Amor de festegiar più voglia avea,
le due sorelle agiunte a Pasitea
cantando di sé cerchio intorno fèro,

tal se fece oggi, e più legiadro e altero,
essendo in compagnia de la mia Dea
e de l'altre doe belle, onde tenea
la cima di sua forza e il summo impero.

Gioiosamente in mezo a lor si stava
voltando le sue ale in più colori,
e sua belleza tutta fuor mostrava.

La terra lieta germinava fiori
e il loco aventuroso sospirava
di dolce foco e d'amorosi odori.

29. Sonnet 24

When She Goes To the Country and Plays Young Women's Games

O noble city, how desolate you are!
Today you are deprived of your true splendor!
Instead, a little stream takes great delight
in having such a treasure on its bank.

I'm going now to where Love waits for me,
having departed in my Lady's company;
Love, that considers all else vile and loathsome,
and always fears of leaving her alone.

Without her I like neither you nor any other;
I do not think I could find peace without her,
not in the Blessèd Isles, nor even in heaven.

Remain, therefore, alone, O gentle city,
since one of your small villages today
so boldly strips you of nobility.

---

the Blessèd Isles: mythical islands of the Atlantic where it is always spring. Cf. poem 82 (4.9).

30. Sonnet 25

As in Idalium's fields or in Cythera's,
if Love's desire were to celebrate,
two sisters joined with Pasithea in song
to form a circle with him in a dance:

So did they dance today, but with more gaiety,
he being in the company of her,
my goddess, and the other two, wherewith
he held the summit of his power and reign.

With joyful pleasure he remained with them,
changing at will the color of his wings,
and showing off his beauty all about.

New flowers sprouted from the happy earth,
and the lucky place began to sigh
with sweet Love's burning and with Love's perfumes.

31

Ben se ha trovato il più legiadro seggio
Amor che fabricasse mai natura;
ed io presumo a scriver sua figura
perché d'ognor nel cor me la vagheggio.

La sua materia è de alabastro egreggio
e d'or coperta è la suprema altura,
sotto a cui splende luce viva e pura
tal ch'io non la scio dir come io la veggio:

ché di cristallo è tutta la cornice,
de ebbano ha sopra uno arco rivoltato;
chi dentro può mirar ben è felice.

Qui sede Amor de raggi incoronato,
dolce cantando a' riguardanti dice:
—Piacer più vago il Ciel non v'ha mostrato.—

32

Perché non corresponde alcuno accento
de la mia voce a l'aria del bel viso?
ch'io faria in terra un altro paradiso
e il mondo ne l'odir di lei contento.

Farebbe ad ascoltarmi a forza intento
ogni animal d'umanità diviso,
e se mostrar potesse il dolce riso,
faria movere e' saxi e star il vento.

Idalium's fields: Idalium or Idalia, modern Dali. "In ancient geography, a town and promontory on the coast of Cyprus, with a temple to Aphrodite, who was sometimes called Idalia." (CH)

Cythera: the birthplace of Aphrodite/Venus. "One of the Ionian Islands. . . . It was near this island that Aphrodite was said to have arisen from the foam of the sea, whence her epithet 'Cytherea.'" (CH)

Pasithea: one of the minor Graces whom the poet treats as one of the three major ones (cf. *Orlando Innamorato*, II.15.52.5).

31. Sonnet 26

There is no doubt that Love has found himself
the finest throne that Nature ever fashioned,
and I presume now to describe its form,
since it is always present in my heart.

The body is of choicest alabaster,
all covered at the highest part with gold,
below which glows a pure and vivid light
that I cannot describe as it appears;

for it is resting in a frame of crystal,
with an arch of ebony above it;
whoever can gaze into it is blessed.

Here Love is seated with a crown of rays,
and, sweetly singing, says to his admirers:
"Heaven's never shown you a finer source of joy."

32. Sonnet 27

Why is it that the sounds made by my voice
can't match the look in her angelic face?
For if they did, I'd make this world a paradise,
and all the world content to hear of her.

I would oblige not only man to listen,
but every beast apart from man as well,
and if I could describe her gracious smile,
I'd move the rocks and make the winds be still.

Ben ho più volte nel pensier stampite
parole elette e nòtte sì süave
che assai presso giugneano a sua belleza;

ma poi che l'ho legiadramente ordite,
par che a ritrarle el mio parlar se inchiave
e la voce mi manche per dolceza.

33

Cantus Rithmo Interciso Continuatus

1. *L'alta vagheza che entro al cor me impose*
con l'amorose ponte il mio volere,
il spirto me sotrage al suo piacere,
ché a lei volando l'alma se desvia:
se stessa oblia, ed io non ho potere
di ratenere il fren come io solia,
ché più non stano da la parte mia
arte né inzegno, forza né sapere.
Hagio quel foco in me che io soglio avere
e quel vedere usato e quella voglia,
ma il poter più tener mie fiame ascose
mi è tolto in tutto, e il ricoprir mia noglia
che un tempo occultamente il cor mi rose,
mentre potei celar, come io dispose.

2. *Già son le rose a la sua fin extrema,*
e pur non scema de mia fiama el fiore,
anzi più caldo ha preso e più vigore,
come più largo il giro or prende il sole.
Ma non mi dole or tanto questo ardore
che me arde il core assai più che non sòle:
sia quel che il Ciel dispone e che Amor vole,
pur che altri non cognosca il mio furore.
Ma che posso io? Ché 'l tempo mostra l'ore,
e il viso amore, e però cerco invano
mostrar di fora ardir, se 'l cor mi trema.
Se pietà non mi porge il viso umano,
e proveda che Amor sì non mi prema,
ancor convien ch'io cridi, non ch'io gema.

How many times my thoughts have been imprinted
with words well-chosen and with pleasant sounds,
that came so close to equaling her beauty!

But, once I have them gracefully in order,
it seems as though my speech cannot repeat them,
as ecstasy deprives me of my voice.

33. Canzone 2

A Song With Internal Rhyme

1. The sovereign beauty that my will impresses
on my heart with passion's pointed arrows
deprives me, as it wishes, of my spirit,
which, flying to her, takes my soul off course.
The soul forgets herself, and I have not
the power to rein it in as once I would,
since I now have as help in my defense
not art nor wit nor strength nor even wisdom.
As always I possess that fire in me,
that same habitual vision and desire;
but what is taken from me is the power
to hide my flame and cover up my woe,
which once in secrecy consumed my heart
while I could hide the fact, as I saw fit.

2. The roses are already at their season's end,
yet the flower of my passion withers not,
gathering instead more vigor and more life,
just as the sun begins its wider course.
But now this ardor that inflames my heart
much more than usual gives no pain to me;
be Heaven's order and Love's wish fulfilled,
as long as others know not of my madness.
But what can I do, since time reveals the hours
and my face my love? It is therefore in vain
that I feign boldness when my heart is trembling.
If her kind face does not show signs of mercy
and thus provide that Love not so oppress me,
I must not only moan, but cry aloud.

3. *Come vuol frema il mare o il ciel intoni,*
ché a tutti e' soni a me dansar convene,
né in zoglia altrui voria cangiar mie pene,
se amirar quel potesse ond'io tanto ardo.
L'ochio fu tardo, e già non se sostene,
ché più non vene il fugitivo pardo;
tenir non posso el cor sanza quel guardo,
ché mal se può tenir chi non ha spene.
Qual capestro qual freno on qual catene,
qual forza tene el destrier ch'è già mosso
nel corso furïoso, ed ha chi el sproni?
Sapiati, alma gentil, che più non posso,
quando convien che alfine io me abandoni:
on che io me mori, on che al guardar perdoni.

4. *Queste cagioni furno al mio fallire,*
se altri vuol dire un fallo il guardar mio;
ma se più mai signor benigno e pio
odì suo servo, odeti mia ragione:
ne la stagione che il mio cor sentio
l'alto desio e dolce passïone,
si lieto el viso vostro se mostrone
che in lui pusi speranza come in Dio.
Fatto se è poi, non scio perché, restio,
e tanto rio e del suo guardo avaro
che il cor degiuno più non può soffrire.
Usato non è lui pascer d'amaro;
perciò li è forza al suo fonte venire,
on a spegner la sétte on a morire.

5. *Se pur languire io debo in questa etate,*
vostra beltate non sarà mai quella,
ch'io scio che non potria cosa sì bella
esser cagion di morte a chi l'adora.
Or ride or plora l'alma tapinella,
d'una facella avampa e discolora:
a voi sta che la viva e che la mora;
voi la regina seti, e lei l'ancella.
Perché s'asconde adunque la mia stella?
perché se cella il mio lume sereno?
Se cor gentil asdegna crudeltate,
come assentite voi ch'io venga meno?
Pur vostra forma è di tal nobiltate
che esser non può ribella di pietate.

3. Let oceans roar at will and heavens thunder,
for I must dance no matter what the sounds;
nor would I change my pain to others' joys,
if I could see the face that makes me yearn.
My eyes delayed and now they suffer for it,
since chance, the fleeing leopard, won't return.
My heart cannot survive without her sight,
for without hope there is no will to live.
What rope, what rein, what links, what force can hold
the steed that has already set itself
upon a furious course, and is spurred on?
Know this, O gentle lady, that I'm done;
when I've surrendered fully to desire,
I'll either die or you'll forgive my gaze.

4. These are the reasons that I give for failing,
if someone wants to call my looking failure;
but, if a merciful and gentle master
did ever hear a servant, hear my reasons.
During the season when my heart succumbed
to Love's desire and to a lover's passion,
your countenance appeared to be so friendly
I placed all hope in it as though in God.
But then, I know not why, it turned away,
grew cold and so reluctant to be seen
that my desirous heart cannot endure it.
His habit's not to feed on bitter woe;
yet he will always go to his own fount,
and there will he assuage his thirst, or die.

5. If I must pine away my youthful days,
your beauty cannot ever be to blame,
for I know that a thing so fair cannot
be cause of death to one who worships it.
My wretched soul first laughs and then it cries,
it brightly burns then flickers like a candle;
On you depends whether she lives or dies.
You are her queen and she your waiting-maid.
Why does my star conceal itself from me?
Why does my tranquil light avoid my sight?
If gentle hearts do scorn all cruelty,
why do you let me fail without concern?
Your manner is of such a noble cast
it cannot be an enemy to mercy.

Ma sia quel che esser vuole: io quel che sono
tutto abandono in vostre braza alfine;
né mia fortuna ha scampo in altro porto.
Abi la terra l'osse mie meschine,
e il cor, che del suo spirto è privo a torto,
vostro fu vivo e vostro sarà morto.

34

Capitalis

Anzelica vagheza in cui Natura
Ne mostra ciò che bel puote operare,
Tal che a sì chiara luce a comperare
Ogni stella del ciel parebbe oscura,
Non si può aconciamente anima dura
In grazïosa vista colorare;
A voi una umiltà ne li ochi appare
Che de pietate ogn'alma rassicura.
A che mostrare adunqua che le pene
Per voi portate sian portate invano,
Ridendo el foco che 'l mio cor disface?
Alma ligiadra, tropo disconvene
Risposta dura a un viso tanto umano:
Aiuto adunque, on morte, qual vi piace.

35

Se cosa bella sempre fu gentile,
né mai mentì Pietade a Gentileza,
ancor sarà che giù ponga l'aspreza
quel magnanimo core e signorile.

Sdegno regal se placca al servo umile,
e in picol tempo se dilegua e speza;
l'ira crudiel e l'odio e la dureza
non han ricetto fuor che in alma vile.

But, be it what it may, I, as I am,
abandon all, at last, to your embrace;
my fortune has no hope of safer ports.
So let the earth possess my wretched bones;
my heart, instead, so wrongfully deprived,
was yours in life, and will be yours in death.

3.10, *the steed*: cf. II.62. A. B. Giamatti treats the theme of 'release and restraint' in the essay cited.

5.14, *enemy of mercy*: "ribella di pietade," echoes Petrarch's "rubella di mercé" (Petrarch 29).

34. Sonnet 28

Acrostic

Angelic comeliness whereby the goddess
Nature shows the skills at her command,
To now compare your luster to the stars
Of heavens overhead will make them pale.
No one can rightly say a cruel spirit
Is suitably attired in pleasing garb;
A look of humbleness is in your eyes
Compelling souls to turn to you for mercy.
And for what purpose might I here reveal
Pains borne for you are borne by me in vain,
Reproved by you with laughter as I burn?
Ah, lovely soul, it does not suit you well,
Responding harshly with so kind a face:
Assistance now, or death, give as you please.

35. Sonnet 29

If every beauteous thing were ever noble,
and Mercy never failed Gentility,
then someday will that grand and lordly heart
yet lay aside its store of bitterness.

Regal disdain before a humble servant
subsides, and soon it fades and breaks apart;
cruel ire and hate and cold hard-heartedness
are only well received by baser souls.

Ma se pur forsi il Ciel novo destino
fatto ha per me, né vuol che io me conforte
de aver mercé dal mio viso divino,

tacito porterò la dura sorte,
e sol, piangendo, me morrò meschino,
per non incolpar lei de la mia morte.

36

Datime a piena mano e rose e zigli,
spargete intorno a me vïole e fiori;
ciascun che meco pianse e' mei dolori,
di mia leticia meco il frutto pigli.

Datime e' fiori e candidi e vermigli,
confano a questo giorno e' bei colori;
spargeti intorno d'amorosi odori,
ché il loco a la mia voglia se assumigli.

Perdon m'ha dato ed hami dato pace
la dolce mia nemica, e vuol ch'io campi.
lei che sol di pietà se pregia e vanta.

Non vi maravigliati perch'io avampi,
ché maraviglia è più che non se sface
il cor in tutto de alegreza tanta.

37

Chorus Triplex Rithmo Interciso

Doppo la pugna dispietata e fera
Amor m'ha dato pace,
a cui despiace   che un suo servo pèra.

Still, if, for me, the Heavens plan a fate
unknown, and will that I'm not comforted
by drawing mercy from her godly eyes,

I'll bear my bitter sentence silently.
Weeping, alone, I'll die a wretched man,
so that my death will not be blamed on her.

36. Sonnet 30

Roses and lilies give me by the handful,
strew round me violets and other blooms,
let all who shed their tears with me in grief
now gather up the fruit of my rejoicing.

Do give me flowers that are white and red;
such colors are well-suited to the day.
Strew all about the fragrances of Love
so that this place and my desire seem one.

My gentle foe has granted me forgiveness
and peace, and she, who boasts and brags of being
so merciful, wants me to go on living.

Don't be amazed that I am all aflame,
for it is more amazing that my heart
is not consumed by so much happiness.

Roses and lilies . . . : cf. Virgil, *Aeneid*, VI.883–84: "Manibus date lilia plenis,/ purpureos spargam flores . . . ," and the theme of an early death. See also Dante, *Purgatorio*, 30.20–21, where the "ministers and messengers of eternal life" prepare for the advent of Beatrice and the departure of Virgil.

37. Ballata 3

Ballata Mezzana with Internal Rhyme

After a fierce and merciless assault
Love has brought me peace,
for he regrets to see his servant perish.

Come più dolce a' navicanti pare,
poi che fortuna gli ha sbatuti intorno,
veder le stelle e più tranquillo il mare
e la terra vicina e il novo giorno,
cotale è dolce a me, che al porto torno
da l'unda aspra e falace,
la chiara face   che mi dà lumera

E qual al peregrin de nimbi carco
doppo notturna pioggia e fredo vento
se mostra al sole averso il celeste arco,
che sol de la speranza il fa contento,
tal quel Sol ch'io credea che fusse spento
or più che mai me piace,
e più vivace   è assai che già non era.

38

Cum Misisset Loculum Auro Textum

Grazïoso mio dono e caro pegno
che sei de quella man gentil ordito
qual sola può sanar quel che ha ferito
e a la errante mia vita dar sostegno,

dono amoroso e sopra l'altri degno,
distinto in tante parte e colorito,
perché non è con teco il spirto unito
che già te fabricò con tanto inzegno?

Perché non è la man legiadra teco?
perché teco non son or quei desiri
che sì te han fatto di beltate adorno?

Sempre ne la mia vita sarai meco,
avrai sempre da me mille sospiri,
mille basi la notte e mille il zorno.

Just as it seems a comfort to all sailors,
after fortune's battered them about,
to see the stars, to see a calmer sea,
and land nearby, and the new day appear,

so am I comforted as I return
to port off harsh and treacherous waves
by that resplendent face that gives me light.

As to a pilgrim burdened by dark clouds,
after a night of rain and chilling winds,
a rainbow shows itself against the sun
and makes him happy by restoring hope,

so does that Sun appear which I thought spent;
it is more pleasing now
and far more brilliant than it ever was.

Just as it seems . . . : cf. *Orlando Innamorato*, III.1.

38. Sonnet 31

After She Sent a Little Gold-Embroidered Purse

You freely-given gift and precious token,
woven for me by that kind and gentle hand
which can, alone, restore what it has maimed
and give some meaning to my aimless life;

You gift of love, more worthy than all others,
distinguished by your rich design and color,
why is there not attached to you that spirit
which made you with such ingenuity?

Why is that graceful hand not here with you?
Why are those same desires not with you now
that made you then so beautifully adorned?

As long as I'm alive I'll have you with me;
you'll always have from me a thousand sighs,
a thousand kisses yours both night and day.

39

Già vidi uscir de l'onde una matina
il sol di ragi d'or tutto jubato,
e di tal luce in facia colorato
che ne incendeva tutta la marina;

e vidi a la rogiada matutina
la rosa aprir d'un color sì infiamato
che ogni luntan aspetto avria stimato
che un foco ardesse ne la verde spina;

e vidi aprir a la stagion novella
la molle erbetta, sì come esser sòle
vaga più sempre in giovenil etade;

e vidi una legiadra donna e bella
su l'erba coglier rose al primo sole
e vincer queste cose di beltade.

40

Ad Luciferum

Rendece il giorno e l'alba rinovella,
che io possa riveder la luce mia;
stella d'Amor che sei benigna e pia,
rendece il giorno che la notte cella.

Tu sei sola nel cielo ultima stella,
per te si sta la notte e non va via:
se non fusse per una, io pur diria
che dispetosa al mondo è chiunque è bella.

Rendece il giorno, ché il desir me strugge,
perché la mia speranza al giorno aspetto
e lo aspettar nel cor dentro me adugge.

Stella crudel c'hai del mio mal diletto,
ché ogn'altra fuor del ciel la luce fugge,
e tu ferma ti stai per mio dispetto!

39. Sonnet 32

I saw the sun one morning rise above
the waves, wearing a cloak of golden rays,
and with such radiant brilliance in its face
that all the sea was set aflame by it;

and then I saw beneath the morning dew
the rose unfold with colors so intense
that any distant eye would have perceived
a fire burning there amid green thorns;

and then I saw the tender shoots of grass
sprout in the first new season of the year
more lovely, as it is in all its youth;

and then I saw a fair and graceful lady
at sunrise picking roses on the green,
surpassing all these other things in beauty.

A Petrarchan vision poem; an example of *ekphrasis*.

40. Sonnet 33

To the Planet Venus, the Light-Bearer

Give us again the day, renew the dawn,
that I may gaze again upon my light,
You, star of Love, so kind and merciful;
give us again the day which night conceals.

You are the final star there in the sky;
because of you night stays and does not flee.
Save for one lady I would surely say
that every lovely thing is full of spite.

Give us again the day, for my desire
consumes me as I wait my hope at dawn,
and waiting casts dark shadows on my heart.

Cruel star that revel in my misery,
the others flee the light and leave the sky,
but you stand firm because you like to taunt me.

41

Questa matina nel scoprir del giorno
il ciel s'aperse, e giù dal terzo coro
discese un spiritel con l'ale d'oro,
di fiame vive e di splendor adorno.

—Non vi maravigliati s'io ritorno—
dicea cantando—al mio caro tesoro,
ché in sé non have il più zentil lavoro
la spèra che più larga gira intorno.

Quanto ablandisse il Celo a voi mortali
che v'ha donato questa cosa bella,
ristoro immenso a tutti e' vostri mali!—

Così cantando quel spirto favella,
battendo mòtti a le sue voce equali,
e tornasi zoglioso a la sua stella.

42

Chi non ha visto ancora il gentil viso
che solo in terra se pareggia al sole,
e l'acorte sembiance al mondo sole
e l'atto dal mortal tanto diviso;

chi non vide fiorir quel vago riso
che germina de rose e de vïole;
chi non audì le angeliche parole
che sonan d'armonia di paradiso;

che più non vide sfavilar quel guardo
che come stral di foco il lato manco
sovente incende, e mette fiamme al core;

e chi non vide il volger dolce e tardo
del süave splendor tra il nero e il bianco,
non scia né sente quel che vaglia Amore.

41. Sonnet 34

This morning as the day began to break
the sky was parted, and a little spirit
with golden wings descended from the third chorus,
adorned with lively flames and with bright splendor.

"Don't be surprised to see me now return,"
said he by means of song, "to my dear treasure,
for that great sphere that turns more widely round
possesses not a sweeter task than this.

How Heaven flattered you poor mortal beings
by giving you so beautiful a thing,
immense amends for all your other ills!"

Thus, singing, does that spirit make his speech,
stressing his steps so that they match his song,
then joyfully returns to his own star.

---

the third chorus: the chorus of angels (principalities) that presides over the third heaven, *i.e.*, the sphere of Venus.

that great sphere: the *primum mobile*, governed by the seraphim.

42. Sonnet 35

Whoever has not seen that gentle face,
the only thing on Earth that's like the Sun,
the proper beckonings, uniquely hers,
and gestures not like those of other mortals;

whoever has not seen her flowering smile
that sprouts from roses and from violets;
whoever has not heard her angel's words
which echo harmonies of paradise;

whoever has not seen that glowing glance,
which, often, like a blazing dart, will burn
the left-hand side, and then ignite the heart with flames;

whoever has not seen the sweet, slow turning
of quiet splendor framed by black and white,
knows not nor feels what worth there is to Love.

43

Somnium Cantu Unisono Trivoco

1. *Ancor dentro dal cor vago mi sona*
il dolce ritentir di quella lira;
ancor a sé me tira
la armonia disusata, e il novo canto
tanto süave ancor nel cor me spira
che me fa audace de redirne alquanto,
abenché del mio pianto
la dolce melodia nel fin ragiona.
Quando l'Aurora il suo vechio abandona
e de le stelle a sé richiama il coro,
poiché la porta vuol aprir al giorno,
veder me parve un giovenetto adorno,
che avea facia di rose e capei d'oro,
d'oro e di rose avea la veste intorno;
cinta la chioma avea di verde aloro,
che ancor dentro amoroso il cor gli morde,
ché l'amor perso eternamente dole.
Indi movendo il plectro su le corde
sì come far si sòle,
la voce sciolse poi con tal parole:

2. *—Quanto Natura imaginando adopra,*
quanto di bello in vista può creare,
ha voluto mostrare
in questa ultima etate al mondo ingrato;
né pòssi a tal belleza acomperare
il mio splendor, che il cielo ha illuminato,
e ciò che fu creato
primeramente, cede a l'ultima opra.
Tanto è questa beltate a l'altre sopra
quanto a noi Marte, e quanto a Marte Jove,
quanto a lui sopra sta l'ultima spera.
Formata fu questa legiadra fera
che paro in terra di beltà non trove,
perché il regno d'Amor qua giù non pèra.

framed by black and white: her eyes. Cf. Petrarch 29.23.

43. Canzone 3

Song About a Dream

1. Still does the sweetest echo of that lyre
resound within the chambers of my heart;
still does that harmony
most rare draw me to it; and that strange song
whispers so softly still within my heart
that it now makes me dare a bit to speak,
although it makes me weep,
of that sweet melody's concluding thought.
When Dawn abandoned her most-ancient mate,
and bid the chorus of the stars return,
wanting the portal opened to the day,
I seemed to see a richly-suited youth
with roses in his cheeks and golden hair,
with raiments trimmed with roses and with gold.
He had his locks bound up with verdant laurel,
and it constantly consumes his love-sick heart,
because he grieves forever his lost love.
Then, as he moved the bow across the chords,
as singers often do,
he gave vent to his voice with just these words:

2. "What, with imagination, she can do,
what beauty for the eyes she can create,
Nature wished to show
to this ungrateful world in these last days.
The splendor that is mine, by heaven painted,
cannot compare to beauty such as hers;
the earlier creation
must cede its place to this more recent work.
This beauty stands as high above all others'
as Mars to us, as Jupiter to Mars,
as heaven's highest sphere to Jupiter.
This fair creation, which can find no match
in beauty here on earth, was made so that
Love's kingdom would not perish here below.

Amor la sua possanza da lei move,
come tu senti e può vedere il mondo,
e più degli altri il cor tuo questo intende.
Quando Amor vien dal suo regno jocondo,
da questa l'arme prende,
perché sua forza sol da lei descende.

3. *Beato il cielo e felice quel clima*
sotto al qual nacque e quella regïone;
beata la stagione
a cui tanto di ben pervenne in sorte;
beato te, che a la real pregione
per te stesso sei chiuso entro a le porte,
ché non pregion, ma corte
questa se de' nomar, se ben se stima;
beati li occhi toi, che vedér prima
quel nero aguto e quel bianco süave
che a l'amorosa zoglia apre la via;
beato il cor che ogn'altra cosa oblia
né altro diletto né pensier non have
fuor che di sua ligiadra compagnia.
Quanto beata è l'amorosa chiave
che apre e dissera l'anima zentile
nel dolce contemplar de gli atti bei!
Fatto è beato e nobile il tuo stile
nel cantar di colei
che in terra è ninfa, e Diva è fra gli Dei.

4. *Quando costei dal cielo a vui discese*
una piogia qua giù cadea de zigli,
e rose e fior vermigli
avean di bel color la terra piena.
Non voglio che per ciò sospetto pigli,
ma al vero in cielo io mi rateni apena,
e in vista più serena
mostrai la zoglia mia di fuor palese.
Jove, che meco a mano alor se prese,
mirava in terra con benigno aspetto,
e fèsse a nostra vista il mondo lieto.
A noi stava summesso ogni pianeto,
fioria la terra e stava con diletto,
tranquillo il mare e il vento era quïeto.

Love gains from her the power that he had,
as you can feel, and as the world can see;
and your heart knows this more than any other.
When Love comes to us from his joyful realm,
he gets his arms from her,
because his strength can only come from her.

3. Blessed is that sky, and fortunate that clime
which saw her born, and fortunate that region!
Blessed is the season, too,
to which so rich a bounty came by chance!
And blessed are you who are enclosed alone
within the portals of that royal prison!
No prison, but a court
it should be called, in any true appraisal.
Blessed are your eyes, which were the first to see
those shades of deepest black and purest white
that open up the way to Love's sweet joys!
And blessed, too, is the heart that does forget
all else, and has no thought and no desire
except those born of her sweet company!
How blessed is the key which Love provides
to open and set free the gentle soul
that sweetly contemplates her charming ways!
Your style is made more noble and is blessed
when singing of the one
who is earth's nymph, and Goddess to the Gods.

4. When that fair lady came to you from heaven,
a shower of lilies fell upon this place;
vermilion blooms and roses
had covered all the earth with their fine hues.
I do not want to rouse your jealousy,
but I, in truth, could hardly stay in heaven,
and in my quiet look
I showed my joy to all without restraint.
Then, Jupiter, who took me by the hand,
looked down upon the earth with kindly eyes,
and all the world grew happy seeing us.
All planets were subservient to us,
the earth came into flower and was gay,
the sea was tranquil and the wind was calm.

Così a noi venne questo ben perfetto,
favorito dal Cielo e da le stelle
più che mai fusse ancor cosa formata.
Questa dal petto l'alma a te divelle:
ma se al ver ben se guata,
mal per te fo cotal beltà creata.

5. *Mal fo per te creata, il ver ragiono;*
sciai che io so Febo e non soglio mentire:
per farti alfin languire
venuta è in terra questa cosa bella.
Misero te che tanto hai da soffrire
da questa fera fugitiva e snella!
Miser, quanta procella
porrà ancor la tua barca in abandono!
E se io de lo advenir presago sono,
nulla ti giova lo amonir ch'io facio,
ché distor non te posso a chi te guida.
Tristo chi d'alma feminil se fida,
acciò che doppo il danno e doppo il straccio
sovente del suo male altri se rida!
Nel foco, che t'arde ora, vedo un giaccio
che te farà tremar l'osse e la polpa,
mancar il corpo e il spirto venir meno.
Non te doler de altrui, ché l'è tua colpa,
e tu lo vidi apieno
che dovevi al desir por prima il freno.—

Così cantava, e querelando al fine
la citera süave sospirava
voce più chetta e nòtte peregrine.
Qual vanitate noi mortali agrava!
Credere al sogno ne la notte oscura
ed al cieco veder dar chiara fede!
Ma benché io non sia sciolto da paura,
il mio cor già non crede
aver del suo servir cotal merzede.

Thus did the perfect good come unto you,
favored by Heaven and by all the stars
more than all others things till then created.
This being plucked the spirit from your breast,
but, if the truth be known,
such beauty was created for your grief.

5. Created for your grief: I speak the truth.
You know that I am Phoebus and lie not:
this lovely thing, in short,
has come to earth to drain you of your strength.
O wretched man, how much you'll have to suffer
because of this evasive, nimble creature!
poor you, how many storms
will ravage yet that little boat of yours!
And, if I can at all foretell the future,
the warning that I give will be no help,
since I cannot divert you from your guide.
Whoever puts his trust in woman's soul
is lost, for, after all the hurt and torment,
he often hears how others mock his grief!
I see now in the flame consuming you
an ice that will cause your flesh and bone to quake,
and make your body fail, your soul grow faint.
Do not blame others, for the fault is yours;
you saw it all quite clearly,
that it was up to you to curb your passion."

So did he sing, and at the end his cithern,
as though lamenting, softly sighed with voice
more tranquil and with notes more rare.
What vanity oppresses mortal beings,
believing in the dreams of darkest night,
and placing all our faith in blinded sight!
But even though I am not freed from fear,
my heart does not expect
to gain that kind of favor for its service.

Somnium cantu unisono trivoco: the heading for this title is not entirely clear. *Unisonus* apparently (it is not how Boiardo usually uses the term) refers to the repetition of rhyme in each stanza; there is no obvious explanation for *trivocus*.

44

Ocio amoroso e cura giovenile,
gesti legiadri e lieta compagnia,
solazo fuor di noglia e di folia,
alma rimota da ogni pensier vile,

donesco festegiar, atto virile,
parlar accorto e giunto a cortesia,
son quelle cose, per sentenzia mia,
che il viver fan più lieto e più zentile.

Chi così vise, al mondo vise assai,
se ben nel fior de gli anni il suo fin colse,
ché più che assai quel campa che ben vive.

Passata zoglia non se lassa mai;
ma chi pòte ben vivere, e non vòlse,
par che anzi tempo la sua vita arive.

45

Tornato è il tempo rigido e guazoso,
che la notte su crese e il giorno manca,
il ciel se anera e la terra se imbianca,
l'unda è concreta e il vento è rüinoso.

Ed io come di prima son focoso,
né per fredura il mio voler se stanca;
la fiama che egli ha intorno sì lo affranca
che nulla teme il fredo aspro e noglioso.

1.9, *When Dawn abandoned her most-ancient mate*: in Homer's *Odyssey* (5.1) Aurora (Dawn) is portrayed as rising each morning from the bed she shares with Tithonus to bring light to gods and mortals. Dreams at dawn were thought to be prophetic.

1.12, *richly-suited youth*: Apollo grieves for Daphne who has been transformed into a laurel tree. Cf. Ovid, *Metamorphoses*, Book One.

3.1ff, *Blessed* . . . : cf. Petrarch 61.

Phoebus: epithet that defines Apollo as god of the sun.

44. Sonnet 36

Love's idleness, the diligence of youth,
some gracious gestures, cheerful company,
escape from boredom and from folly's grip,
a soul removed from every wicked thought,

the merriment of women, deeds of men,
wise conversation joined by courtesy,
these are the very things, as I can tell,
that make our lives much richer and more joyful.

Whoever lived like this lived very well,
even though he met his end while in his prime,
for who lives well lives more than any other.

A past joy is a joy that's never lost;
but one who could live well and yet refuses,
would seem to steer life's craft to shore too soon.

Verse 12: cf. *Orlando Innamorato*, I.12.14.8.

45. Sonnet 37

The weather has now turned severe and damp,
the nights grow longer as the days grow short,
the sky is blackened and the Earth turns white,
the water's frozen and the wind is bitter.

Yet I, just as before, am all aflame,
nor is my will diminished by the cold;
the flame surrounding him so bolsters him
that he does not fear the harsh and biting cold.

Io la mia estate eterna haggio nel petto,
e non la muta il turbido Orïone
né Iàde né Pliàde né altra stella.

Scaldami il cor Amor con tal diletto
che verdegiar lo fa d'ogni stagione
che il suo bel Sole a li ochi mei non cella.

46

Flos Frigore Fractus

Che non fa il tempo infin? Questo è quel fiore
che fu da quella man gentile accolto,
e sì legiadramente ad oro involto
che eterno esser dovea di tanto onore.

Or secco, sanza foglie e sanza odore,
discolorito, misero e disciolto,
ciò che gli diè Natura il tempo ha tolto,
il tempo che volando afretta l'ore.

Ben se assumiglia a un fior la nostra etate,
che stato cangia da matino a sera,
e sempre va scemando sua beltate.

A questo guarda, disdegnosa e altera:
abi, se non di me, di te pietate,
aciò che indarno tua beltà non pèra.

I bear eternal summer in my breast,
and fierce Orion cannot alter it,
nor can the Hyades or Pleiades.

Love fills my heart with such delight and warmth
that it stays ever green in any season,
as long as its fair Sun still greets my eyes.

Orion, Hyades, Pleiades: a constellation and two star clusters that are most easily seen in the evening hours in the Winter months.

Orion ("Light of Heaven"): the great, handsome and boastful hunter of mythology mentioned in Homer's *Iliad*.

Hyades: daughters of Atlas and Aethera, and half-sisters of the Pleiades; a V-shaped cluster of five stars that outline the head of the constellation Taurus, the Bull (Zeus in the form of a bull). They are the "rainy stars" because in the Mediterranean they rise in the eastern sky in autumn (the rainy season).

Pleiades: the Seven Sisters, daughters of Atlas and Pleione; the seven stars form the Bull's shoulder. Their rising in May, it is said, announced the advent of the sailing season to ancient mariners. Thus, it is always summer in the lover's heart.

46. Sonnet 38

A Flower Shattered by the Cold

What, after all, can time not do? This flower
is the one picked by that kind and gentle hand,
and bound so gracefully with strands of gold
that, honored so, it should have lived eternally.

Now, dry, without its fragrance or its leaves,
discolored, pitiful, and free of bonds,
what Nature gave it time has soon removed;
that time which, rushing, makes the hours fly.

Our life is also something like a flower,
with its condition changing dawn to dusk,
with all its beauty waning as it goes.

Beware of this, you proud and haughty lady:
have pity now, if not on me, then on yourself,
in order that your beauty not be wasted.

47

Con qual piogia noiosa e con qual vento
Fortuna a lo andar mio si fa molesta!
Gelata neve intorno me tempesta
aciò che io giunga al mio desir più lento.

Ed io del ciel turbato non pavento,
ché per mal tempo il bon voler non resta,
ed ho dentro dal cor fiamma sì desta
che del guazoso fredo nulla sento.

Stretto ne vado in compagnia de Amore,
che me mostra la strata obliqua e persa
e fatto è guida al mio dritto camino.

Or mi par bianca rosa e bianco fiore
la folta neve che dal ciel riversa,
pensando al vivo Sol che io me avicino.

48

Io non scio se io son più quel ch'io solea,
ché 'l mio veder non è già quel che sòle;
veduto ho zigli e rose e le vïole
tra neve e giazi a la stagion più rea.

Qual erbe mai da Pindo ebbe Medea?
qual di Gargano la figlia del Sole?
qual pietre ebbe ciascuna e qual parole
che dimostrasse quel ch'io mo' vedea?

Io vidi in quel bel viso primavera,
de erbetta adorna e de ogni gentil fiore,
vermiglia tutta, d'or, candida e nera.

Ne l'ultima partita stava Amore
e in man tenea di fiame una lumera
che l'altri ardea ne li ochi, e me nel core.

47. Sonnet 39

With what a vexing rain and with what wind
does Fortune now impede me on my way!
She whips cold snow into a storm around me
to slow me down in reaching my desire.

But I am not afraid of troubled skies,
foul weather does not weaken my resolve;
I have a flame so vivid in my heart
that I don't feel the humid cold at all.

I make my way in Love's close company;
he shows which is the lost and twisted way,
and is the guide that keeps me straight on course.

The heavy snow that pours down from the skies
seems like white roses and white buds to me
when thinking of the living Sun that I am near.

Cf. poem 45 and the Provençal poet Bernart de Ventadorn's *Tant ai mo cor ple de joya* ("I have my heart so full of joy,/ that it confuses me./ The chill of winter seems/ like white, red and yellow flowers to me . . .").

48. Sonnet 40

I don't know if I'm still what I once was;
my way of seeing things is not the same,
for I've seen lily, violet and rose
amid the snow and ice of our worst season.

What herbs from Pindus did Medea have?
What did Sun's daughter get from Gargan's peak?
What magic stones, what words did either get
that showed to anyone what I have seen?

I saw fair springtime in that lovely face,
adorned with green and every noble bloom,
vermilion, gold, and black and white her colors.

And then I saw that Love was also standing there,
and in his hand he held a burning light
which shone in others' eyes, and in my heart.

49

Quando ebbe il mondo mai tal maraviglia?
Fiamma di rose in bianca neve viva,
auro che 'l sol de la sua luce priva,
un foco che nel spirto sol se impiglia,

candide perle e purpura vermiglia,
che fanno una armonia celeste e diva,
una altereza che è d'orgoglio schiva,
che ad altro che a se stessa non sumiglia.

Questo è il monstro ch'io canto sì giolivo,
dal qual lo inzegno e la alta voce piglio,
di cui sempre ragiono e penso e scrivo.

Questa è la augella da l'aurato artiglio,
che tanto me alcia che nel cielo arivo
a rivederla nel divin conciglio.

Pindus: a mountain range in Greece.

Medea: the enchantress who fell hopelessly in love with Jason and helped him accomplish his seemingly impossible task with the aid of a magic ointment of invulnerability.

Sun's daughter: Circe, also an enchantress in Greek mythology; sometimes said to be the sister of Medea who (unlike Medea) uses her magic powers for evil purposes. She often transformed her adversaries into monsters and animals. She figures prominently in the story of Odysseus.

Gargan's peak: Monte Gargano or the Gargano peninsula in Apulia; not far from Circe's island home in the Adriatic.

a burning light: his lady's eyes.

49. Sonnet 41

When has the world beheld so great a wonder?
A rose's flame alive in pure-white snow,
gold that deprives the sun of its bright light,
a fire that only catches in one's soul;

a rich vermilion and the whitest pearls
create a harmony which is divine;
a pride which is opposed to haughtiness
and bears resemblance to no other form.

This is the wonder that I praise so joyfully
from which I take my voice and inspiration,
of which I always think and write and speak.

This is the she-bird with the golden talons
that raises me so high I see her beauty
reflected there in Heaven's holy council.

A portrait of his lady.

the she-bird with the golden talons: a possible reference to the tale of Ganymede, who was transported to Olympus by Zeus transformed into an eagle (*aquila*, "eagle," being feminine in Italian). However, neither Virgil nor Ovid mentions golden talons.

50

Epthalogos Cantu Per Suma Deducto

1. *Quella amorosa voglia*
che a ragionar me invita
in rime ascose e crude
di lungi a la mia diva,
doni soccorso a la mia stanca mente,
poiché me fa parlare
come Madona fosse a me presente.

2. *Candida mia columba,*
qual è toa forma degna?
Qual cosa più somiglia
a la toa gran beltate?
Augella de l'Amor, segno di pace,
come deb'io nomarti,
che nulla cosa quanto te me piace?

3. *Arbosel mio fronzuto*
dal paradiso còlto,
qual forza di natura
te ha fatto tanto adorno
di schieto tronco e de odorate foglie,
e de tanta vagheza
che in te racolte son tutte mie voglie?

4. *Gentil mia fera e snella,*
agile in vista, candida e ligiera,
sendo cotanto bella,
come esser puote in te mai mente altera
né de pietà ribella?
Però se in cosa umana il mio cor spera,
tu sola in terra èi quella.

5. *Lucida perla colta ove se coglie*
di precïose gemme ogni richeza,
dove l'onda vermiglia abunda in zoglie
e sopra el lito suo le sparge entorno,
serà giamai ventura
che a me dimostri sì benigno il volto,
che da te speri aiuto?

50. Canzone 4

A Song in Seven Stanzas of Seven Verses

1. That amorous desire
that bids me to address
my Goddess at a distance
in crude and obscure verses,
may it give succor to my wearied mind,
helping to make me speak
as though my Lady were before me now.

2. Oh say, my snowy dove,
what form is worthy of you?
What thing does most resemble
your all-surpassing beauty?
You female bird of Love, you sign of peace,
what name shall I give you,
since nothing pleases me as much as you?

3. My leafy little tree,
captured from paradise,
what hidden power in nature
made you so well-adorned
with flawless trunk and leaves
so fragrant, with such beauty
that my desires are all contained in you?

4. My gentle, slender creature,
so sharp-eyed, light and candid,
being so beautiful,
how can it be that you possess a mind
that's proud and merciless?
Hence, if my heart's hope is in something human,
that something's you alone.

5. You shining pearl, found where the greatest wealth
of precious gems is ever to be found,
where crimson-colored waves abound with joys
and scatter them about upon the shores,
will chance someday allow
that you reveal a kinder face to me,
that I hope aid of you?

6. *Vago fioreto, io non ho vista audace*
che fissamente ardisca de guardarti;
perciò tua forma e il tuo color se tace,
ché tanta è tua belleza e nobiltate,
e di tal maraviglia,
che esser da noi cantata se disdegna,
e chiede magior trumba.

7. *Canzon, il cor mio lasso ormai se pente*
sua dona ad altro più rasumigliare,
ché sua beltate immensa no 'l consente.
Lassa che Amor con sua man la descriva
tra le tre Ninfe nude:
la voce lor diversamente unita
dimostri tanta zoglia.

51

Quello amoroso ben de ch'io ragiono
tanto è in sugetto nobile e soprano
che dimostrar no 'l pò lo inzegno umano,
però che al ciel non giunge il nostro sono.

Unde io la impresa più volte abandono,
vegendo ben che io me affatico invano,
ma pui, cacciato da desir insano,
nel corso già lassato ancor me sprono.

Così ritorno a ragionar d'amore
con mente ardita e con la voce stanca,
da ragion fiaco e punto da speranza.

Di questo pasco il deboleto core,
or di luce vermiglia ed or di bianca,
ché quel pensiero ogni diletto avanza.

52

Qualunque più de amar fu schiffo in pria
e dal camin de Amor più dilungato,
cognosca l'alegreza del mio stato,
e tornerase a la amorosa via;

6. O lovely flower, my sight's not bold enough
to dare to look at you with steady eyes;
I, therefore, do not praise your form and color,
since so much beauty and such nobleness,
so marvelous to see,
disdain the humble song I offer them,
and seek a brighter trumpet.

7. O song, my tired heart renounces all
attempts comparing her to other things,
because her boundless beauty won't allow it.
To Love's own hand he leaves it to describe her
with the three unclothed nymphs;
let their rich, varied voices, joined in song,
present such joyfulness.

51. Sonnet 42

That quality of Love of which I speak
abides in such a rare and noble being
that human wit cannot explain its nature,
because our human song does not reach heaven.

Thus do I so often quit the task,
seeing too well my struggle is in vain;
but then, pursued by a mad desire I spur myself,
once more to follow that abandoned course.

And so I turn to speak again of love
with a burning mind and with a tired voice,
weakened by reason and pricked on by hope.

This is the pasture of my faintish heart,
a light, sometimes vermilion, sometimes white,
because that thought surpasses every pleasure.

52. Sonnet 43

Whoever shied away at first from loving
and then was driven farther from Love's path,
let him but see the happiness I know
and he'll turn back upon the lover's way.

qualunque in terra ha più quel che ei disia,
di forza, senno e di belleza ornato,
qualunque sia nel mondo più beato,
non se pareggia a la fortuna mia:

ché il legiadro desire e la vagheza
che dentro mi riluce nel pensiero
me fan tra l'altre gente singulare.

Tal che io non stimo la indica richeza
né del gran re di Sciti il vasto impero,
che un sol piacer de amor non può aguagliare.

53

La smisurata ed incredibil voglia
che dentro fu renchiusa nel mio core,
non potendo capervi, esce de fore,
e mostra altrui cantando la mia zoglia.

Cingete il capo a me di verde foglia,
ché grande è il mio trionfo, e vie magiore
che quel de Augusto on d'altro imperatore
che ornar di verde lauro il crin si soglia.

Felice bracia mia, che mo' tanto alto
giugnesti che a gran pena io il credo ancora,
qual fia de vostra gloria degna lode?

Ché tanto de lo ardir vostro me exalto
che non più meco, ma nel ciel dimora
il cor che ancor del ben passato gode.

Whoever has what he desires most,
and is adorned with strength and wit and grace;
whoever in this world may be most blessed,
must not compare his fortune to my own,

because the sweet desire and sense of pleasure
that are reflected in my every thought
make me unique among all other persons,

so that I value neither Indian riches
nor the endless realm of Scythia's king,
which cannot equal one of love's delights.

Scythia: to the Greeks, the country between the Carpathian mountains and the Don river; later southern Russia. "There the group to which, strictly speaking, the term Scythian should alone apply, first founded a kingdom—Royal Scythia—on the lower reaches of the Dnieper." (*OCD*)

53. Sonnet 44

The boundless and incredible desire
that had been held a captive in my heart,
no longer fitting in that place, bursts forth,
and, singing, shows my joy to everyone.

So gird my head for me with leaves of green,
for great is now my triumph, and far greater
than that known by Augustus and like rulers,
whose locks are often wreathed with verdant laurel.

O happy arms that reached so high just now
that I hardly can believe that it is true,
what worthy praises are there for your glory?

I'm so exalted by your daring deed
my heart, which still rejoices over it,
no longer lives with me, but dwells in Heaven.

Cf. Ovid, *Amores*, II.12 and the closing ballad of day eight of Boccaccio's *Decameron*, which this poem imitates (*SC*, *U*).

54

Ben se è ricolto in questa lieta danza
ciò che può far Natura e il Cielo e Amore;
ben se dimostra a' nostri ochi di fuore
ciò che dentro dal petto avean speranza.

Ma quella dolce angelica sembianza
che sempre fu scolpita nel mio core,
è pur la stella in cielo, in prato il fiore,
che non che l'altre ma se stessa avanza.

Il süave tacer, il star altero,
lo accorto ragionar, il dolce guardo,
il perregrin dansar ligiadro e novo,

m'hano sì forte acceso nel pensiero
che sin ne le medole avampo ed ardo,
né altrove pace che in quel viso trovo.

55

Sazio non sono ancora e già son lasso
de riguardar il bel viso lucente,
che racender poria l'anime spente
e far l'abisso d'ogni noglia casso.

Qual alma più villana e spirto basso
de lo amoroso foco ora non sente,
che fuor vien de quelli ochi tanto ardente
che può scaldar d'amor un cor di sasso?

Fiamelle d'oro fuor quel viso piove
di gentileza e di beltà sì vive
che puon svegliare ogni sopito core.

Da questa gentil lampa se commove
quanto parlando mostra e quanto scrive,
quanto in sé coglie il mio pensier d'amore.

54. Sonnet 45

Gathered together in this merry dance
are all that Nature, Love and Heaven combine;
what hope had kept alive inside my breast
has been presented now before our eyes.

Indeed, that sweet, angelic face of hers,
which always had been sculpted in my heart,
is, too, that star above, that flower afield
that honors others and itself as well.

Her sweet decorum and her noble bearing,
her subtle reasoning and her gentle glance,
her novel, lively dancing all about,

have kindled such a fire within my thought
I'm burning to the marrow of my bones,
and find no peace except within her gaze.

Nature, Love and Heaven combine: "Nature, which created the body; Heaven, from which the soul descended; Love, which caused such beauty to be inflamed by it." (*ST*)

55. Sonnet 46

I have not had my fill, although I'm weary
from gazing at her lovely, radiant face,
which could rekindle an expired soul
and empty Hell's abyss of every pain.

What lowly spirit or what barbarous soul
is there that now feels not the amorous flame
which issues from those eyes so ardently
that it can warm a heart of stone with love?

Those eyes pour forth their little golden flames
so filled with beauty and nobility
that they can waken any stifled heart.

As much of love as my own thoughts can reap
and then display in speaking and in writing,
proceeds directly from this noble light.

56

Chorus Duplex Unisonus

Chi crederebbe che si bella rosa
avesse intorno sì pungente spine?
Chi crederebbe ascosa
mai crudeltate in forme sì divine?

Merita tal risposta la mia fede?
Convense a cortesia
scaciar da sé colui che mercé chiede?

Forsi de lo arder mio tanto non crede?
Ma già la fiamma mia
fatta è tanto alta che ciascun la vede.

Obliquo fàtto e mia fortuna ria,
da qual cagion procede
che a me costei sia cruda, a l'altri pia?

Ma sia, se vuol, crudele: io non poria
mai desperar mercede,
né abandonar quel che il mio cor desia.

Perfetto amor ogni dispetto oblia:
serà ancor tempo forsi anci il mio fine
che a mie pene meschine
pace conceda l'alma grazïosa.

57

Io sono e sarò sempre quel ch'io fui,
e se altro esser volesse, io non potrei:
lo amor, la fede e tutti e' penser mei
e tutta mia speranza ho posta in vui.

Né dar poriame, se io volesse, altrui,
né loco né credenza trovarei;
sansel gli omini in terra, in cielo e' Dei
dove raposta è la mia spene e in cui.

Servo me vi son fatto, e non mi pento,
né pentirò giamai, se 'l foco e l'onde,
se con le nube non fa pace il vento,

56. Ballata 4

A Ballata Grande with Recurrent Rhyme

Who would believe that such a lovely rose
could be surrounded by such prickly thorns?
Who would believe that cruelty
would ever hide in such a heavenly form?

Is such an answer due my faithfulness?
Does courtesy require
that one who asks for mercy be rebuffed?

Perhaps she thinks my passion's not so great?
And yet my flame has grown
so high by now that everyone can see it.

Oh unjust fate, and fortune so unkind!
What reason does require
that she be cruel to me, and kind to others?

But let her, if she will, be cruel; I never
could lose hope of mercy,
nor abandon what my heart desires.

A perfect love dismisses all abuses:
perhaps before my end there still is time
to let that gracious soul
confer her peace on my grim suffering.

57. Sonnet 47

I am and always will be what I was,
and, wanting to be otherwise, I couldn't,
for I have posited my love, my faith,
and all my thoughts, and all my hope in you.

I couldn't surrender freely to another;
nor would I be received or be believed.
On earth men know it, the gods in heaven too,
just where my hope is hidden, and in whom.

Your servant I've become; I do not now
nor ever will regret it; not till fire
and water, clouds and wind declare a peace;

se 'l sol la luce al giorno non asconde,
se in guerra non congiura ogni elemento,
se 'l mar la terra e il ciel non se confonde.

58

Come esser può che a nui se obscuri il sole
per così poca nube e poco obietto?
Come puote esser che 'l benigno aspetto
non se dimostra a noi pur come il sòle?

Se sua sia la cagione, assai me dole;
se mia, vie più di doglia ha il gran dispetto.
O voglia ardente, o disïoso affetto,
come conduci altrui dove ei non vole!

Nui pur vediamo il cielo e le sue stelle,
la luna, il sole, e ne' celesti chiostri
il vago lampegiar de gli alti segni:

Dio fece al mondo le sue cose belle
per dar più de diletto a li ochi nostri:
e tu de esser mirata te desdegni?

59

Se 'l mio morir non sazia il crudo petto,
ribella de pietade, or che più chiedi,
poi che condutto son, come tu vedi,
che sol da morte il mio soccorso aspetto?

Ben pòi del mio languir prender diletto,
ma non sarà giamai quel che tu credi,
che discaciar me possi dai toi pedi
per sdegno, per orgoglio, on per dispetto.

until the sun denies the light to day,
until all elements conspire in war,
until the sea and earth and sky are blended.

An example of *adynaton.* "In Gr. and L. literature the two most common varieties are the 'sooner-than type' bringing out that the impossible will come true sooner than that which is mentioned by a person will take place, and the 'impossible count' type referring to the numbers of sands on the shore, the stars in the sky, pebbles on the beach, waves in the sea. . . . [They were] abundantly revived by Petrarchists all over Europe." (*EPP*) A variant form was popular among the Provençal poets and was used by Petrarch. Cf. Giraut de Bornelh's *Un sonet fatz malvatz e bo* and Petrarch 134.

58. Sonnet 48

How can the sun be so obscured for us
by clouds so thin and by so small a thing?
How is it that the kindly countenance
does not reveal itself, as is its wont?

If she's to blame, it grieves me very much;
if mine's the fault, more painful the contumely;
O ardent wishes, O desirous passion,
how you do lead one where he would not go!

We rightly see the sky and all its stars,
the moon, the sun, and, in celestial cloisters,
the lovely spark of all the other wonders.

God made all things of beauty in this world
to give a greater pleasure to our eyes,
and you would now disdain to be admired?

59. Sonnet 49

If my death can't sate your cruel breast,
what more do you ask, you enemy of mercy,
since I am martyred so, as you can see,
that I expect relief from Death alone?

Well may you take delight in my undoing,
but never will it be as you may think,
that you can bar my being at your feet
by means of anger, pride, or spitefulness.

Teco sarà il mio core e morto e vivo,
né lungo tempo cangiarà desio,
se in mille forme l'anima mutasse.

Se del tuo amore a torto ben son privo,
se discaciato a torto, e che posso io?
Ma chi poria mai far che non te amasse?

60

Fin qui me è parso fresca rosa il foco,
fresca rogiada il lacrimar de amore,
süave vento è parso al tristo core
il suspirar, e il lamentar un gioco.

Or più nel gran martìr non trova loco
il cor dolente e l'anima che more,
la anima aveza a stare in quello ardore
che dentro la consuma a poco a poco.

Misero mio pensero, a che pur guardi?
Guardar dovevi alor, quando alla rosa
la man porgesti, e paventar le spine.

Ch'or pur, lasso, comprendo, abenché tardi,
che da giovenil alma e desïosa
lo amor non se cognosce insino al fine.

Finis

My heart, alive or dead, will be with you,
nor will it change its passion over time,
even though my soul would change a thousand times.

If I am wrongfully denied your love,
and wrongfully expelled, what can I do?
But who could ever halt my loving you?

---

you enemy of mercy: cf. 33.5.14.

60. Sonnet 50

Till now the fire has seemed a budding rose
to me, the tears of love fresh morning dew;
my sighs have seemed a gentle breeze to my
sad heart, my lamentations but a game.

Now, in this martyrdom my doleful heart
and dying soul no longer find a home,
not even my soul, accustomed to this flame
that inwardly consumes it bit by bit.

Why do you now stand guard, O wretched thoughts?
You should have guarded when you let my hand
reach for the rose, and should have feared its thorns.

So now, though late, alas, I understand
that when a soul is youthful and desirous
it cannot know what Love is till the end.

End of Book One

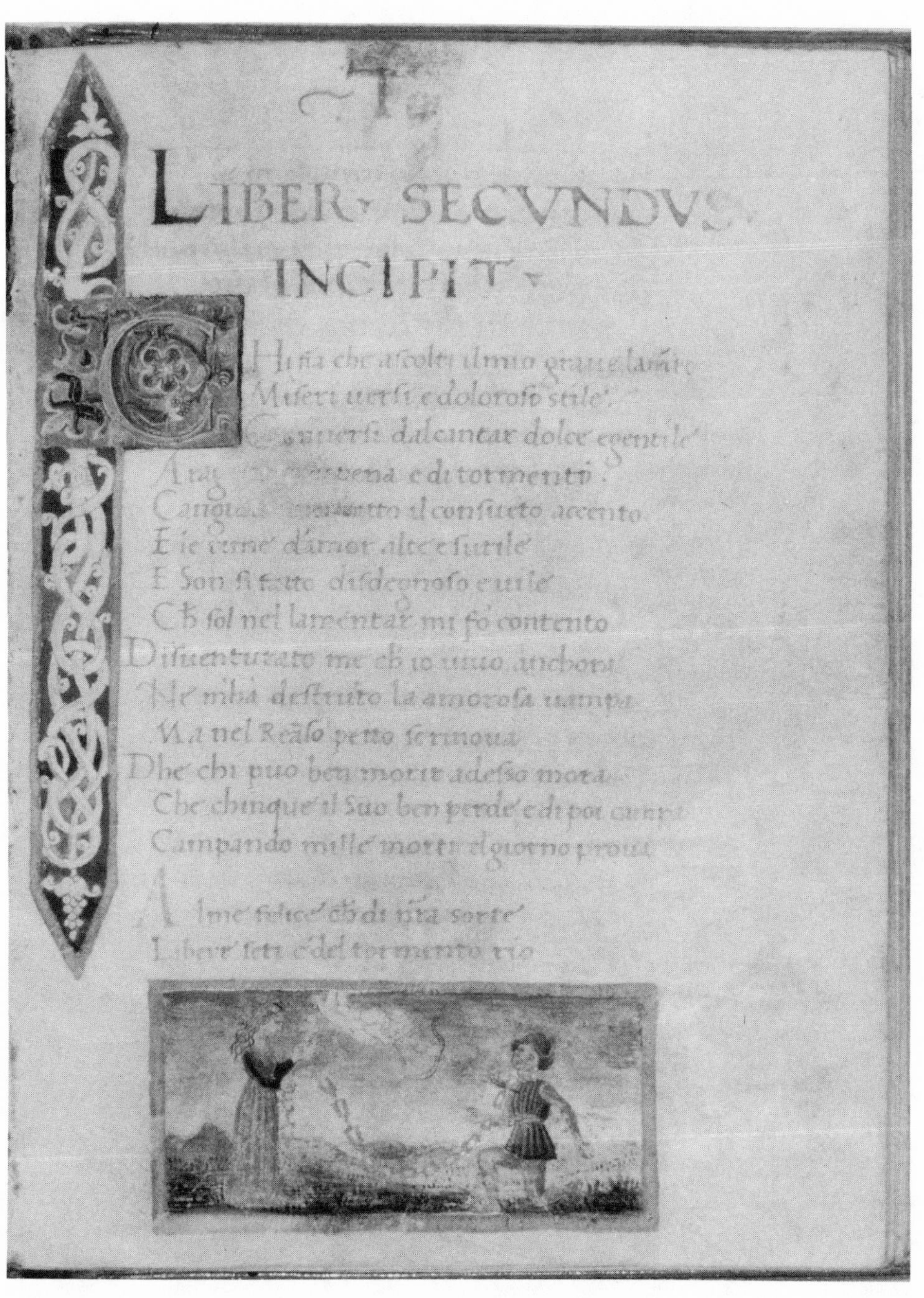

Biblioteca Nazionale Marciana (Venezia), MS. It. IX,545 (= 10293), f. 31r

Amorum Liber Secundus Incipit

61

Chi fia che ascolti il mio grave lamento,
miseri versi e doloroso stile,
conversi dal cantar dolce e gentile
a ragionar di pena e di tormento?

Cangiato è in tutto il consüeto accento
e le rime d'amor alte e sutile;
e son si fatto disdegnoso e vile
che sol nel lamentar mi fo contento.

Disventurato me, che io vivo ancora,
né m'ha destrutto la amorosa vampa,
ma nel rearso petto se rinova!

Deh, chi può ben morir, adesso mora:
ché chiunque il suo ben perde e dipoi campa,
campando mille morte el giorno prova.

62

Alme felice, che di nostra sorte
libere seti e del tormento rio,
fugeti Amor, e per lo exemplo mio
chiudeti al suo venir anti le porte.

Men male è ogni dolor, men mal è morte
che il cieco labirinto di quel dio;
credeti a me, ché experto ne sonto io,
che cerco ho le sue strate implexe e torte.

Fugite, alme felice, il falso amore,
prendendo exemplo de la mia sagura,
stregneti il freno al desïoso core.

Beginning of Book Two

61. Sonnet 51

Who is there that will hear my grave lament,
my wretched verses, and my doleful style,
converted from a sweet and gentle song
to messages of torment and of pain?

My usual tone has been completely changed,
as have my love-rhymes, once sublime and light;
and I've become so bitter and so base,
I find contentment only in laments.

It's my misfortune to be still alive;
I have not been destroyed by passion's flame,
but it rekindles in my oft-burned breast!

Let him who can die well accept his death;
for one who loses all, and then lives on,
in living dies a thousand deaths each day.

62. Sonnet 52

You happy souls, all you who are still free
of our grim fate and of our baleful torment,
flee Love, let my lot serve as your best guide;
secure your doors before he reaches you.

Less harsh are other pains, less harsh is death
than that god's dark and gloomy labyrinth;
believe me, for in this I am well versed,
since I have searched his winding, tortured paths.

Flee, happy souls, from love's deceptiveness,
taking my own misfortune as your cue;
pull hard the reins that curb your yearning hearts.

Prendeti exemplo, e prendavi paura,
ché il caso è più crudel tanto e magiore
quanto saliti più seti in altura.

63

Dove deb'io le mie querele ordire?
dove deb'io finire e' mei lamenti?
Da gli passati oltragi on da' presenti?
dal nuovo duol on dal primo languire?

Ché destinato ho al tutto de scoprire
l'aspra mia noglia e i dolorosi stenti;
forsi pietà ne avran qualche altri genti
odendo la cagion del mio morire.

Questo riposo fia de mia fatica,
e fia de l'almo afflita alcun conforto
al smisurato duol che 'l cor me inchiava,

se alcun sarà che sospirando dica:
—Questa donna crudiel diede a gran torto
amara pena a chi dolce la amava.—

64

Voi che intendeti tanto il mio dolore
quanto mostrar lo può mia afflitta voce,
mirati a quel ardor che 'l cor mi coce,
se mai nel mondo pena fu mazore.

Per dritto amar e per servir di core
son preso, flagellato e posto in croce,
e servo un cor sì rigido e feroce
che me tormenta in guidardon de amore.

Né il Ciel prende pietà del mio martìre
né pietà prende Amor che 'l cor mi vede
né quella che è del mal prima cagione.

Quanto felice a quel saria il morire
che pena in doglia, e altri non gli crede
né porta al suo penar compassïone!

Make use of my example—be afraid:
the greater and more painful is the fall,
the more you climb to reach a higher place.

63. Sonnet 53

Where should I start in stating my complaints?
How should I put an end to my laments?
With past offenses or with present wrongs?
With newer grief or with my early pining?

I am determined to expose completely
my bitter anguish and my painful trials;
perhaps some others will have pity when
they hear the reason given for my dying.

This will be consolation for my toil,
and for my anguished soul a remedy
against the wanton pain that pounds my heart,

if someone, sighing, will be heard to say:
"This cruel woman did unjustly give
but bitter pain to one who loved her sweetly."

64. Sonnet 54

All you who comprehend so well my pain,
as much of it as my grieved voice can show,
think of the passion that consumes my heart,
and if the world has known worse suffering.

For steadfast love and service from the heart,
I'm seized and whipped and placed upon a cross;
I serve a heart so rigid and so fierce
it trades the gift of pain for that of love.

Not Love, who sees my heart, nor Heaven above
expresses pity for my martyrdom,
nor she who is first cause of all my ills.

How happily would death arrive for one
who dwells in sorrow; yet no one believes
or brings compassion to his suffering.

65

E' miseri pensieri ancora involti
nel foco de la antiqua vanitate,
membrando il tempo e le cose passate
ed al lieto zoir dove son tolti,

me son radutti intorno al cor sì folti
di pianti e di querele disusate
che un saxo farian romper di pietate,
ma ben non trovan chi sua pena ascolti.

Ché il cor per longa doglia è fatto un marmo
né e' pietosi pensier se tene avanti,
ma disdegnoso intorno a sé gli scaccia.

Onde io la vita mia più non risparmo,
ma giorno e notte me consumo in pianti
per far questa crudel del mio mal sazia.

66

Corus Sinplex

Dapoi ch'io son lassato
da quello amore che già me fu jocondo,
che degio far più sconsolato al mondo?

Tempo è ben da morir, anci è passato;
morir dovea in quel punto
che da me se divise l'alma mia.

Or qui, contro a mia voglia, pur son giunto,
misero, abandonato
fuor che da vita, e lei lasciar voria.

Ahi, crudel sorte e ria,
come deposto m'hai da cima al fondo!
Doppo il primo morir manda il secondo!

65. Sonnet 55

My wretched thoughts, which are enveloped still
by flames born of that ancient vanity,
remembering the times and things now past
and all the joy from whence they have been plucked,

have crowded 'round my heart so densely filled
with unaccustomed cries and strange laments
they'd cause a rock to rupture with despair,
but cannot find one soul to hear their wails.

For constant grief has turned my heart to stone,
and does not keep compassion's thoughts close by,
but chases them disdainfully away.

So I no longer seek to spare my life,
but waste myself both day and night in tears,
to sate this unkind woman with my grief.

66. Ballata 5

Ballata Mezzana

Since I have been forsaken
by that love that was so full of joy for me,
why go on living so disconsolate?

The time to die has surely come; no, passed:
I should have died back when
my soul became divided from my self.

So now, against my will, I've reached this point,
a wretch, abandoned by all
except by life—the one that I would leave.

Alas, cruel, wicked fate,
from highest peaks you've forced me to the depths!
So send, after the first, a second death!

The time to die has come: cf. Petrarch 268.2.

67

—Se pianti né sospiri Amor non cura,
né per chieder mercé pietà se aquista,
a che più querelarsi, anima trista,
e farci vita breve e fama oscura?

Tacita passi nostra gran sciagura,
ché tal beltà per noi mal fòra vista,
se eterno in questa vita ne contrista
e ne l'altra lo onor e il Ciel ne fura.—

—Deh, come leve n'escon le parole!
come e' fatti a seguir son gravi e lenti!
come altri ben conforta chi non dole!

De tanto mal non vòi che io me lamenti
né che io contrasti a quel che il Ciel non vole:
ma taci tu che del mio mal non senti!—

68

Dapoi che Amor e lei pur vol che io pèra,
lei che me occide in guiderdon de amore,
altro rissor non trova il tristo core
che il lamentarsi da matino a sera.

Così dal bianco giorno a notte nera
sfogo piagnendo l'alto mio dolore,
che sempre lamentando vien magiore,
poiché soccorso da Pietà non spera.

Indi de pianto li ochi mei son pieni
sempre, e di voce sospirosa il cielo,
e de rime dogliose le mie carte;

e saran sempre, insin che 'l mortal gielo
il caldo spirto mio da me non parte,
ché ben son gitti e' mei giorni sereni.

67. Sonnet 56

"If Love has no respect for tears and sighs,
and pity is not gained by begging mercy,
why, melancholy Soul, go on complaining,
thus shortening life and letting fame be dimmed?

Let's let our great misfortune pass in silence;
seeing such beauty will have been our ruin
if, in this life, it constantly brings grief,
and robs us in the next of Heaven and honor."

"Alas, how light the words are as they issue!
How ponderous the deeds, and slow to follow!
How one who suffers not is quick to comfort!

You want me not to rail at so much sorrow,
and not object for all that Heaven denies?
No, you be still, for you don't feel my pain!"

A dialogue with his Soul.

68. Sonnet 57

Since she and Love both want to see me perish
(she, who slays me in exchange for love!),
my saddened heart cannot find other refuge
except in its lamenting day and night.

From daylight's brightness to the black of night
I ease my deep-felt grief with woeful weeping,
because laments are always more pronounced
when one no longer hopes for Pity's aid.

My eyes, therefore, are always full of tears,
and all the sky contains my sighing voice,
and all my pages bear my doleful rhymes;

So shall it be, until the chill of death
has driven my ardent spirit out of me,
for surely all my tranquil days are gone.

69

Aequivocus

Tanto è spietata la mia sorte e dura,
che mostrar non la pòn rime né versi,
né per sospir on lacrime che io versi
costei se intenerisse on men se indura.

Passan le voce, e il duolo eterno dura
ne' spirti che a doler tutti son versi;
dal ciel la luna pòn detrare e' versi,
né mover pòn questa alma ferma e dura!

Per questo odio le rime e il tristo canto,
nel qual dolendo ormai tropo me atempo
né porgo al mio dolor alcun aiuto.

Odio me stesso e il mio cantare, e canto
rime forzate per vargare il tempo,
e con la voce il suspirar aiuto.

70

Ingrata fiera, ingrata e scognoscente
de lo amor che io te porto e te portai,
vedi a che crudo stracio giunto m'hai,
ingrata fiera, fiera veramente.

Se la dureza tua pur non si pente
di voler consumar mia vita in guai,
mira nel viso mio se ancora assai
de li ochi tristi son le luce spente;

mira, crudel, se ancor non ha' ben colto
del mio languire, e la mia tanta pena,
e il piagner tal che più piagner non posso;

mira che più non ho colore in volto
né spirto in core, e non ho sangue in vena
né umor ne li ochi né medolla in osso.

69. Sonnet 58

An Equi-vocal Poem

My fate is so inflexible and harsh
it cannot be conveyed by rhyme or verse,
nor do the sighs and tears that I pour out
move her to pity me or be less cruel.

The voices die but mourning will endure
in all those souls that are in anguish versed;
the moon can be pulled from the sky by verses,
but they can't move this soul so fierce and hard.

I, therefore, hate my rhymes and my sad song,
in which, alas, while grieving, I grow old;
nor do I bring relief to suffering.

I hate my song and my own self; I sing
forced rhymes to pass away the time,
and with my voice my sighing I relieve.

An Equi-vocal Poem: here, in the Italian text, the same rhyme-words are used with varied meanings, while in sonnet 79 (poem 83) the meanings do not change (*SC*).

70. Sonnet 59

Ungrateful beast, ungrateful and unthankful
for the love I bore and still do bear,
see now to what cruel torture you have led me,
ungrateful beast; you truly are a beast!

If your hard-heartedness does not regret
wanting to have me waste my life in woe,
look, nonetheless, into my face and see
whether the light of my sad eyes is spent.

See, cruel Lady, if you've understood
my languishing, the depth of pain I feel,
such weeping that I can no longer weep.

See that I have no color in my face,
no spirit in my heart, no blood or tears
in veins or eyes, no marrow in my bone.

71

Cantus Intercalaris Rithmo Intersecto
(Ternarius Enim Tetralogon Dividit)

1. *Se il Cielo e Amore insieme*
destinan pur ch'io mora
e gionta è l'ora che mia vita incide,
queste mie voce extreme
almanco sieno intese
e sian palese a quella che me occide.
Ma a che, se lei se 'l vede e se ne ride?
Ché aperta è ben mia doglia
a quella fiera che 'l mio cor conquide;
ed essa, che mi spoglia
e vita e libertade,
non ha pietade del martìr ch'io sento.
Insensata mia voglia!
Ché doler mi convene
e sazo bene che io mi doglio al vento.
Odi, superba e altera, le mie pene,
odi la mia rason sol una volta,
prima che morte al crudo fin mi mene.

2. *Se a te non è quella memoria tolta*
che aver solea quella anima gentile,
se la tua mente al tutto non è involta,
come è scordato il dì quarto de Aprile,
quandro mostrasti aver tanto diletto
de lo amor mio, che adesso è tanto vile?
Tardi ho chiarito il turbido suspetto
che finte erano alor tue parolette,
finta la voce e finto il dolce aspetto.
Deh, siano ambe due chiuse e maledette
le orechie mie che odirno tue parole
e il simplice voler che gli credette!
Con rose fresche e con fresche vïole
lassai gelarmi il sangue ne le vene,
che or dentro al cor giazato sì me dole.

71. Canzone 5

Discontinuous Song in Tercets and Quatrains with Intersecting Rhyme

1. If Heaven and Love together
do destine me to die,
and the hour is near
that will cut short my life,
at least let these last words
of mine be understood,
let them be known
to her who wants me dead.
But why, —if, seeing them, she merely laughs?
For my suffering is clear
to that untamed beast that vanquishes my heart;
and she, who takes away
my life and liberty,
does not show pity
for the torment that I feel.
Oh what a foolish passion!
For I am made to wail,
and well I know
I wail into the wind.
Now hear my grieving, proud and haughty lady,
and listen to my reasoning just this once,
before death leads me to its bitter end.

2. If the memory your gentle soul once had
has not been taken fully from you now:
if your remembrance is not all obscured,
how can you have forgotten April fourth,
when you appeared to take such open pleasure
from the love I offered, which you now despise?
Too late did I expose the dark suspicion
that then your gentle words were merely feigned,
as were your tone of voice and charming ways.
Alas! Let both my ears that heard your words
be sealed and damned, and let be damned as well
my simple will that gave them so much credence.
I let fresh roses and fresh violets
turn all the blood that's in my veins to ice,
which now so pains me in my frozen heart.

Odi, superba e altera, le mie pene,
odi la mia rason solo una volta,
prima che morte al crudo fin mi mene.

3. *Tu m'hai lassato prèsso, e tu dissolta*
prendi vagheza del mio lamentare
che fa doler ogn'altro chi l'ascolta.
Ben te dovria lo arbitrio sol bastare,
che Amor te ha dato, de mia morte e vita,
ma l'un né l'altro non posso impetrare.
Tu tieni in ghiazo l'alma sbigotita,
il cor nel foco, il mio pensiero al vento,
né mia compagnia vòi, né mia partita.
A te par forsi un gioco il mio tormento,
che fresca te ne stai fra l'erba e il fiore,
né pòi sentir il gran fervor che io sento.
Mostrar pur te potess'io dentro al core,
ché, s'tu fussi di marmo, io tengo spene
che io te faria pietosa al mio dolore.
Odi, superba e altera, le mie pene,
odi la mia rason solo una volta,
prima che morte al crudo fin mi mene.

4. *Alma fallita e stolta,*
che segui ed hai seguito
chi t'ha tradito   sempre in falsa vista,
il tuo pensier rivolta,
e lassa questa luce
che te conduce   a notte oscura e trista.
Arme di Marte o inzegno di sofista
non pòno altrui mai tòre
la libertà, che co il voler se acquista.
Alma carca de errore,
che credi aver sofrenza
a la potenza   immensa, ben sei paza.
Or non sciai tu che Amore
la tua libertà tene?
E le catene   sue chi le dislaza?

Now hear my grieving, proud and haughty Lady,
and listen to my reasoning just this once,
before death leads me to its bitter end.

3. You've left me in my bonds, and you, unbound,
find your delight in hearing me complain,
while others, hearing me, are moved to tears.
The power alone which Love has given you
to grant me life or death should satisfy,
but my entreaties gain me neither one.
You've cast my poor, bewildered soul in ice,
my heart on flames, my thoughts upon the winds;
you neither want my presence nor my absence.
To you my torment may seem just a game,
as you sit coolly poised 'mid grass and flowers,
nor can you feel the fervor that I feel.
If I could let you see into my heart,
I'd have some hope, although you were of stone,
of making you responsive to my pain.
Now hear my grieving, proud and haughty Lady,
and listen to my reasoning just this once,
before death leads me to its bitter end.

4. Deceived and foolish soul,
that chased, and still now chase,
the one that has betrayed
with false appearances,
your thought rebels against you,
abandoning this light,
which leads you toward
a dark and mournful night.
The arms of Mars, or a clever sophist's wit,
cannot deprive another
of liberty gained by an act of will.
O soul weighed down by error,
thinking you can withstand
the mighty power
of Love, you're truly mad.
Do you not know that Love
controls your liberty?
And who will loose
the chains with which he binds?

Odi benigna adunque le mie pene,
odi li preghi mei solo una volta,
prima che morte al crudo fin mi mene.

5. *Prima che morte giunga, un poco ascolta*
con quella aria serena e dolce vista
che ha già del corpo mio l'anima tolta.
Se mai pietate per servir se aquista,
per ben servir con amore e con fede,
acquistata l'ha ben questa alma trista.
E se non l'ha acquistata, sua mercede
gli è retenuta, e dimanda ragione
a chi la tene ed aver se la crede.
Deh, cangia la ustinata opinïone,
candida rosa mia, rendime pace,
che mercé te dimando in genochione.
Soccorri a questo cor che se disface,
che per te sola lassa ogni altro bene
e sempre a' piedi toi languendo giace.
Odi benegna adunque le mie pene,
odi gli preghi mei solo una volta,
prima che morte al crudo fin mi mene.

6. *L'anima mia smarita e in sé racolta*
aspetta per risor quella risposta
che se conviene a sua fede, che è molta.
Quinci ha del viver la speranza posta,
stimando pur che non sarai disdire
quel che, campando lei, nulla a te costa.
E s'tu volessi forsi sostenire
la cosa in lungo, sapi e credi certo
che lungamente non porò soffrire.
Quanto ho possuto, tanto ho più sofferto;
tanto ho sofferto che l'alma ne crida
per non mostrarti il mio cor tutto aperto.
Nel tuo benegno viso ancor se anida
il spirto lasso; a quel sol se ratene
la debol vita e sol in quel se fida.
Odi benegna adunque le mie pene;
odi gli preghi mei solo una volta,
prima che morte al crudo fin mi mene.

Now hear my grieving and be kind to me,
and listen to my humble plea this once,
before death leads me to its bitter end.

5. Before death reaches me, I pray you listen
with that tranquil air and sweet appearance
that have deprived my body of its soul.
If ever mercy were obtained through service,
this anguished soul has surely earned its due
by serving well with love and faithfulness;
and if it has not gained its share of mercy,
it's wrongfully withheld; my soul demands
an explanation from the one who hoards it.
Do change your obstinate opinion, please,
my snowy rose, and give me back my peace,
for I am begging mercy on my knees.
Come, give assistance to this failing heart,
which has, for you, scorned every other prize,
and, languishing, is always at your feet.
Now hear my grieving and be kind to me,
and listen to my humble plea this once,
before death leads me to its bitter end.

6. My soul, withdrawn, discouraged and confused,
awaits the comfort given by the answer
its abounding faithfulness deserves.
In this it places all its hope of life,
hoping you will not know how to refuse
that which, though saving it, will cost you nil.
And, if by chance your aim is to prolong
this thing, I hope you know and do believe
that I'll not long endure the suffering.
I've suffered just about as much as possible;
so much so that my soul cries out because
it can't expose my heart to you completely.
My weary spirit seeks its refuge, still,
in your kind face; my failing life remains
attached to it, and has faith in no other.
Now hear my grieving and be kind to me,
and listen to my humble plea this once,
before death leads me to its bitter end.

7. *Se la vita me è tolta*
e per tua cagion manco,
il marmo bianco occulti il tuo fallire.
Così rimanga involta
la causa ne le tombe,
né mai rimbombe chi me fa morire.
Non voglio che per me se hagia a sentire,
né mai per mie querele,
né odito sarà mai per mio martìre.
—Qui giace quel fidele—
dirà mia sepultura,
—che un'alma dura pinse a mortal sorte.
Ben sei, lettor, crudele,
se lacrime non doni,
e le cagioni attendi de sua morte.—

72

Se quella altera me volesse odire
che tien le orechie al mio duol sì serate,
faria sentire un lago de pietate
nel misero contar del mio martìre.

Come potrebb'io lunga istoria ordire,
dal tempo che io perdei mia libertate,
dil grave gioco e de la crudeltate
che ognor me occide e vetami il morire!

7. If I'm deprived of life
and die because of you,
may the marble's whiteness hide
your cruel offense to me.
Thus may the cause remain
concealed deep in the tomb,
nor ever heard the name
of her who slays me.
I do not want to have it heard from me,
by way of my complaints,
nor will my sorrow cause it to be heard.
"Here lies that faithful man
(so shall my tomb declare)
whom a harsh soul
spurred to a grievous end.
You, reader, are quite cruel
if you don't shed some tears,
knowing the cause
that brings him to his death."

A number of compositions in Giusto de' Conti's *La bella mano* (numbers 147–149 and 151 in particular) may have served as the metrical model for this canzone. Mengaldo (*LBL*, 236) cites number 149, which is composed exclusively of tercets, as the likely model. I have followed Scaglione in presenting stanzas 1, 4, and 7 as sets of quatrains in the translation, but have kept the format of Mengaldo's Italian text to show that they can be read as sets of tercets with internal rhyme. The intersecting rhyme is like that of *terza rima*.

2.4, *April fourth*: the poet alludes on other occasions to having fallen in love in the spring; a day on which the lady gave him some sign of returning his affection.

72. Sonnet 60

If that haughty one who keeps her ears so sealed
against my mournful cry would only want to hear,
I'd bring her to compassion's deepest waters
with the sad recounting of my martyr's tale.

And what a lengthy history I could write,
beginning with the day of freedom's loss,
and with the cruel and painful game
which slays me slowly and denies me death!

Faria pietate a l'alme oscure e nigre,
dove a gran pena mai mercé se impetra,
ne le tenebre inferne orrende e basse;

faria pietate a un cor crudel de tigre,
a un crudel cor di drago, a un cor di petra;
faria pietate a lei, se me ascoltasse.

73

Più veloce che cervo o pardo o tigre,
più veloce che augello on che saetta,
fugito è ogni mio ben con tanta fretta
che io son tardo a seguir, benché già migre.

Spietate Parche, al mio troncar sì pigre,
come fugetti sempre chi ve aspetta,
ed a cui più nel mondo star diletta
drizati il viso e le man impie e nigre!

Alor viver dovea quando fiorire
vidi mia spene e lo amor mio novello,
libero ancor da scognosciuti inganni:

anci in quel tempo pur dovea morire,
ché ben felice e fortunato è quello
che pò fugir per morte tanti affanni.

74

Io ho sì colma l'alma de' lamenti
formati da lo extremo mio dolore,
che se io potesse ben mostrarli fore
li ochi piagner faria che morte ha spenti;

e benché io li abia forsi ancor depenti
ne la mia fronte in palido colore,
non sono intesi dal mondano errore,
né a dimostrar sua noglia son potenti.

I'd move the darkest-shaded souls in Hell,
where mercy hardly ever penetrates,
to pity in their deep and horrid gloom.

I'd move a tiger's savage heart to tears,
a dragon's cruel heart, a heart of stone;
I'd make my lady weep, if she would listen.

73. Sonnet 61

Much faster than a tiger, deer or leopard,
much faster than an arrow or a bird,
my happiness has fled with so much speed
that, even dying now, I cannot match the pace.

You spiteful Fates, so slow to end my life,
oh how you flee the ones who wait for you,
yet raise your heads and dark and wicked hands
to those who would most happily live on!

I should have lived back when I saw my hope
was flourishing, and when my new-born love
was yet unfettered by unknown deceits.

I, rather, should have died back in those days;
for one who can escape such trials by death
is truly fortunate and truly blessed.

You spiteful Fates: Greek *Moerae*, Roman *Fata* or *Parcae*; "they are Klotho, Lachesis, and Atropos: they distribute to mortal people what people have, for good and for evil." (Hesiod, *Theogony*, 905ff.)

74. Sonnet 62

My soul's so overflowing with laments
wrought by the endlessness of pain,
that, if I could express them to the world,
I'd make the eyes that Death has sealed shed tears.

And though I have them painted on my brow
in all of my complexion's pallid hues,
they are not understood by earth-bound souls,
nor do they have the power to show their grief.

Così meco rimanga nel mio petto
la angoscia mia, poi non posso mostrarla
né far noto ad altrui quel che mi dole:

perché, se io me conduco nel conspetto
de quella per cui formo le parole,
voce non ho né ardir pur di guardarla.

75

E' lieti soni e il bel dansar süave,
li abiti adorni e le legiadre gente
tanta tristeza danno a la mia mente
che ogn'altra noglia li forìa men grave.

Crudeli Idii, fu ben che già non ave
in odio e' canti e il suon tanto spiacente;
or parmi ogni alegreza un stral pungente
che in trista angoscia il cor dolente inchiave.

E son d'altrui zoir sì róto e lasso
ch'io porto invidia non che a li animali,
ma priego il Ciel che me converta in sasso.

Quai doli a le mie pene fieno equali?
ché io son in festa, e tengo il viso basso,
e porto odio a me stesso ne' mie' mali.

76

Misero me, che ogn'altro in lieta festa,
in lieti soni e danzie se diletta
e l'alma mia pensosa sta dispetta,
né dove è gente alegra mai se aresta.

Come stanco nochier, che da tempesta
afflitto a la rivera il corpo getta,
e benché l'unda mite se rasetta,
pur rasettata ancora gli è molesta,

il suon rumor, la danzia un andar sciolto,
il candido color mi pare adusto,
e vil quel guardo che altri ha tanto caro:

So let my anguish stay locked in my breast,
since I cannot express it to the world
or make my suffering well known to others:

because I find when I am face to face
with her for whom I fashion all my words,
I have no voice, nor dare to look at her.

75. Sonnet 63

The cheerful music and the graceful dance,
the splendid clothes and all the happy folks
create such depths of sadness in my mind
that any other pain would be less harsh.

Cruel Gods, time was when I did not detest
those songs and sounds that now displease me so;
now every joy seems like a piercing dart
that pins my aching heart to bitter grief.

And I'm so tired of others' joyfulness
that I don't even care to be a beast,
but beg that Heaven turn me into stone.

What suffering shall ever match my pain?
In gay festivity my head hangs low,
and I despise myself for all my woes.

76. Sonnet 64

Oh wretched me, the others all delight
in cheerful sounds of music and in dance,
while my unhappy soul remains apart
and never mingles with the happy crowd.

I'm like a weary helmsman, tempest-tossed,
who throws himself exhausted on the shore,
and, though the gentle waves are calm again,
still finds the water is disquieting.

To me the music's noise, the dance disordered
movement, and the color white seems parched;
that gaze so dear to them is vile to me.

così lo infermo da la febre colto
perde il sentire e lo usitato gusto,
e quel che è dolce altrui gli pare amaro.

77

Chorus Sinplex

A che più tanto affaticarti invano,
pensier insano? Quella che tu amavi,
e per cui tu cantavi,
te fuge come scognosciuto e strano.

Che meco ragiono io, misero lasso?
Come ancor quello amore
non me fosse nel core
che sempre vi de' star, se sempre vivo!

Se ella ha il mio cor da sé bandito e casso,
ben lo terà in dolore,
ma non che n'esca fore
amor, né che di lei possa esser schivo.

Piagnendo penso ciò, piagnendo il scrivo;
ché questa disdegnosa e gentil fera
tanto più se fa altiera
quanto più vede il servo esser umano.

78

O Cielo! o stelle! o mio destin fatale!
o sole a' dui Germani insieme giunto,
che in ora infausta ed infelice punto
me solvisti da l'alvo maternale!

Lo arbitrio contra voi nulla mi vale,
che libro meco fu da Dio congiunto;
anzi son sì da voi sforzato e punto
che, vedendo il mio ben, seguo il mio male.

Ma chi altri ne incolpo io se non me stesso?
E del mio fàtto a torto mi lamento,
ché io per me son ligato, e nacqui sciolto.

Just so the feverish invalid will lose
his sense of smell and usual sense of taste;
what others say is sweet to him seems bitter.

77. Ballata 6

Ballata Grande

Why go on wearying yourselves in vain,
you crazy thoughts? The one you used to love,
the one who made you sing,
avoids you now as though you were a stranger.

Poor wretch, what am I saying to myself?
As though that love were not
still there within my heart,
where it must stay as long as I'm alive!

If she has banned my heart from being near her,
she'll surely make it grieve,
but she can't drive my love
from it, nor force my heart to want to shun her.

Crying, I think these thoughts; crying, I write;
because this gentle but disdainful beast
is all the haughtier
the more she sees her servant's docile ways.

78. Sonnet 65

O Heaven above! O stars! O destiny!
O sun arriving in the Twins' domain,
that set me free to leave my mother's womb
at that unhappy point and luckless hour!

My will, that God had granted me as free,
is useless to me in opposing you;
indeed, I am so stung and weakened by you,
seeing what's good, I choose what does me harm.

But whom am I to blame if not myself?
I wrongfully complain of my sad fate,
for I, born free, have put myself in bonds.

Io non dovea tornar sì spesso spesso
a riveder quel che il veder m'ha tolto:
tardi il cognosco e tardi me ne pento.

79

Chi crederà giamai ne l'altra etade
(se in altra etade duraran mie voce)
che il foco, che in tal pena il cor mi coce,
non sia confinto e fuor di veritade?

Poco han di fede in noi le cose rade,
perché in forma süave un cor feroce,
in abito gentil l'animo atroce
son disusata e nova qualitade.

Ma pur è giunto insieme per mio male
quel che più mai non giunse la Natura,
benegna faza e di mercé ribella.

Qual novo moto e sopranaturale,
qual nobil sido aposto in parte oscura
tanto crudel la fece e tanto bella?

80

Itevi altrove, poiché il mio gran dolo
per voi non manca, o versi dolorosi;
versi ove ogni mio senso e cura posi,
itevi altrove, e me lasiati solo.

I should not have returned so frequently
to see the one who robbed me of clear sight;
I slowly see my error, and repent.

---

the Twins' domain: in the constellation Gemini (the twins Castor and Pollux); astronomical observation would put the poet's birth sometime in June or July, even accounting for the five centuries that have passed since the poem was written. (The sun currently passes through Gemini between June 21 and July 21, and the phenomenon known as 'precession' causes a displacement of the sun by one constellation approximately every two thousand years.) By reference to the astrological zodiac (a displacement of one constellation) rather than on the actual position of the sun, the poet would have been born in May or June (cf. *SC*, *U*).

79. Sonnet 66

Who will dare believe in later times
(if my words endure to later times)
that the fire that burns my heart so painfully
is not fictitious and beyond the truth?

We often disbelieve the rarer things,
because an untamed heart in gentle guise,
a savage mind attired in noble garb,
are of a strange and unfamiliar kind.

And yet, to my misfortune, we find joined
what Nature never has conjoined again:
a gentle face that is compassion's foe.

What sort of strange and supernatural force,
what noble star lost in obscurity,
made her so cruel and yet so beautiful?

80. Sonnet 67

Be gone, you doleful verses, for you fail
to lessen all the suffering I feel;
Verses in which I put my every thought
and care, be gone and let me be alone.

Voi già levasti il mio pensier a volo
quando furno e' mei giorni più gioiosi;
or che Fortuna e Amor me son retrosi,
ite, che a voi e a me stesso me involo.

Soletto piagner voglio il mio dolore,
ché ben soletta al mondo è la mia pena,
né pari in terra trova né magiore.

Chi me darà di lacrime tal vena
che agual se mostri nei mei pianti fore
a la cagion che a lacrimar mi mena?

81

Solea spesso pietà bagnarmi il viso
odendo racontar caso infelice
de alcuno amante, sì come se dice
di Piramo, Leandro e di Narciso.

Or sono in tutto da pietà diviso,
e porto invidia a lor beata vice,
ché, de lo amor scorgendo la radice,
vedo che il lor finir fu zoglia e riso.

Quel morì sotto il celso, e quello in mare,
quello a la fonte fu converso in fiore,
e Tisbe ed Ero e il suo desir fu sieco.

Qual duol al mio se puote assumigliare?
ché mi torei di vita esser già fore,
se pur sperasse morto averla meco.

You caused my thoughts to soar as though in flight
back when my days were filled will joyfulness;
now that Love and Fortune are against me,
be gone, for I would hide myself from me and you.

I want to mourn my suffering alone,
because my anguish roams the world alone,
finding no equal or superior.

Where will I find so great a gush of tears
that I can equal in my outward wails
the inner cause that leads me to such weeping?

81. Sonnet 68

Once pity often bathed my face with tears
hearing someone recount a woeful tale
about a lover, like the ones that tell
of Pyramus, Leander and Narcissus.

But now I'm thoroughly immune to pain,
and envy them their blessèd love-affairs,
for, looking at the roots of their desire,
I see that their result was joy and laughter.

One died beneath a mulberry; one died
at sea; one, by a fount, became a flower;
and Thisbe, Hero and self-love were there.

What suffering can be compared to mine?
For I would gladly choose to leave this life
if I could hope, in death, to have her near me.

Pyramus, Leander and Narcissus . . . Thisbe, Hero and self-love: cf. Ovid, *Metamorphoses*: Pyramus killed himself, thinking his beloved Thisbe dead; Thisbe killed herself upon finding Pyramus near death. Leander, the lover of Hero, swam the Hellespont nightly to visit her, but perished one night when he had no light to guide him; Hero drowned herself in the sea after learning of Leander's death. Narcissus, the handsome youth who spurned the love of Echo and thus caused her to waste away to nothing but a sound, wasted away himself and died of self-love because he could not leave his own reflection seen in a pool of water.

82

Alegoria Cantu Monorithmicho
Ad Gentiles Marietam Et Genevram Strottias

1. *Donne gentile, a vui ben se convene*
odir ciò che ragiona il tristo core,
novellamente preso da lo errore
che non l'occide e fuor di vita il tene.
A voi per parlar vosco se ne vene,
gentil donne e pietose,
che non seti orgogliose
come colei che spreza odir sue pene;
e bench'ormai desperi in terra aita,
piacer avrà che sua ragion sia odita.

2. *Odite come preso a laci d'oro*
fu il giovenil desir, che non sapea
che occidesser gli presi, anci credea
starsi zoioso fra quel bel lavoro.
Non avia visto a guardia de il tesoro
tra l'erbe il frigido angue,
tal che ancor ozi il sangue
nel rimembrar me agiela, e discoloro:
non avia visto il cor lo ascoso drago,
tanto d'altro mirar fatto era vago!

3. *Dolce m'è a rimembrar il tempo e il loco,*
e racontarlo a voi, come io fu' preso,
abenché il mio diletto in foco acceso,
e in giazo sia tornato ogni mio gioco.
Parrami pur che nel parlar un poco
se alenti il dolor mio,
e il gelato disio
vigor riprenda dal suo antiquo foco,
perché ne la memoria pur me aquieto,
ramentandomi il tempo che fu lieto.

4. *Splendeami al viso il ciel tanto sereno*
che nul zafiro a quel termino ariva,
quando io pervenni a una fontana viva
che asembrava cristal dentro al suo seno.

82. Canzone 6

An Allegorical Song for the Gentle Ladies Marieta and Genevra Strozzi

1. It truly does behoove you, gentle ladies,
to hear the tale which my sad heart now tells
as he succumbs again to error's ways,
which, though not killing it, deny it life.
To you, compassionate and gentle ladies,
it comes, to speak to you,
for you are not as proud
as she who deigns not hear its woeful plaint;
and though it now despairs of help on Earth,
it would be pleased to have its story heard.

2. So hear how youthful passion was ensnared
by golden strands, not knowing that they killed
their prisoners; it thought instead to find
its happiness within that well-wrought trap.
It had not seen the precious treasure's guard,
the cold snake in the grass
which, thinking back on it,
still chills my blood and causes me to blanch.
My heart, so smitten by another sight,
had failed to see that dragon hidden there.

3. To me, remembering the time and place
and telling you how I was caught is sweet,
even though my pleasure turned to fire,
and all my joyfulness was changed to ice.
It seems to me that as I speak of it
my pain is somewhat lessened
and my chilled desire
regains some vigor from its ancient flame,
because I find my peace in memories,
recalling by-gone days when I was happy.

4. The sky was shining so serenely on me
no sapphire can compare to it in beauty,
just as I came upon a living fountain
that seemed to be pure crystal at its center.

Verdegiava de intorno un prato pieno
di bianche rose e zigli
e d'altri fior vermigli,
tal che ne la memoria mia rendéno
queste Isole Beate, là dove era,
dove se infiora eterna primavera.

5. *A primavera eterna era venuto,*
al chiaro fonte che ridendo occide,
quando tra l'erba e' fior venir me vide
a lo incontro un destrier fremente e arguto.
Frenato era di fiamma, e bianco tutto,
e un fanciullo il regea
che tal ardir avea
che forza non curava o inzegno astuto;
custui con dardi caciando una fera
me fiè partir dal loco dove io era.

6. *Sì che vagando per bon tempo andai*
per quei bei campi e incogniti paesi,
sinché al prato arivai, dove eran tesi
e' laci che se ordirno per mie' guai.
Quel cavalier che io dissi, sempre mai
or dietro or nanti andando,
e talor saetando,
sfavilava da li ochi accesi rai;
ma io che tenea il scudo de Minerva
ridea secur la sua virtù proterva.

7. *Misero me, ché il tropo mio fidare*
di quella adamantina mia diffesa
me impose il carco adosso che or sì pesa,
e che in eterno mi farà penare.
Sprezando de il fanciulo il saetare,
co il scudo me copria,
e per sventura mia
li ochi a' bei laci d'or veni a voltare,
che mai più bella cosa vide il sole,
benché ogni giorno intorno al mondo vóle.

8. *L'esca atrativa sua, che fuor mostrosse*
di dolce umanità, mi fece sete
de pormi per me stesso ne le rete
de le qual più giamai mia vita scosse.

About it was a verdant field filled full
of lilies and white roses
and other crimson blooms,
so beautiful a place, there where I stood,
my mind compared it to the Blessèd Isles,
where spring remains in bloom eternally.

5. I had, there, come upon eternal spring,
before the crystal fount that, laughing, kills,
when facing me amid the grass and flowers
I saw a spirited and high-strung steed.
His bridle was like flame, and he pure white;
a boy was riding him
who had such confidence
he neither feared his strength nor craftiness.
That boy, hunting a wild beast with arrows,
forced me to leave the place where I had been.

6. So I went wandering for quite some time
about those lovely fields and unknown places,
until I came upon a meadow where
the snares that were to be my doom were laid.
That knight of whom I spoke before approached
from front and then from back,
at times with arrows flying,
and always with bright flashes in his eyes.
But I who held Minerva's shield in hand
just laughed securely at his bold attack.

7. Oh wretched me, placing my trust to much
in that impervious defense of mine,
I set upon myself the burden that I bear,
and which will make me grieve eternally.
Disdainful of that youth and of his arrows,
I hid behind my shield,
and my misfortune was
I turned my eyes toward lovely golden strands
fairer than anything the sun has seen
even flying round the world each day.

8. Her lure, which on the surface seemed to be
composed of sweet humanity, urged me
to throw myself upon the netted strands
from which it's never let my life shake free.

Quel falso caciator alor se mosse
in vista sì süave
che io gli deti la chiave
del core e dissi:—lo cedo a le tue posse,
né contra a te più mai diffesa prendo:
eccoti il scudo a terra, a te mi rendo.—

9. *Così dicëa, e sì me apparechiava*
possar per sempre ne li eterni odori
che de l'erbe gentile e dai bei fiori
süavemente il loco fuor spirava;
ma mentre che a le rose me apresava
(ancor tutto me agielo
ne la memoria, e il pelo
ancor se ariza, e il viso se dilava)
scorsi una serpe de si crudel vista
che sua sembianza ancor nel cor me atrista.

10. *Questa superba, con la testa alciata,*
disperse in tutto quel piacer che io avea,
tal che l'alma che lieta se tenea
de esser più mai contenta è disperata.
Smarita ancor de intorno pur se guata
se potesse fugire;
ma e' gli convien morire,
con tal groppo se stessa se è anodata;
con tal nodo è agropata e tanto forte
che, così presa, aspetta la sua morte.

11. *Narato v'ho cantando la ragione*
del mio grave tormento, donne care;
e se pietose alcun duol vi pò fare,
doveti aver del mio compassïone.
Se alcun dirà che mia sia la cagione
de questo aspro languire,
a quel poteti dire
che contro Amor lui venga al parangone,
e provi qual sapere on qual forteza
un cor gentil diffenda da belleza.

That faithless hunter then revealed to me
a countenance so sweet
that I gave him the key
to my heart and said: "I cede before your power,
nor will I ever seek defence against you;
my shield is down, I yield myself to you."

9. Thus did I speak and then prepare myself
to rest forever amid the eternal fragrances
exhaled so sweetly by that charming place
from tender grass and from its lovely flowers.
But just as I drew nearer to the roses
(the memory of it
still chills me now, my hair
still stands on end, my face is washed of color),
I saw a serpent with so cruel a stare
that even now its image grips my heart.

10. That arrogant one, with its head raised high,
dispelled at once the pleasure I had felt,
so that my soul, once always so content,
despairs of ever knowing joy again.
Bewildered still, it looks about itself
to see if it can flee;
but it must surely die
for having tied itself so full of knots;
it is so tightly tied with such hard knots
that, captured so, it waits for its own death.

11. Dear ladies, I have given you in song
the reason for the torment that afflicts me;
if any sorrow can evoke compassion,
mine surely ought to make you pity me.
If anyone should say the fault is mine
for so much suffering,
you ought to answer him
that he should test himself against Love's power,
and demonstrate what wisdom or what strength
can guard a gentle heart from beauty's lures.

Marieta (Marietta) and Genevre (Ginevra) Strozzi were probably relatives of Boiardo on his mother's side. Cf. poem 120.

83

Monologus

Li usati canti mei son volti in pianto,
e fugiti quei versi ch'io solea
usar ne la stagion ch'io non credea
che in dona crudeltà potesse tanto.

Ma poich'io vedo il suo venen pur tanto
multiplicar vie più che io non credea,
lasciato quel zoir che aver solea,
convien che io me consumi in tristo pianto.

Così intervene a chi pon troppo spene
in legereza feminile, e a cui
crescendo ognor disio manca la spene.

Pur voria ancor sperar, ma non scio in cui,
poiché tradito m'ha quella mia spene:
dil che, se io vuò dolermi, non ho a cui.

84

Ad Guidonem Scaiolam

Tieco fui preso ad un lacio d'or fino,
gentil mio Guido, e tieco ad uno iscoglio
roppi mia nave, e sol di ciò mi doglio,
che tieco ancor non compio il mio camino.

2.6, *the cold snake in the grass*: jealousy. Virgil, *Eclogues*, III.93: "frigidus . . . latet anguis in herba." Cf. poem 111.

4.2: cf. *Orlando Innamorato*, II.8.41.2.

4.9, *Blessèd Isles*: cf. poem 29.

5.6, *a boy*: Cupid.

6.9, *Minerva's Shield*: the shield used by Perseus to avert Medusa's fatal glance.

83. Sonnet 69

Monologous

My former songs have turned into complaints,
and gone are all the verses that I used
back in the season when I did not think
that a woman's cruelty could be so great.

But seeing that her venom has increased
much more than I could ever have believed,
abandoning the joy that once was mine,
I must consume myself in sad complaints.

This happens to the one who trusts too much
in the fickleness of woman, and to him
who, as desire grows, soon loses hope.

I want to trust someone, but don't know whom,
since I have been betrayed by my one hope:
tell her that my complaint has no one's ear.

Monologous: literally, one-worded; the same six rhyme-words are used throughout. Unlike sonnet 59 (poem 69), the meaning of each rhyme-word here remains constant.

My former songs: cf. Petrarch 152.

84. Sonnet 70

To Guido Scaiola

With you, my gentle Guido, I was caught
in a fine gold snare, and dashed my ship with you
upon a reef, and have but one regret:
that I no longer share one road with you.

Io nel diserto, e tu stai nel giardino;
tu favorito, ed io pur come soglio;
io come vuoli, e tu non come voglio,
prendi la rosa, dove io prendo il spino.

Più me ne duol, perché più de ira aduna
colui che nudo sta nel litto solo
e suspirando guata l'unda bruna,

che quel che vide cento nave in stolo
sparte con sieco e rotte da fortuna,
ché par che l'altrui mal ralenti il duolo.

85

Intercisus

Qual cervo è sì vivace, on qual cornice,
on qual fenice   che si rinovella,
che solo ad ella   reparar se lice,
come se dice,   ché lo ardor la abella;

qual pianta è quella   de antica radice,
che da pendice   mai non se divella;
qual ninfa snella   ne la età felice
de l'oro in vice,   e mo' di nostra stella,

che mi rivella   in così lunga etade
tal crudeltade   come ha questa fiera,
che tanto è altera   de la sua belleza

che Amor dispreza   e spreza umanitade,
né mai Pietade   fu ne la sua schiera,
anci è bandiera   e capo d'ogni aspreza?

86

De qual sangue lernèo fu tinto il strale,
di qual fiel di ceraste o anfisibena,
il stral che il cor mi punge in tanta pena
che altra nel mondo a quella non è equale?

I'm in a desert, you are in a garden;
you find favor, I go on as always;
I'm as you want me, you're not as I want you;
where you pluck roses, I grasp only thorns.

This pains me more, because the one who stands
alone and naked on the shore and looks
at darkened waves and sighs, is angrier

than one who sees a hundred ships piled up
like straw with his, and battered by misfortune:
it seems another's ills cut down his grief.

Poem 18 is also dedicated to Guido, but the tone is different.

85. Sonnet 51

A Sonnet with Internal Rhyme

What stag is there so full of life, what raven
or what phoenix that renews itself,
for it alone, they say, can be reborn,
because the flame restores its youthful beauty;

what plant is there that has an ancient root
that never is uprooted by decline;
what nimble nymph lived in the golden age,
or lives today beneath our golden sun,

that showed such cruelty for so long a time
as has been shown to me by this one beast
that is so filled with pride by her own beauty

that she despises Love and slights humanity,
and never kept compassion in her company,
but is, instead, the symbol of hard-heartedness?

86. Sonnet 72

With what Lernaean blood is that dart tinged,
or with what Amphisibene or Cersate venom,
that dart that fills my heart with so much pain
that nothing in the world compares to it?

Ognor se va più dilatando il male
e sparso è già el venen per ogni vena,
tanto che a forza al crudo fin mi mena,
né arte de Apollo a tal ferita vale.

Non vale arte de Apollo a la mente egra,
ché l'alma sciolta ha pena assai magiore
e più diletto, e più teme e più spera.

Scioca dunque la mia che se ralegra
scioglier dal corpo per scioglier d'amore,
ché, sciolta, fia pur serva a questa fiera.

87

Ad Amorem Interogatio

—Qual possanza inaudita on qual destino
fa, Signor mio, che te rivegia tale,
che hai li ochi al petto e al tergo messo l'ale
e fuor de usanza porti il viso chino?

De unde venuto sei, per qual camino,
a rivedermi nel mio extremo male,
sanza l'arco dorato e sanza il strale
che me ha fatto a me stesso perregrino?—

—Io vegno a piagner teco, e teco ascolto
il tuo dolore e la tua sorte dura,
che da lo abito mio sì m'ha rivolto.

The suffering grows worse with every hour,
the deadly poison runs through all my veins,
compelling me to die a cruel death;
nor can Apollo's arts heal such a wound.

Apollo's arts aid not the grieving mind,
for the unfettered soul knows greater pain
and greater joy, and fears and hopes much more.

Mine is, therefore, but foolish to rejoice,
leaving the body to be free of love,
since, free, it will be slave to her no less.

Learnaean blood: one of the labors of Hercules was to slay the Lernaean Hydra. He used its venemous blood to poison his arrows.

Amphisibene or Ceraste: serpents from Lucan's description of the plagues of Lybia (*Pharsalia*, 708–21).

Apollo's art: a multi-talented Olympian divinity, Apollo was skilled in various arts, including healing, prophecy, and the aversion of evil and misfortune.

the grieving mind . . . an unfettered soul: neither the torment of the body nor that of the disembodied spirit is appeased by Apollo's arts. Apollo was also seen as a death-delivering warrior or destroyer, as suggested by traditional epithets and one possible etymological derivation of his name ("to destroy").

87. Sonnet 73

Questions Put To Love

"What unknown power or destiny, My Lord,
makes you appear before me in this way,
with eyes upon your breast and wings laid back,
with head bowed in so strange a way?

Whence did you come, and following what path,
to visit me in my extreme dismay,
without your golden bow, without the shaft
that's made of me a stranger to myself?"

"I come to weep with you, and hear from you
about your sorrow and your cruel fate,
which has so altered me in my demeanor.

Tu sei tradito ed io dal più bel volto
che al mondo dimostrasse mai Natura:
questo a te il core, a me lo strale ha tolto.—

88

Item Ad Eundem

—Se dato a te mi sono in tutto, Amore,
a cui di te me degio lamentare?—
—Al Cielo, al mondo ed a me, s'el ti pare
che a' mei sugetti son iusto signore.—

—Il Ciel non me ode, il mondo è pien de errore,
e tu non degni e' miseri ascoltare:
pur noto al Cielo, al mondo e a te vuò fare
che nel tuo regno m'è rapito il core.—

—Nel regno mio non dir, ché in così trista
parte non regno, né regnar poria,
benché a te paia si gioiosa in vista.

Questa superba che il tuo cor disvia,
meco contende spesso, e tanto aquista
che io me disprezo e la possanza mia.—

89

Chorus Semisonus

Fu creato in eterno da Natura
mai voler tanto immane
fra l'unde caspe on ne le selve ircane?

Qual tigre in terra on qual orca nel mare,
che tanto crudel sia
che a costei ben si possa assumigliare?

You have been betrayed, and so have I,
by the fairest face that Nature put on Earth:
from you she stole your heart, from me my shaft."

Cf. poem 19.

88. Sonnet 74

The Questioning Continues

"If I, Love, have surrendered all to you,
to whom shall I address complaints of you?"
"To Heaven, to the world, or, if you like,
to me, for I'm a just lord to my subjects."

"Heaven does not hear me, error fills the world,
and you won't deign to listen to the wretched;
yet I'd have you, the world and Heaven note:
my heart has been imprisoned in your realm."

"Say not my realm, for in so sad a place
I do not reign, nor could I ever reign,
although to you it seems a joyful sight.

That haughty one that leads your heart astray
has often challenged me and showed such strength
that I distrust myself and my own power."

89. Ballata 7

Ballata Maggiore

Did Nature ever bring into the world
a will so fiercely cruel,
mid Caspian waves or in Hyrcanian woods?

What tiger here on Earth, what orc at sea
is there so cruel
that it could possibly compare to her?

Vuol questo il Ciel e la sventura mia,
che io sia forzato amar quel viso altero?
Ché, a confessar il vero,
tanto più l'amo quanto più me è dura.

90

Tra il Sonno e Amor non è tregua né pace,
ché quel riposo e questo vuol fatica,
il foco l'uno e l'altro umor nutrica,
quel crida e piagne e questo eterno tace;

l'un sempre vola e l'altro sempre jace,
questo la cura soglie e quello intrica,
a l'un la luce, a l'altro è l'umbra amica,
pigrizia a quel diletta, a questo spiace.

Quïete universal de gli animali,
che domi e tigri e rigidi leoni,
né pòi domar un amoroso core,

come la notte sempre me abandoni,
come èi del petto mio bandito fore,
perché io non abia sosta nei mie' mali!

Is this the will of Heaven and my misfortune,
that I be forced to love that too proud face?
For, if I may confess,
the more she's cruel, the more I love her.

---

mid Caspian waves: *Mare Caspium* or *Mare Hyrcanium* to the ancients, in what is now the area of the south central Soviet Union that borders on Iran. "The prevalent winds of the Caspian blow from the south-east, usually between October and March, and from the north and north-west, commonly between July and September. They sometimes continue for days together with great violence, rendering navigation dangerous and driving the sea-water up over the shores." (*EB*, V.454) Such conditions would, presumably, breed fierce creatures.

Hyrcanian woods: "Hyrcania. An ancient district of Asia, south of the Caspian Sea . . . called *Virkana*, or 'Wolf's Land,' in Old Persian." (*EB*, XIV.210) Cf. Boccaccio, *Teseida*, VIII.26.1–2 (*U*).

orc: a legendary sea-monster sustained by human victims. Such a creature figures prominently in the story of Perseus and Andromeda (Cf. Euripides, *Andromeda*): Angered by Cassiopeia's boast that she is more beautiful that the sea-dwelling Nereids, Poseidon sends a sea-monster to ravage her husband's kingdom. Cepheus, the king, learns that he can appease Poseidon only by exposing Andromeda to the horrible creature. She is, therefore, chained to a rock at the edge of the sea. Happily, Perseus sees her, falls instantly in love with her, and saves her from the monster after gaining her father's consent to their marriage. Cf. *Orlando Innamorato* (III.3, the story of Lucina) and *Orlando Furioso* (VIII.51ff.), where Ariosto describes the orc as one of the sea-creatures sent by Proteus to ravage the island of Ebuda, and as a monster that feeds on the flesh of young maidens.

90. Sonnet 75

With Sleep and Love there's neither truce nor peace,
for one seeks rest, the other only toil;
one feeds on flame, the other feeds on humors,
one cries and moans, the other's ever silent.

One always flies, the other's in repose,
one thrives on calm, the other thrives on intrigue;
the light befriends the one, and shade the other,
the sloth that pleases one annoys the other.

Universal quiet of all beasts,
who tame the tigers and ferocious lions,
and yet cannot subdue a loving heart,

how quickly you abandon me at night,
how easily you're banished from my breast,
so that I have no respite from my woes!

91

Se alcun per crudeltà de Amor sospira,
percosso da Fortuna e Zelosia,
legia lo affanno e la sventura mia,
ché in me l'altrui dolor se spechia e mira.

Soverchio dolo a lamentar me tira,
ché tolto me è quel ben che aver solia:
colei che la mia vita in man tenia,
sanza ragion vèr me se è volta in ira.

Né scio se la fallace finga forse
el sdegno e 'l crucio, per tenire in cima
e far altrui del mio languir contento.

Non scio, né de ciò el cor mio mai se accorse;
ma se esser pur dovesse, io voria prima
morir non de una morte, ma di cento.

92

Ormai son giunto al fine, ormai son vinto,
né più posso fugir né aver diffesa;
quel desir che tenea mia voglia incesa
è da geloso nimbo in tutto extinto.

Deh, che dico io? ché si m'ha il cor avinto
questa indovuta e inaspetata offesa,
che l'alma che vagava adesso è presa,
in tutto è préssa e posta in labirinto.

Chi mi trarà già mai del cieco errore?
Ché il filo è róto e róta è quella fede
che era de lo errar mio conforto e duce.

Più non spiero pietà, non più mercede,
abandonato, solo, e sanza luce,
né meco è più se non il mio dolore.

91. Sonnet 76

If someone sighs because he finds Love's cruel,
and is assailed by Fortune and by Jealousy,
then let him read of my unhappy fate,
for other's pains are mirrored in my own.

Excessive sorrow leads me to lament,
for I have lost the joy that once was mine;
the one who held my life within her grasp
has turned in anger, without cause, against me.

Nor do I know if that deceitful lady
feigns abhorrant anger to hold high
and please another with my suffering.

I do not know, nor was my heart aware of it;
but if it happened to be true, I'd want
to die no single death, but die a hundred.

92. Sonnet 77

I'm at the end at last, at last defeated,
unable to defend myself or flee;
the desire that kept my passion once aflame
has been extinguished by a jealous cloud.

Alas! What am I saying? This undue
and unexpected hurt so grips my heart,
my soul, which wandered free before, is trapped;
it's trapped and placed within a labyrinth.

Who'll ever lead me from blind error's way,
now that the thread is broken, and the trust,
which were my guide and comfort in my erring?

I have no hope of pity, nor of mercy,
abandoned and alone and without light,
with no companion but my suffering.

---

labyrinth: of jealousy.

the thread is broken: Ariadne fell in love with Theseus and helped him kill the Minotaur by giving him a ball of thread that would guide him (magically) into the center of the Labyrinth and out again. The thread had come from Daedalus, builder of the Labyrinth.

93

Qual fia il parlar che me secondi a l'ira
e corresponda al mio pianto infelice,
sì che fuor mostri quel che 'l cor mi dice,
poiché fòri il dolore a forza il tira?

Pur vedo mo' che per altrui sospira
questa perfida falsa e traditrice;
pur mo' lo vedo né inganar me lice,
ché l'ochio mio dolente a forza il mira.

Hai donato ad altrui quel guardo fiso
che era sì mio ed io tanto di lui
che per star sieco son da me diviso?

Hai tu donato, perfida, ad altrui
le mie parole, e' mei cinni, il mio riso?
O iustizia, dal ciel riguarda a noi!

94

Tetrasticus Cantus Quater Ordine
Quatuor Rithmis Comutato

1. *Rime inaudite e disusati versi*
ritrova il mio disdegno,
ma nel novo rimar non toca il segno
sì che al par del dolor possa dolersi.
Le voce perse indarno, i passi persi,
il perso tempo in la fiorita etade,
e tutto quel che per costei sofersi,
fan di me stesso a me tanta pietade
che un nimbo lacrimoso il cor me invoglia,
e poi da li ochi cade
né lascia fuor uscir l'ardente noglia.

93. Sonnet 78

What words are there that can express my anger
and correspond to my unhappy tears
revealing thus the dictates of my heart,
since suffering draws them out of me by force?

I see now that her sighs are for another,
perfidious, lying traitress that she is;
I see it clearly now, deception fails,
for now my anguished eye is forced to see.

Have you bestowed on him your steady gaze
which was so part of me and I of it
that, longing to join it, I am disjoined?

Have you, deceiver, freely given him
my words, my nods, the laughter that was mine?
O Justice, look from heaven down on us!

94. Canzone 7

A Song of Four Rhymes in Four Stanzas

1. Unheard of rhymes and unfamiliar verses
are what my anger finds,
but in this new rhyme does not hit the mark
so well that its lament can match my pain.
The needless waste of words, the wasted steps,
the time I wasted when in youthful bloom,
and all the suffering I've endured for her,
evoke in me such pity for myself
my heart is flooded by a storm of tears,
that, falling from my eyes,
prevent my burning sorrow from escaping.

2\. *E pur così confuso a scoprir vegno*
quel che già ricopersi,
e così gli ochi e il cor hagio conversi
a chi me impose il peso che io sostegno.
Dove è quel tuo felice e lieto regno,
falace Amor? falace, ove è la zoglia
che me se imprometteа per fermo pegno?
Miser colui che per te si dispoglia
il proprio arbitrio e la sua libertade,
con sperar che si soglia
per tempo o per pietà tua crudeltade!

3\. *Ahi, lasso me, che questo più me adoglia,*
che sapendo io toa penta falsitade,
sapendo come rade
volte del seme tuo frutto si coglia,
lassai portarmi a la sfrenata voglia,
e tardi doppo il danno li ochi apersi,
tardi, ché più non fia che indi me stoglia.
Ma per qual cor gentil quai laci fersi
giamai con tanto inzegno,
quando io stesso a mia voglia me copersi
nel nodo che mostrava sì benegno?

4\. *Chi avria creduto mai che tal beltade*
fosse sì cruda? E che sì ferma voglia
fosse poi come foglia,
mostrando grave fuor sua levitade?
Coperto orgoglio e finta umanitade
fôr quei che me pigliar senza rategno,
e che m'han posto in tal captivitade.
Fanciul protervo perfido e malegno,
che da li ochi mei versi
quel duol de che il mio cor fu tanto pregno,
parti a mia fede questo convenersi?

Crudele istelle e cieli a me perversi
che fuor creasti in lei tal nobiltade
che il perfido suo cor non pò vedersi;
crudele istelle, che tal novitade
creasti al mondo per mia eterna doglia,
mostratime le strade
che a voi ne venga e da costei mi toglia.

2. So is it that, confused, I now reveal
what earlier I hid;
So is it that I've turned my eyes and heart
upon the one who made this burden mine.
Where do I find your cheerful, happy realm,
deceitful Love? Where is the joy, false friend,
you promised me upon your solemn pledge?
I pity anyone who, for your sake,
gives up his own free will and liberty,
hoping that either time
or pity will decrease your cruelty!

3. Alas, what pains me more than anything
is that, though knowing of your veiled deceit,
and knowing how few times
one gathers fruit from all the seed you sow,
I let unbridled passion sweep me off,
not opening my eyes to harm 'til later,
too late then to release me from its hold.
When was a snare made for a gentle heart
as cleverly as that,
as when I willingly took up the noose
that was as far as I could tell so harmless.

4. Whoever would have thought that such great beauty
could be so cruel? Or that so firm a will
could be so like a leaf,
covering its levity with weightiness?
A hidden pride and false civility
are what took hold of me without restraint
and placed me in such cruel captivity.
You insolent, perfidious, cruel child,
who cause my eyes to gush with all that pain
by which my heart was filled to overflowing,
does this seem to you to suit my faithfulness?

Cruel stars and heavens that have turned against me,
that outwardly gave her so much nobility
that her perfidious heart is hidden by it;
cruel stars, that introduced this novel wonder
to the world to my unending grief,
reveal to me the paths
that lead to you and may take me from her.

95

Fu forsi ad altro tempo in dona amore,
forsi fu già pietade in alcun petto,
e forsi di vergogna alcun rispetto,
fede fu forsi già in feminil core.

Ma nostra etade adesso è in tanto errore
che dona più de amar non ha diletto,
e di dureza piena e de dispetto,
fede non stima né virtù né onore.

Fede non più, non più ve è de onor cura
in questo sexo mobile e fallace,
ma volubil pensiero e mente oscura.

Sol la Natura in questo me despiace,
che sempre fece questa crëatura
o vana troppo, o troppo pertinace.

96

Superiori Eadem Respondens Desinentia

Ben cognosco oramai che il mio furore
non ha più freno on di ragion obietto:
il sdegno mio, che un tempo fu concetto,
è pur con chiara voce uscito fore.

Perdon vi chiezo, donne, se il dolore
ha fatto trabocar qualche mio detto,
ché Veritade e Amor me n'ha constretto:
quella me è amica, e questo me è signore.

Certamente altrui colpa o mia siagura,
che a torto a mio parer l'alma mi sface,
al iusto lamentar me rassicura.

Donati al mio fallir, donne mie, pace,
ché a tacer tanto duolo è cosa dura,
e poco ha doglia chi dolendo tace.

95. Sonnet 79

Perhaps there was a time when a woman loved,
perhaps compassion then filled someone's breast,
and modesty was something to respect,
and faithfulness dwelt in a lady's heart.

But now our age is bent so much on error,
that a woman takes no pleasure in love's ways,
and, being filled with cruelty and contempt,
care not for virtue, honor or affection.

No longer is there honor and affection
in this inconstant and deceptive sex,
but rather a deceiving mind and fickle thoughts.

Nature displeases me in this alone,
that she created this one being to be
too easy or too steadfast in her ways.

96. Sonnet 80

Same Rhyme Scheme as Above

I am now well aware that my mad passion
cannot be curbed and has no reasoned goal;
my anger, that was once a mere conceit,
has made its exit with a hearty voice.

I beg forgiveness, ladies, if my pain
has caused me to speak out too hastily,
for Truth and Love are what, in fact, coerced me:
the one's my friend, the other is my master.

Another's cruel offence or my misfortune,
which wrongfully, I think, consume my soul,
convince me that my grief was justified.

Forgive, I beg you, ladies, my transgression,
for silencing such pain's a bitter task,
and silent sufferers must suffer little.

97

Qual soccorso mi resta, on qual aiuto,
se chi aiutar mi pote non soccore?
Pur me destino de lasciare amore,
prima che 'l corpo mio sia sfatto in tuto.

Hagio gli incanti di quel vechio arguto
chi regea Bactra, ed hagio de lo umore
di Lete inferna, e la radice e il fiore
che fece Ulisse a Circe scognosciuto.

Ma in che me affido, lasso! Che arte maga
soglia da amore? E non sciolse Medea
con l'erbe scite e' canti di Tesaglia.

Lei non pòte saldar l'ardente piaga
che avea nel cor, con quanto ella sapea,
ché contro Amor non è forza che vaglia.

97. Sonnet 81

What comfort is there, or what help, for me,
if the one who could give aid to me does not?
Indeed my plan is to abandon love,
before my flesh is totally corrupted.

I know the spells of that old, clever man
who ruled at Bactra, and I have some water
from infernal Lethe, and the root and flower
that made Ulysses stay unknown to Circe.

Alas, what do I hope! That magic arts
can undo love? When with her Scythian herbs
Medea could not break Thessalian spells?

She could not hope to heal the burning wound
within her heart, with everything she knew,
for there's no force that can stand up to Love.

---

old, clever man: Sheikh al Aodin or Sheikh al Jabal, the Old Man of the Mountain(s), Chief of the Assassins (Hashishin), a secret society formed in the eleventh century. The Sheikh used the intoxicating power of *hashish* to induce his faithful to carry out his commands. Marco Polo speaks of him in his book of travels.

Bactra: capital of Bactria in ancient Persia.

infernal Lethe: in Greek mythology, the river of forgetfulness in Hades. Its waters caused those who drank them to forget their previous existence. For Dante it was to be found in the Earthly Paradise on the mountain of Purgatory, and for others (e.g., Ariosto) elsewhere.

the root and flower: given to Ulysses by Hermes, and allowing Ulysses to resist her spells.

Medea . . . : even though she was herself an enchantress, Medea could not cure herself of her passion for Jason.

Scythian herbs: from the land of the Scyths, who were Nature worshipers. Herodotus reports (*Histories*, IV.74) that the Scyths derived great pleasure from inhaling the intoxicating fumes of charred hemp seeds.

Thessalian spells: Thessalian witches were legendary in antiquity. Plato reveals (*Gorgias*, 513a) that they had the power to pull down the moon from the sky. Medea's love was for Jason.

98

Chorus Disiunctus

Deh, non mostrar in vista
che 'l mio languir ti doglia, disleale,
ché 'l cor tradito più se ne contrista
e più cresce il suo male.

Questo tuo divo, a cui nullo altro è equale,
rida la pena mia
e stiasi in segnoria
di te, poiché de onor nulla te cale.

Ma, se vendetta il danno a levar vale,
non fia lunga la lista
de lo amor vostro, ché il pensier ti vola,
né lui fu mai contento de una sola.

99

Misero quivi e sconsolato e solo
me son radutto per fugire Amore,
se fugir pòsse quel che se ha nel core,
per piagner, per languir, per star in dolo.

Così mei cari amici, a voi me involo
per non vi apartegiar nel mio dolore,
che a l'alma trista dà tanto terrore
che aperte ha l'ale per fugirse a volo.

Viver voglio così, così morire,
poiché piace ad Amor che così viva,
e che così tra saxi amando pèra.

Quella crudel che la mia vita schiva
farà pur sazia la sua mente altera,
se parte del mio dol potrà sentire.

98. Ballata 8

Ballata Grande

Don't feign, alas, with looks,
unfaithful lady, that my suffering pains you,
for the more my heart, betrayed, succumbs to grief,
the more its torment grows.

This god of yours, to whom no other's equal,
let him mock my pain,
and let him have his lordship
over you, who give no thought to honor.

But, if revenge can wipe away the hurt,
the history of your love
will not be long, for you have fickle thoughts,
and he has never been content with one.

This god of yours: the suitor she favors over the poet.

99. Sonnet 82

Disconsolate, alone and miserable,
I've taken refuge here to flee from Love,
if one can flee what's carried in one's heart,
by crying and by dwelling on my grief.

So, dear friends, I hide myself from you,
in order not to share with you my pain,
which brings such terror to my saddened soul
that it has spread its wings and taken flight.

I want to live this way and die this way,
since Love is pleased to see me living so
and perishing for love amid the rocks.

That cruel one who disdainfully avoids me
will surely satisfy her own proud mind
if she will hear but part of my complaint.

100

Voi, monti alpestri (poiché nel mio dire
la lingua avanti a lei tanto se intrica,
e il gran voler mi sforza pur ch'io dica),
voi, monti alpestri, oditi il mio martìre.

Se Amor vol pur che suspirando expire,
Amor che in pianto eterno me notrica,
fàtti voi noto a quella mia nemica,
nanti al mio fin, che io vuò per lei morire.

Voi me vedeti sol con lento passo
ne' vostri poggi andarmi lamentando
de li ochi mei, non già del suo bel viso.

De li ochi mei se dole il cor mio lasso
che il religarno in foco e in giazo, quando
scoprirno a lui quel volto e il dolce riso.

101

Fuòr per bon tempo meco in compagnia
gióvanni lieti e liete damigelle;
piaquerme un tempo già le cose belle,
quando con la mia età lo amor fioria.

Or non è meco più quel che solia:
solo il languir da me non se divelle,
e solo al sole e solo a l'alte stelle
vo lamentando de la pena mia.

Ripe de fiumi e jogi di montagne
son or con mieco, e son fatto selvagio
per boschi inculti e inospite campagne.

Qualor al poggio on nel fresco rivagio
me assido, del mio mal conven me lagne,
ché altro rissor che lamentar non hagio.

100. Sonnet 83

You, high mountains (since my tongue gets twisted
when I try to speak while in her presence,
when my great passion forces me to speak),
You, high mountains, hear my martyr's tale.

If Love insists that I expire sighing,
Love, that nurtures me with endless plaints,
may you make known to her, my enemy,
before my end, that I would die for her.

You see me slowly wandering alone
about your hills complaining all the while
about my eyes, and not her lovely face.

My weary heart is vexed by my own eyes,
which fettered him with fire and ice, when they
revealed her face and her sweet smile to it.

You, high mountains: the Petrarchan motif of seeking solace in Nature.

101. Sonnet 84

For a good long while all my companions were
young gentlemen of cheer and cheerful damsels;
There was a time when things of beauty pleased me,
when love, together with my youth, was flourishing.

But now my company is not the same,
for suffering alone does not abandon me,
and only to the sun and stars above
do I go on complaining of my pain.

The banks of rivers and the mountain crests
are with me now; and I've become a savage
lost in unmarked woods and untilled fields.

And when I stop to sit upon a hill
or in the coolness of a river's bank,
I cry, because I have no other solace.

102

Ben è fallace il sogno, e falso il segno
che se dimostra a lo animo sopito:
quella crudel che a torto m'ha tradito
come sembrava mo' di cor benegno!

—Or pui tener—dicea—per fermo pegno
lo animo mio, che sempre è teco unito,
né da te per tuo crucio è mai partito
né mai se partirà per tuo disdegno.

Vedi che adesso a consolarti vengo,
adesso che il venir non m'è interditto,
né contro a te quel cor che credi tengo.—

Così diceva, e sì con viso fitto
parea parlar che lacrimar convengo
d'ognor ch'io lo rimembro al cor afflitto.

103

Con che dolce concento insieme accolti
se vano ad albergar quei vagi occelli,
vegendo come l'umbra il mondo velli
e i ragi del gran lume in mar involti!

Felici ocei, che de ogni cura sciolti,
a riposar ne giti lieti e snelli!
Or par che 'l mio dolor se rinovelli
quando è la notte e non è chi l'ascolti.

E come l'aria intorno a noi se imbruna
così dentro se anera il pensier mio,
nel rimembrar de le passate offese.

Qui tutte le rivegio ad una ad una:
sua finta umanità, suo pensier rio
che se coperse sì quando mi prese.

102. Sonnet 85

False is the dream and just as false the figure
that comes before a mind that's dulled by sleep:
oh how affectionate she seemed just now,
that hurtful one that wrongfully betrayed me.

"You may now take as solemn pledge," she said,
"all my affection, which is always with you,
nor has it ever fled despite your anger,
nor will it ever flee though scorned by you.

You see that now I've come here to console you,
now that my coming has not been denied,
nor is my heart, as you have claimed, against you."

These were her words; and with so false a face
did she appear to speak that I must always cry
when I remind my grieving heart of it.

103. Sonnet 86

With what sweet harmony those lovely birds
fly off together to their place of rest,
seeing how the shade has veiled the earth
and the great sun's rays absorbed into the sea!

You happy birds, set free from every care,
you cheerfully and swiftly find repose!
Just now, it seems, my painful song returns
when it is night and no one's here to listen.

And as the air that is about us darkens,
so too do all my thoughts within turn black
as I remember all her past offenses.

I see them all again here, one by one:
her feigned humanity, her devious thought,
with which she cloaked herself when snaring me.

Mandrialis Cantu Dimetro Rithmo Intercalari

1. *Se io paregiasse il canto ai tristi lai,*
qual già fece Arïone
a la temenza de li extremi guai,
forsi così faria compassïone
al veloce delfin questo cantare,
tanta pietade ha in sé la mia ragione!
Qual monstro sì crudel nel verde mare
che non tornasse a tanto mal pietoso,
se il mio dolor potesse dimostrare?
Qual animal tanto aspro ed orgoglioso
e qual bellua sì immane che dolere
non fèssi del mio stato doloroso?
Farebbe a' saxi tenereza avere
del mio cordoglio e le cime inclinarsi
de' monti e a' fiumi il suo corso tenere.
Ogni cosa potrebbe umilïarsi,
se non quella spietata che non cura
per prieghi on per pietà benigna farsi,
ma per li altrui lamenti più se indura.
Adunque, poiché il cielo a noi se oscura
e il gran pianetto la sua luce asconde,
posso dolermi intra le verde fronde
e dar al ciel le mie voce meschine;
ché così lamentando il tempo passa
che a me dilunga lo aspettato fine,
benché cantando il mio duol non mi lassa,
né lasserà, per quel ch'io creda, mai.

2. *Or cominciamo gli dolenti lai*
qua sotto l'aier bruna,
rincominciamo e' canti pien di guai.
Diceti, stelle, e tu, splendida luna,
se mai nei nostri tempi o ne' primi anni
simile a questa mia fu doglia alcuna.
Diceti se più mai cotanti affanni
sofferse uom nato per amar con fede,
guiderdonato poi di tanti inganni.
Voi ben sapeti che la mia mercede
m'è dinegata e ritenuta a torto;
sasselo il Ciel con voi, che il tutto vede.

104. Madrigal 2/Canzone 8

A Madrigal Song in Tercets and Quatrains

1. If I compared my song to sad complaints,
like those of Arion,
born of the fear of his impending death,
perhaps in doing so I could arouse
compassion in the nimble dolphin's breast,
for just so moving is the cause I plead!
What monster in green seas is there so cruel
that it would not respond to such a wrong
if I could demonstrate my suffering?
What animal so wild and fiercely proud,
what beast so savage as not to grieve for me
because of seeing how I'm forced to grieve?
I'd make the rocks respond with tenderness
to my suffering, and make the mountain tops
bow down, and rivers hold to course.
Every thing there is could be more humble,
except that hurtful one who heeds no prayer
and is not moved to kindness by compassion,
but rather hardens with another's sorrow.
And so, because the sky grows dark above,
and that great planet hides its light from us,
I vent my sorrow here among green leaves,
and cast my doleful words up to the skies,
for, so lamenting, I can pass the time
that keeps me from the end that I foresee,
though, while I sing, grief still remains with me,
nor, as I see it, will it ever leave.

2. Let's now begin our sorrowful laments
here under night's dark sky,
let's now begin again our songs of woe.
Do tell me, stars, and tell me, splendid moon,
if ever in our times or long ago
there was a torment similar to mine.
Do tell me if a man born true to love,
but then rewarded by so much deceit
has ever suffered so much grief as I.
You know full well that mercy's been denied,
and that it's wrongfully withheld from me;
and Heaven, that sees all, must know it too.

Sapete ben con qua' losenge scorto
fosse ne la pregion, là dove invano
aspettando mercé, son quasi morto.
Sapete come fuor me aparbe umano
quel guardo che me incese a poco a poco
di quel fervor che tanto è fatto insano
che lo arder suo dimostra in ogni loco.
Bench'ormai più non ardo, ch'io son foco,
ché nulla trova più che arder mi possa
la fiamma che m'ha roso e' nervi e l'ossa,
e sanza nutrimento vive ancora.
Sarà quel giorno mai ch'io veda extinto
questo foco immortal? sarà quel'ora
ch'io veda il cor mio libero e discinto
di laci ove io me stesso me legai?

3. Laci di bei crin d'or che in tanti lai
me faceti languire,
tenendomi legato in pianto e in guai,
come potrò mia noglia ad altri dire,
che me teneti in tal captivitade
e non lassati apena ch'io sospire?
Odite, selve, e prendavi pietade
del mio dolor che a tutti è disequale,
che sia in la nostra on fusse in altra etade.
Tu, che hai de la mia mano il bel signale,
arbor felice, e ne la verde scorza
inscritta hai la memoria del mio male,
strengi lo umor tuo tanto che si smorza
quel dolce verso che la chiama mia,
che ognor che io il lego a lacrimar mi forza.
Non è più a me, no, no, quel che solia,
ché la crudel Fortuna me l'ha tolta,
anci sua legereza e sua folia
che a la promessa fede ha dato volta;
né più mei prieghi o mia rason ascolta
che ascoltin questi tronchi sanza senso.
Oh noglia scognosciuta, oh male immenso,
che tanto è grande e par che altri no 'l veda!
Ché assai minor angoscia ha un cor dolente
quando si dole e par che altri gli creda;
ma io, che ho le mie pene sì patente,
credenza on fede ancor non gli trovai.

You know with what allurements I was led
into that prison where I nearly died
while waiting for some mercy to be shown.
You know how human in appearance was
that gaze that slowly filled me with a fervor
turned so much into a mad obsession
that it shows its passion everywhere.
By now I burn no more, although I'm fire,
because the flame that's charred my nerves and bones
finds nothing left in me to be consumed,
and yet lives on without new nourishment.
Will there be a day when I shall see
this immortal fire quenched? And will
the hour come when my heart is loosed and free
of bonds with which I freely bound myself?

3. Bonds of lovely golden locks that make me
languish in such wailing,
keeping me bound in tears and misery,
how shall I speak to others of my anguish
if you keep me bound so very tight
you hardly leave me room to sigh?
Listen, woodlands, pity me my pain,
which is unequal to all other kinds
that be in this or were in other times.
You, lucky tree, that bear the lovely sign
made by my hand, and bear on your green bark
the memory of all my ills inscribed,
concentrate your humours in the wound,
let that sweet verse that calls her mine be gone,
for every time I read it I must cry.
No longer is she what she was to me,
no, no, cruel Fortune's taken her away,
or rather her own fickleness and folly
overturned her promise of fidelity.
No longer does she listen to the pleas
that these insensate tree trunks must hear.
Oh unimagined grief, oh endless sorrow,
so great and yet, it seems, unseen by others!
For an anguished heart is filled with far less grief
when it laments and seems to be believed;
but I, who bear my pain so openly,
have not yet found belief or faith for it.

4. *Debo tacer adunque questi lai*
che l'alma mia sostene?
Debo io tacere e consumarme in guai?
Doglia mi forza e parlar mi convene,
ché più non pò tenere il tristo petto,
colmo de affanno e di soverchie pene.
E poiché a me rapito è quello aspetto,
quel dolce aspetto che mia vita incese,
parlar a l'aria e al vento haggio diletto.
Tu che li mei desir senti palese,
aura süave che in questa rivera
con le tremante foglie fai contese,
sentendo quale io sono e quale io era,
non che tu ne dovristi esser pietosa,
ma Borea, di natura alpestra e fera.
Già me vedesti in faccia più gioiosa,
se te rimembra ben, ch'io te aspettava
fatta dal spirto suo più grazïosa,
quando io sua forma, e lei sua fede amava.
Lasso, che il lamentar non mi disgrava
da quel peso crudel che l'alma incarca:
sì come il perregrin che l'alpe varca,
che al più salir più prende di fatica,
così più de tristeza al cor me aduce
il mio cantar e più di duol me intrica,
e non ho pòssa quando il mondo ha luce
né quando il sol sottera asconde i rai.

5. *Tu dai riposo, notte, ai tristi lai*
de tutti li animali,
e doni smenticanza a tutti e' guai;
tu, notte, le fatiche a zascun cali;
ed io, ne l'umbra tua distesso in terra,
non prendo posa dai mei eterni mali:
ma alor più se rinfresca la mia guerra
quando per te se copre il nostro polo
che sotto il suo emispero il giorno serra;
alor mi vedo sconsolato e solo,
e porto invidia a ogni animal terreno
che alor se aqueta e non sente il mio dolo.
Dormen li ocelli in fronda al ciel sereno,
le fere in bosco e ne' frondusi dumi,
nei fiumi e' pesci e dentro al salso seno.

4. Must I then silence these laments of mine
in which my soul finds sustenance?
Must I be silent and consumed by sorrow?
My grief compels me and I'm forced to speak,
my melancholy breast can hold no more,
for it is filled with woe and too much pain.
And since the sight of her is snatched from me,
that lovely face that kept my life aflame,
I'm now content to speak to the air and wind.
You who hear of my desire so openly,
sweet, gentle breeze, that are contending here
upon this bank with all the trembling leaves,
hearing of what I am and what I was,
it's not of you that I expect compassion,
but Boreas, of a wild and savage nature.
You saw me once with a far more joyful face,
if you remember well, while waiting for you
to be made more pleasing by her gracious breathing,
when I loved her and she loved her fidelity.
Alas, complaints do not unburden me
of the cruel weight that bears upon my soul:
just like the traveller that scales the Alps,
who is all the more fatigued the more he climbs,
so does my singing fill my heart with sadness,
and confound me with continued suffering,
so that I can find no rest when there is light
nor when the Sun conceals its rays below.

5. You, night, bring rest to the melancholy plaints
of every living being,
and grant forgetfulness to every care;
you, night, do lessen every creature's labor;
yet I, who am reclining in your shadow,
can find no rest from my eternal ills:
instead, my own war is renewed again
just when your darkest shadows cloak our pole
so that its hemisphere seals out the day;
just then I see myself disconsolate,
alone, and I envy every earthly being
that then finds peace and does not share my grief.
Birds sleep on boughs beneath a tranquil sky,
and beasts in forests and in leaf-packed dens,
and fish in rivers and in the salty seas.

Ed io, pur ne li antichi mei costumi,
la notte umido ho il viso, umido al sole,
perché mia vita tosto se consumi,
poiché quel cor spietato così vole.
Ben sei, notte, crudel, se non ti dole
del mio dolor e de mia pena acerba,
che me vedi jacer pallido a l'erba,
né poter impetrar morte con preghi.
Odi tu adunque il mio lamento amaro,
e fa che il tuo poter non me se neghi,
fa a coste' in sogno manifesto e chiaro
quanto ora l'amo e quanto già l'amai.

Misero, lasso, a che cotesti lai
raconto e i crudi stenti
a chi nulla sentir può de mie' guai?
lo spargo al cielo invano e' mei lamenti,
a l'aura e a' boschi invano odir mi facio,
invano a l'umbre sanza sentimenti.
Tu sola, che potevi il stretto lacio
lassar alquanto, te prendi vagheza
vedendo con qual pena io me disfacio.
Che maledetta sia quella dureza
che te è nel cor gelata, e il falso amore
che agiunse a crudeltà tanta belleza!
Maledetto esca in pianti quello umore
de li ochi mei, che se invaghì si forte
de il tuo bel viso e che lo mostrò al core!
Tu m'hai, fera crudel, a mortal sorte
condutto, e pur sembiante ancor non fai
che te piaza on rincresca la mia morte:
ché assai minor forìan mei tristi lai,
se i' credesse de averti
fatta pietosa alquanto de' mie' guai,
on ver, morendo, un poco compiacerti.

Yet I, persisting in my same old ways,
still bathe my face with tears both day and night,
because my life is quick to be consumed,
since her inhuman heart still wants it so.
You, night, are truly cruel if you don't share
with me my sorrow and my bitter pain,
for you see me lying, pale, upon the grass,
unable to solicit death with prayers.
I beg you listen to my bitter cry,
let not your powers be denied me,
and make it clear to her by way of dreams
how much I've loved her and do love her still.

Alas, oh wretched me! Why do I sing
these lays and tales of woe
to one who does not want to hear me grieve?
I scatter these laments on the air in vain,
in vain I make the dawn and forests hear me,
in vain I speak to shadows without feelings.
You alone, who could have loosed the snare
a bit, find your delight in seeing how,
and with what pain, I tear myself apart.
Damned be that stubborness that's frozen solid
in your heart, as well as that false love
that joined such beauty to such cruelty!
Let from my eyes pour forth as wretched tears
that cursèd humor that did love so much
your pretty face it showed it to my heart.
You've led me, savage creature, to a fatal end,
and still you give no outward sign to tell
if my death is pleasing or if you regret it:
I'd have far fewer mournful lays to sing
if I were to believe
that I had made you pity me in grief,
or that, by dying, I had pleased you some.

You, lucky tree: cf. poem 153 for the *topos* of writing on trees.

105

Se Amor me fosse stato sì gioioso
come il crudel m'ha sempre a torto offeso,
avrebbe del mio foco un fiume acceso
e il ciel intorno a me fatto amoroso.

Ma il canto mio fu sempre doloroso,
a noglia, a pianti, a lamentar inteso,
e se lieto il mostrai quando io fui preso,
fume al principio il mio dolor nascoso.

Sì me abagliava quella incesa voglia
che assai pur mi parea di poter dire
del dolce tosco unde avea l'alma piena.

Or voria ben cantar, ma la gran doglia
la voce me combate in tal martìre
che, non ch'io canti, ma sospiro apena.

106

Mira quello ocellin che par che senta
de la tua pena, misero mio core,
e tieco insieme piagne del tuo ardore,
piagne cantando, e tieco se lamenta.

Come esser può che il Cielo e Amor consenta
che a ogni animal rincresca il mio dolore,
se non a lei, che mostra pur di fore
umana vista e di pietà dipenta?

Sola non cura il mio tristo languire,
e sola il può curar, ché solo a lei
il mio vivere è in mano e il mio morire.

Or vedi, altiera, quanto crudel sei,
ché a pietà non ti move il mio martìre
che fa con meco lamentar li occei.

105. Sonnet 87

If Love had ever been as kind to me
as he has been offensive by his cruelty,
he would have burned a river with my fire
and made the air around me glow with passion.

But my song was always full of sorrow,
intended for laments, and grief, and weeping;
and if it seemed more cheerful when I first was struck,
my suffering, back then, was hidden from me.

That kindled passion blinded me so much
I thought it quite a lot to merely speak
of that sweet poison that had filled my soul.

Now I would like to sing, but my great pain
assails my voice with such relentlessness,
not only can't I sing, I barely sigh.

---

not only can't I sing: cf. *Orlando Innamorato*, II.31.49.8.

106. Sonnet 88

Look at that little bird that seems to share
your suffering with you, my aching heart,
and weeps with you because of your own passion;
in singing weeps, and, weeping, mourns with you.

How can it be that Heaven and Love consent
to let my sorrow trouble every beast,
and yet leave her untouched, though she may show
a kindly face that's painted by compassion?

She, only she, ignores my lanquishing,
and she alone can cure it; she alone
has in her hands the power of life and death.

Now see, my haughty one, how cruel are you
who are not moved to pity by my pain,
which causes even birds to mourn with me.

Cf. Petrarch 353.

107

Ombrosa selva, che il mio dolo ascolti
sì spesso in voce rotta da sospiri,
splendido sol, che per li eterni giri
hai nel mio lamentar più giorni volti,

fiere selvage e vagi ocei, che sciolti
seti da li aspri e crudi mie' martìri,
rivo corrente, che a doler me tiri
tra le ripe deserte e i lochi incolti;

o testimoni eterni de mia vita,
odeti la mia pena e fàtti fede
a quella altiera che la aveti odita.

Ma a che? se lei che tanto dolor vede
(ché pur mia noglia a riguardar la invita)
vedendo istessa a li ochi soi non crede!

108

Per l'alte rame e per le verde fronde
non ho mie voce al tutto messo invano,
ché il senso a li ocelleti è fatto umano
tanto che il nome tuo non se nasconde.

Né sol gli ocei, ma ancor le petre e l'onde
hanno pietà del mio dolor insano,
e il fiume apresso e il monte di lontano
come io soglio chiamar così risponde.

Perché me stesso ingano alcuna volta,
e parlo sopra l'onde a le pendice,
poiché fortuna e sdegno te m'ha tolta.

Alor son quasi nel mio mal felice,
ché quella alpestra ripa sì me ascolta
che l'ultime parole me ridice.

107. Sonnet 89

O shaded grove, that listens to my plaint
so often interrupted by my sighs;
O splendid Sun, that's cloaked so many days
with my laments in your eternal rounds;

O savage beasts and gentle birds, unbound
by my too cruel and bitter martyrdom;
O rushing Brook, that draws me to my wailing
on deserted shores and in untended fields;

O immortal witnesses to my sad life,
please listen to my grief and then make known
to that proud lady that you've heard it all!

But why, if she, who sees the magnitude of pain
(my anguish surely beckons her to look),
does not believe her eyes in seeing it?

108. Sonnet 90

I have not cast my verses all in vain
amid the highest branches and green leaves,
for their meaning's been revealed to all the birds
so that your name is not unknown to them.

Not only birds, but even rocks and waves
have pity on me in my maddening pain;
and the nearby river and the distant hill
respond to me as I call out to them.

That's why I do deceive myself at times,
and call across the waters to the slopes,
since fortune and disdain have taken you.

Then am I nearly happy in my grief,
for that wild hillside listens with such care
that it repeats my final words to me.

109

Chorus Iunctus

Come esser può che in cener non sia tutto
il corpo mio, che un tal ardor consuma
che avrebbe il mar d'ogni liquor asciuto?

Miser, non vedi come eterna piova
te stilan gli ochi e il cor dolente fuma,
che arder non pote, e sua doglia rinova?

Per mia pena si prova,
per mio exemplo se aluma
quanto di mal si trova

quel petto ch'è cresciuto
ne la inferna lacuma
quanto più fu pasciuto;

e la pena di quel che 'l foco ha dato,
che a un saxo religato
un ucel sempre pasce
di sua mirabil fibra che rinasce.

110

Con tanta forza il gran desir me assale
che ogn'altra pena è a sostener minore:
dica chi vuole, il tutto vince Amore,
né al suo contrasto è in terra cosa equale.

109. Ballata 9 (Ballata Maggiore)

A Dance Song Linked by Rhyme

How is my body not reduced to ash
when it's consumed by a flame that is so great
that it would dry the sea of all its waters?

Don't you see, you wretch, how your eyes drip
eternal rain while your grieved heart just smolders,
since it can't burn, and so renews its anguish?

By my grief is shown,
by my example seen,
in how much pain is found

that breast that ever grew
in the infernal pit,
the more it was devoured;

and the pain of the one who gave us fire,
who is bound upon a rock
while a bird feeds constantly
on his wonderous liver that grows back again.

This *chorus* is a kind of ballad with *iunctus* probably referring to the linking of the tercets with the same middle rhyme [ABA, CBC, CBC, ABA] (*SC*).

that breast that ever grew: by Virgil's account Tityus, the son of Jupiter and Elara, is the foster-child (*alumnus*) of Earth killed by Apollo and Diana for trying to rape Latona. Sibyl describes to Aeneas his punishment in the Underworld (*Aeneid*, VI. 595ff.): "And also one might see Tityon . . . whose body stretches over nine full acres; and a monstrous vulture strikes repeatedly his undying liver with its hooked beak, and his entrails are rich with torment."

the one who gave us fire: Prometheus was punished by Zeus for stealing fire from the gods and bringing it to earth. Zeus had him bound to a rock and sent an eagle each day to devour his liver, which, because Prometheus was himself immortal, regenerated itself at night.

110. Sonnet 91

My great desire assails me with such force
that every other pain is borne more easily;
whatever one may say, Love conquers all,
no earthly thing is equal to this power.

Fugito ho l'ozio, e quel fugir non vale,
e fugio lei, né fugio il mio furore;
sol può dar vita al tramortito core
la vista che è cagion di tanto male.

E' corenti cavalli e i cani arditi,
che mi solean donar tanto diletto,
mi sono in tutto dal pensier fugiti;

ciò che solea piacermi, ora ho a dispetto,
e lo esser mio distinguo in dui partiti:
on arder quivi, on giazar nel suo aspetto.

111

Qual si move constretto da la fede
de' tesalici incanti il frigido angue,
e qual si move trepido ed exangue
il mauro cacciator che il leon vede;

tal il mio cor, che a la sua pena rede,
si move sanza spirto e sanza sangue
e giela di paura e trema e langue,
perché de aver più pace mai non crede.

Egli è constretto a gire, e gir non vole,
ma contro al suo voler Amor il tira
perché il dolor antico se rinove.

Lui cognosce che ei va di neve al sole,
e più non pò, ma lacrima e sospira,
e paventoso il passo lento move.

I've fled from idleness to no avail;
I flee from her but not from my own fury.
My wounded heart can only be revived
by the sight of her, the cause of so much ill.

The galloping horses and eager hounds
that gave me so much pleasure in the past
have fled completely from my every thought.

I now despise what once I found so pleasing;
my life is now divided into two:
I burn while here, or freeze when in her presence.

Love conquers all: cf. Virgil, *Eclogues*, X. 69: "Omnia vincit amor: et nos cedamus Amori." Cf. *Orlando Innamorato*, I.5.17.8; II.9.47.5.

Verses 9–11: cf. *Orlando Innamorato*, I.12.11.1–3.

111. Sonnet 92

Just as the icy serpent moves constrained
by the power of Thessalian incantations,
and as the Mauretanian hunter moves,
trembling and fearful when he sees the lion;

so moves my heart, of blood and spirit drained,
when he returns to his same suffering
and chills with fear and trembles and grows faint
because he thinks to have no peace again.

It is compelled to go and yet resists,
but Love obliges it against its will
so that its ancient anguish is renewed.

It goes like snow beneath the sun,
but can't do more than shed its tears and sigh
and fearfully move on with faltering steps.

---

the icy serpent: Virgil, *Eclogues*, III.93: "frigidus . . . latet anguis in herba." Cf. 82.2.6

Thessalian incantations: cf. poem 97.

Mauretanian: from Mauretania, the north-western part of the African continent; land of the Moors.

112

In questo loco, in amoroso riso
se incominciò il mio ardor, che resce in pianto:
tempo fallace e ria fortuna, quanto
è quel ch'io son da quel che era diviso!

Quivi era Amor con la mia donna assiso,
né mai fu lieto e grazïoso tanto;
alor questa aula de angelico canto
sembrava e de adorneza un paradiso.

Quanto a quel tempo questo se disdice!
Di questa corte è mo' bandito Amore,
sieco Alegreza e Cortesia fugita;

ed io qui rinovello il mio dolore,
ché il loco dove io sono or me ne invita
per rimembranza del tempo felice.

113

Non più losenghe, non, che più non credo
a' finti risi e a tue finte parole;
non più, perfida, non, che non ti dole
del mio morir, al qual tardi provedo.

Già me mostrasti, ed or pur me ne avedo,
rose de verno e neve al caldo sole:
l'alma tradita più creder non vole,
né io credo apena più quel che ben vedo.

Così avess'io ben li ochi chiusi in prima,
come Ulisse le orechie a la Sirena,
che se fiè sordo per fugir più male.

così avess'io davanti fatto stima,
come dapoi, del duol che al fin mi mena!
Ché il pensar doppo il fatto nulla vale.

112. Sonnet 93

In this very place, with love-filled laughter,
my ardor, which is now a plaint, was born;
deceitful time and wicked fortune, how
distant am I now from what I was!

Here Love sat with my lady at his side,
and never was he happier, more gracious;
this hall then seemed to fill with angels' songs
and was adorned as though a paradise.

How different is the present from the past!
For now Love has been banished from this court,
and Joy and Courtesy have fled with him;

and I here now renew my suffering
for the place itself invites me to the task
in memory of all those happy times.

In this very place: presumably, the court of Sigismondo d'Este at Reggio.

113. Sonnet 94

No, no more flattery, for I believe
no more in your feigned smiles and your false words;
no, no more, false friend, because my death,
which I am late to counter, does not grieve you.

You showed me then, and I now still regret it,
roses in winter, snow beneath the sun;
A soul, betrayed, no longer would believe,
and I but scarce believe what my eyes see.

Oh would that I had shut my eyes back then,
just as Ulysses sealed his ears to the Sirens' song,
becoming deaf to flee a greater evil!

Oh would that I had sensed before, as after,
the suffering that leads me to my end,
for after-thoughts are not of any value!

114

Lo Idaspe, il Gange e l'Indo agiaceranno
là sotto il Cancro nel cerchio focoso,
e nel spirar di Bora furïoso
gli monti Iperborèi rinverdiranno;

Quando gli Sciti il sol più longe avranno
vedrassi in neve il monte Cassio ascoso;
e nel tempo più fredo e più guazoso
Istro, la Tana e Araxe fumaranno.

Qual cosa fia che non muti Natura?
Li orsi nel mare e li delfin ne l'alpe
vedremo andar, la luna dov'è il sole,

la terra molle e l'unda farsi dura,
il tigre dama e il lince farse talpe,
se io costei fugio e lei seguir me vole.

Sirens' song: in Homer's *Odyssey* (12.39, 184) the Sirens are sweet-voiced sea creatures that live on an island near Scylla and Charybdis. "In Hellenistic art and literature they are representative of music almost as much as Muses." (*OCD*)

just as Ulysses sealed his ears: as Homer tells the story, Odysseus sealed the ears of his crew with wax while he listened to the Sirens' song with impunity by having his companions tie him to his mast (*Odyssey* 12).

114. Sonnet 95

The Hydaspus, Ganges, and the Indus river
will lie there under Cancer's fiery circle,
and with the furious blowing of the Bora
the northern mountains will turn green again.

When the Scythians have the Sun at greater distance,
Mount Cassius will be seen covered with snow;
and in the coldest and the dampest times
the Ister, the Tana and Aras will smoke.

What thing is there that Nature cannot change?
We'll see the bears go out to sea, and dolphins
to the Alps, the moon replace the Sun,

the earth grow limp, the water's waves grow firm,
the tiger made a deer, the lynx a mole,
when I'd flee her or she would follow me.

Hydaspes: a tributary of the Indus, now called Jeloum.

Bora: a fiercely cold wind that blows north across the Adriatic.

When the Scythians . . . : in summer.

Mount Cassius: Jebel Akra in Syria (Mount Casius in antiquity) or, as (*SC*) suggests, a mountain near Pelusium in Egypt. In any event, under normal conditions neither would be covered with snow in summer.

the Ister . . . Aras: from Latin *Ister*, the lower Danube; *Tana*, Latin *Tanais* or modern Don river; *Aras*, Latin *Araxes*, a river in Armenia.

115

Semisenarii

*Sì come canta sopra a le chiare onde
il bianco cegno, gionto da la morte,
fra l'erbe fresche, e l'ultime sue voce
più dolcemente de adornar si forza,
forsi per far al Ciel qualche pietade
dil suo infelice e doloroso fine:*

*così ancor io, davanti che il mio fine
me induca a trapassar le infernal onde,
poiché non ho soccorso da Pietade,
voglio cantar inanzi a la mia morte
quel duol che il cor mi serra e sì mi forza
che il passo chiude a le mie extreme voce.*

*Oh, che fossero odite queste voce
da quella altiera che mi caccia al fine
de la mia vita, e che lassar mi forza
il suo bel viso, prima che ne l'onde
di oscura Lete me bagnasse morte!
Forsi gli soverria di me pietade.*

*Deh, come credo che giamai pietade
tochi colei per lamentevol voce
che non si placa e vede la mia morte?
Crudel stella de Amore, è questo il fine
che convien a mia fede? Ove son l'onde
che di lavar tal machia abin mai forza?*

*La tua perfidia a lamentar mi forza,
fera fallace e vuota di pietade,
abenché io sapia che al rio vento e a l'onde
del mar turbato geto queste voce.
Ma che, se pur me ascolti? ché già al fine
del tanto sospirar me aduce morte.*

*Fosse pur stata alora questa morte,
quando lo amor mio stava in summa forza,
ché nel tempo gioioso è meglio il fine.
Adesso che mancata è ogni pietade,
cerco con prieghi e con pietose voce
placare a l'aria il vento, il foco a l'onde.*

115. Sestina

Sexains

Just as the white swan sings on crystal *waves*
when he is met upon his way by *death*,
amid fresh greenery, as his last *sounds*
to ornament more sweetly he will *strive*
perhaps to move the Heavens to show *pity*
because of his unhappy, painful *end*,

just so do I still want (before my *end*
compels me to traverse infernal *waves*,
considering I have no help from *Pity*),
to sing, before I reach my hour of *death*,
of suffering that seals my heart and me so *strains*
it bars the issue of my dying *sounds*.

Oh that the proud one were to hear the *sounds*,
the one who hurts me to the very *end*
of life, and her sweet countenance *makes me*
forsake before I am cast in the *waves*
of dismal Lethe, bathed by the hand of *Death*!
Perhaps she would be overcome by *pity*.

Alas! How can I ever think that *Pity*
will touch her when she hears my plaintive *sounds*,
if she's not moved by witnessing my *death*?
Cruel star of Love, is this the worthy *end*
my faithfulness deserves? Where are the *waves*
that can obliterate this stain by *force*?

To shed my tears your treachery does *force me*,
false and beastly creature void of *pity*,
well knowing to the bitter wind and *waves*
of seas in turbulence I throw these *sounds*.
Your listening matters what? For to the *end*
of all my sighing I am led by *Death*.

If only it had come back then, this *Death*,
back when my love possessed its greatest *force*,
for better comes in joyful times the *end*.
Now that there is a total lack of *pity*,
I try with prayers and with my piteous *sounds*
to calm the dawn, the wind, the fire and *waves*.

Pietose farian l'onde   a la mia morte
queste mie voce,   e non pòno aver forza
porre in costei pietade   del mio fine!

116

Oggi ritorna lo infelice giorno
che fu principio de la mia sagura,
e l'erba se rinova e la verdura
e fassi il mondo de bei fiori adorno.

Ed io dolente a lamentar ritorno
de Amor, del Cielo, de mia sorte dura,
che adesso infiama la vivace cura
che se agelava al cor dolente intorno.

El tempo rivien pur, come era usato,
fiorito alegro lucido e sereno,
di nimbi raro e di folta erba spesso;

ed io son da quel che era sì mutato,
de isdegno, de ira e sì de angoscia pieno
che il giorno riconosco, e non me stesso.

Compassion to the *waves*, upon my *death*,
will these *sounds* bring; yet they have not the *force*
to make her *pity* me, nearing the *end*.

Just as the white swan sings: the legendary Swan's Song; Aristotle says: "They are musical, and sing chiefly at the approach of death; at this time they fly out to sea, and men, when sailing past the coast of Libya, have fallen in with many of them out at sea singing in mournful strains, and have actually seen some of them dying." (*Historia Animalium*, Book IX.12, 615a–615b) The reference here is certainly to Cygnus, who died of sorrow and was transformed into a swan after his friend Phaeton fell to his death into the Eridanus, a mythical river of antiquity said to have had its source in the Elysian Fields of the Underworld; it has most often been identified with the Po river of Boiardo's homelands in northern Italy. See Book Two of Ovid's *Metamorphoses*.

infernal waves: the river Acheron, the river of sorrow in Hades which the souls of the dead had to bathe in or cross.

dismal Lethe: see poem 97.

Cruel star of Love: the planet Venus.

116. Sonnet 96

Today returns that most unhappy day
that was the very source of my misfortune,
while the grass renews itself with all things green,
and the world adorns itself with lovely blooms.

And I, in anguish, will complain again
of Love, of Heaven, of my bitter fate,
for now the vivid passion in my heart
that had grown cold is bursting into flame.

The season, as it always has, returns,
bedecked with flowers, cheerful, bright, serene,
and rarely clouded, always thick with grass.

And I'm so different from the way I was,
so full of anger, anguish, and disdain,
that I can recognize the day, but not myself.

An anniversary poem.

117

Già per lo equal suo cerchio volge il sole
lasciando il fredo verno a le sue spalle,
e per li verdi colli e per le valle
son le rose odorate e le vïole.

Ma tu non vedi come se ne vóle
il tempo leve, misero mortale,
che stai pur fermo ne lo usato male,
e dei perduti giorni non ti dole.

Recordite, meschin, chi in tal stagione
il tuo Fattor per te sofferse pena
per liberarti de eterna pregione.

Io più non posso, perché error mi mena
dove io non voglio, e la stanca ragione
contro a la fresca voglia ha poca lena.

118

Sovente ne le orechie mi risona
una voce sotil che me ramenta
gli falli andati e dice che io me penta,
perché a' pentuti il suo Signor perdona.

Io, come quel che pur non abandona
la veste incesa e del foco paventa,
ho nel mio core ogni virtù sì spenta
che nulla assente a la ragion che il sprona.

Lasso mio core e simpliceto e fole,
che traportar te lassi a quel desio
che a molti ha tolto e a te la vita tole,

convèrtite, convèrtite al tuo Dio:
ché se lui per camparti morir vòle,
e tu te occidi, ben sei più che rio.

117. Sonnet 97

The sun is turning in its equal rounds
while leaving winter's chilling cold behind,
as the fragrant roses and the violets
appear in valleys and on greening hills.

But you don't see how swiftly nimble time
flies on, you wretched mortal who remain
so firmly planted in your usual woe,
and you don't mourn the passing of lost days.

Remember, wretch, that in this very season
your Creator suffered so much pain
to free you from an everlasting prison.

I can do no more, since error leads me
where I would not go, and my tired mind
has little strength to fight against fresh passion.

---

in its equal round: the vernal equinox (now March 22), when the sun appears to cross the celestial equator into the northern hemisphere, and day and night are of equal length.

your Creator suffered: like Petrarch's narrator, the poet here identifies his own suffering with that of Christ. The poem in an interior dialogue, with the poet responding to himself in the final tercet.

118. Sonnet 98

My ears do often echo with the sound
of a quiet voice that calls to mind again
my past transgressions, bidding me repent,
because the Lord forgives the penitent.

I, like one who does not tear away
his burning clothes though terrified of fire,
have a heart so drained of all resolve
it won't respond at all to Reason's spurring.

My tired, foolish and unthinking Heart,
that let yourself be drawn to that desire
which has taken others' lives and now takes yours,

convert, convert yourself and turn to God:
for if He willed his death to rescue you,
and you destroy yourself, you're more than evil.

119

Le bianche rose e le vermiglie e i fiori
diversamente in terra coloriti,
e le fresche erbe coi süavi odori,
e li arborselli a verde rinvestiti,

solveno altrui ben forsi da' rancori,
e rinverdiscon gli animi inviliti;
ma e me più rinovelano e' dolori
piante fronzute e bei campi fioriti:

ch'io vedo il mondo, da benigne stelle
adorno tutto in sua novella etade,
mostrar di fuor le sue cose più belle;

e la mia fera da sua crudeltade
né da la sua dureza mai se svelle,
né il dolce tempo fa dolce pietade.

120

Capitalis Duplex

Gentil Madonne, che veduto aveti
Mia vita incesa da soperchio ardore,
E ciò che fuor mostrar m'ha fatto Amore,
Ardendomi vie più che non credeti,
Non scio se nel parlar mio ve accorgeti
Remoto da me stesso esser il core;
E spesso, per aver tal parte fore,
Io me scordava quelle che voi seti.
Voi sete in voce in vice di sirene,
Ed io vi parlo con rime aspre, e versi
Rigidi, e nuote di lamenti piene.
Trarami forsi ancor mia Dia di pene,
E canti scoprirò ligiadri e tersi:
Alora avreti quel che a voi convene.

Finis

119. Sonnet 99

The roses, white and red, and other blooms
that fill the earth with every shade and hue,
the fresh, fresh herbs with delicate aromas,
the shrubs and saplings cloaked again in green,

perhaps can free some others of their rancour,
and restore the spirits of despondent souls,
but as for me green plants and flowered fields
simply renew my sorrow even more:

for I see that the world, adorned with lucky stars
in its new season, shows for all to see
those things of hers that are most beautiful;

yet my fierce lady never is set free
of her hard-heartedness and cruelty,
nor does the season's sweetness bring sweet mercy.

120. Sonnet 100

Double Acrostic

Gentle Ladies, you who have beheld
My life inflamed by my excessive ardor,
Even all that Love has made me do,
Arousing passion's flame more than you know:
No, words alone may not reveal just how
Remote my heart is from my very self;
Except that often, since I lost my heart,
I have forgotten what you mean to me.
Voices like yours remind me of the Sirens',
Especially when I declaim harsh rhymes, and
Rigid verses, notes filled with laments.
That Goddess may yet free me from this pain,
Eventually I may sing happy songs:
And then you'll have the homage you are due.

Gentle Ladies: The poet's cousins, Genevre and Marieta Strozzi. Cf. poem 82.

End of Book Two

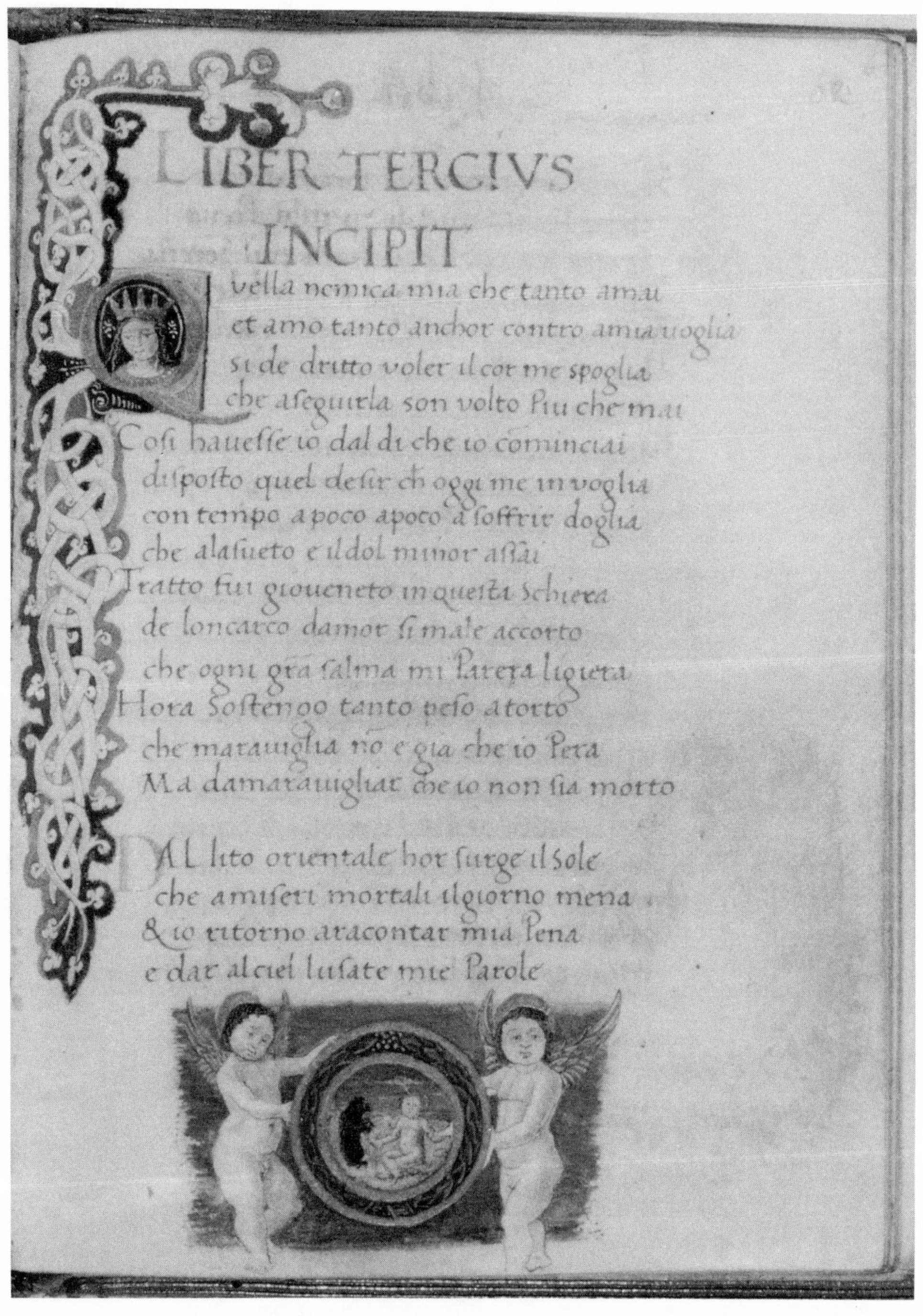

LIBER TERCIVS
INCIPIT

Quella nemica mia che tanto amai
et amo tanto anchor contro amia uoglia
si de dritto voler il cor me spoglia
che aseguirla son volto Piu che mai
Cosi hauesse io dal di che io cominciai
disposto quel desir ch oggi me invoglia
con tempo apoco apoco a soffrir doglia
che alasueto e il dol minor assai
Tratto fui giouenetto in questa schiera
de loncarco damor si male accorto
che ogni grā salma mi Pareça ligiera
Hora Sostengo tanto peso atorto
che marauiglia nō e gia che io Pera
Ma damarauigliar che io non sia morto

DAL lito orientale hor surge il Sole
che amiseri mortali il giorno mena
& io ritorno aracontar mia Pena
e dar al ciel lusate mie Parole

Biblioteca Nazionale Marciana (Venezia), MS. It. IX,545 (= 10293), f. 62r

Amorum Liber Tercius Incipit

121

Quella nemica mia che tanto amai
ed amo tanto ancor, contro a mia voglia,
sì de dritto voler il cor me spoglia
che a seguirla son volto più che mai.

Così avesse io, dal dì che io comminciai,
disposto quel desir che oggi me invoglia
con tempo a poco a poco a soffrir doglia,
ché a l'asüeto è il dol minor assai.

Tratto fui gioveneto in questa schiera,
de lo 'ncarco d'Amor sì male accorto
che ogni gran salma mi parea ligiera.

Ora sostegno tanto peso a torto
che meraviglia non è già che io pèra,
ma da maravigliar che io non sia morto.

122

Dal lito orïentale or surge il sole
che a' miseri mortali il giorno mena;
ed io ritorno a racontar mia pena
e dar al Ciel l'usate mie parole.

Se Amor ingrato e ria fortuna vole
che ne la vita mia, de nimbi piena,
sperar non possa un'ora più serena,
ben a ragion quest'alma se condole.

Beginning of Book Three

121. Sonnet 101

That enemy of mine I once so loved,
and still do love so much, so strips my heart,
against my will, of its own firm resolve
that I must, more than ever, follow her.

Oh would that, from the day that I began,
I had disposed of that desire which now
with time but slowly spurs me on to suffer,
for pain is less to one grown used to it.

I was drawn into this lover's band when young,
so unaware of how much Love demands
that every burden seemed like naught to me.

I now unjustly bear so great a weight
it's not a wonder that I'm perishing;
the wonder is I'm not already dead.

122. Sonnet 102

The sun that brings the day to wretched man
now rises up above the eastern shore,
and I turn again to telling of my woes
and letting Heaven hear my time-worn words.

If ungrateful Love and my misfortune will
that I may not hope for a time of greater peace
in this life of mine, filled with tempestuous clouds,
my soul, indeed, has every right to grieve.

Anzi a gran torto se lamenta e adira
l'anima fol, che al generoso foco
ardendo sì süave se disface.

Piagne cantando e ridendo sospira,
in lieto affanno, in lacrimoso gioco,
pena sì dolce che penar li piace.

123

Prima cagione a l'ultimo mio male,
dritto vïagio del mio torto errore,
stilla fresca pietade a tanto ardore,
ché altro rimedio al mio scampo non vale.

Ben cognosco me stesso, e non son tale
che potesse fugir dal mio Signore:
egli è d'alto ardir pieno, io di terrore,
io grave e inerme, ed egli ha il dardo e l'ale.

Io no posso fugir, né fugir voglio,
ché tanto libertà prezar non degio
quanto il bel laccio d'or che il cor me anoda.

E se captivo in sua pregion me vegio,
dico palese, e vuò che il mondo m'oda,
che non d'Amor, ma sol di te mi doglio.

124

Dovunque io son se canta e se sospira,
di spene si ragiona e di paura;
or pietosa sembianza, or vista dura
a tempo me rafrena, a tempo agira.

Crudeltà me contrasta, Amor me tira
a la preda gentil che il cor me fura;
ed ella or mi spaventa, or me asicura,
or mi dà pace, ed or meco se adira.

And yet the senseless soul that is undone
by burning sweetly in a generous flame
does wrong to seethe with anger, and lament.

It wails when singing and it sighs with laughter,
it dwells in happy woes and tearful joy,
in such sweet sorrow that it likes to suffer.

123. Sonnet 103

First cause of what will be my final doom,
straight way that leads me into twisted error,
please douse my flaming ardor with fresh pity,
for no other remedy can save me.

I know myself too well, I am not one
that could escape the power of my Lord:
He's filled with passion's flame, and I with terror,
I'm slow, unarmed, while he has darts and wings.

I cannot flee, nor do I want to flee,
for I do not hold my liberty as dear
as that fine loop of gold that binds my heart.

And if I see me captive in his prison,
(I say this openly so all may hear)
it's not of Love, but you that I complain.

First cause: the poet's lady.
my Lord: Love.

124. Sonnet 104

Wherever I may be, I sing and sigh,
and speak of hope and speak as well of fear;
at times with mercy's look, at times with hostile eyes,
she draws me near or stops me from approaching.

Cruelty bars my way and Love directs me
toward the gentle prey that steals my heart;
at times she frightens me, at times she reassures,
at times she offers peace, at times it's anger.

Ardo entro a un giazo sì splendido e puro,
che in tanta pena sol per lui mirare
iacio nel foco, e non mi scio partire.

Donne amorose, per Amor vi giuro
che e' non ha il mondo, in quanto cinge il mare,
viver sì dolce, on sì dolce morire.

125

Se in morïente voce ultimi pregi
han forcia di pietade in alcun core,
odi la voce de un che per te more,
crudiel, che al fin ancor mercé mi negi.

Tu me vedi morir, e non ti piegi,
o cor di pietra, a l'ultimo dolore;
e sai che altro non priego il Cielo e Amore
che da le membre l'anima dislegi.

Ma nulla vien a dir, ché Idio destina
il fine a tutti li animanti in terra,
né, perché io preghi, a' mei prieghi declina.

Dona tu pace adunque a tanta guerra,
ché ben fia tropo mia vita meschina
se tu pietade e il Ciel morte mi serra.

126

Quel fiamegiante guardo che me incese
e l'osse e le medole,
quelle dolce parole
che preson l'alma che non se diffese,

volto han le spalle, e me co il foco intorno,
anzi dentro dal petto, han qui lasciato,
a le insegne d'Amor preso e legato,
né speranza mi dan di suo ritorno.

Così, stando captivo, il lungo giorno
tutto spendo in pregiera;
così la note nera,
mercé chiamando a quella che mi prese.

I burn within an ice so pure and bright
that, while my staring causes me great pain,
I lie in flames not knowing how to flee.

Enamored ladies, I do swear by Love
the world, all that the sea surrounds, contains
no sweeter life than this, no sweeter death.

125. Sonnet 105

If in a dying voice these final prayers
can stir compassion in another's heart,
do hear the voice of one who dies for you,
Cruel lady, who deny me mercy to the end.

You see me die and are not moved at all,
to ease my dying pain, O heart of stone;
you know I ask no more of Heaven and Love
but to release my soul from fleshly limbs.

But prayers are valueless, for God decides
the destiny of every living thing,
and does not heed my prayers because they're prayers.

May you, therefore, bring peace in this great war,
for life will be too full of grief for me
if Heaven bars me death, and you compassion.

126. Ballata 10 (Ballata Grande)

That burning glance that set me all aflame
down to my bones and marrow,
those sweet and tender words
that seized my soul, defenseless where it stood,

have turned away and left me captive here,
beneath Love's standard, caught and bound,
engulfed in flames, or rather filled with fire,
and with no hope of seeing them return.

And so do I, a prisoner, now spend
the whole day long in prayer;
thus do I spend black night
begging for mercy from the one that snared me.

127

A l'ultimo bisogno di mia vita
Non dinegati aiuto al core infermo;
Tutte altre vie son rotte, ogni altro scermo,
Ogni rimedio, ogni altra spene è gita.
Ne la vostra pietà sol spero aita,
In voi soletta ogni speranza fermo;
Altri che voi da l'amoroso vermo
Campar non pote l'anima ferita.
Adesso che vedeti farmi giaza
Per quel fredo crudiel che v'è nel core,
Rencresavi che io manchi in tante pene.
Amar vi voglio, e che non vi dispiaza
Richiegio in guiderdon di tanto amore:
A voi ciò poco, a me fia summo bene.

128

La fiamma che me intrò per li ochi al core
consuma l'alma mia sì dolcemente
che apena il mio morir per me si sente,
tanto süave infuso è quello ardore.

Come colui che in sonno dolce more
morso da l'aspe, e con l'ochio languente
rifiuta il giorno, e la torpida mente
senza alcun senso perde ogni vigore;

così ancor io, del mio dolce veneno
pasciuto, vo mancando a poco a poco,
né posso del mancar prender sospetto:

ché, abenché io senta il spirto venir meno,
non cerco per campar spegner il foco,
per non spegner con seco il mio diletto.

127. Sonnet 106

As one last favor in this life of mine,
No, don't deny your aid to my sick heart;
The other roads are blocked, and every shelter;
Other cures and other hopes are gone.
Now my only hope is your compassion,
In you alone I place my every hope;
And, without you to help, my wounded soul
Cannot escape Love's worm and its effect.
And as you watch me turning into ice,
Paled by the bitter cold that's in your heart,
Regret, at least, my dying in such pain.
All that I want is to love you, and the sole
Reward I ask is that it not displease you,
A little thing for you, the greatest good for me.

Another acrostic spelling the name Antonia Caprara, without the usual title *Capitalis*.

128. Sonnet 107

The flame that entered me and reached my heart
by passing through my eyes, consumes my soul
so sweetly that I hardly know I'm dying,
so gently has that fire been kindled there.

Like one who dies, when bitten by the asp,
in a pleasant sleep, and with his failing eyes
renounces day, while his numbed and sluggish mind,
deprived of all sensation, loses strength;

just so do I continue dying bit by bit
for having fed upon my own sweet venom,
nor am I quite aware of this slow death:

for, while I feel my spirit growing weak,
I do not quench the fire to save my life,
in order not to quench my joy as well.

129

Duolmi la mia sventura, e più mi dole
che mostrar non la può la pena mia;
anzi la mostro, e più la mostreria
se me ascoltasse chi ascoltar non vole.

Feci mia doglia nota in cielo al sole,
in mar a gli delfin già per folia,
e lamentai de la fortuna ria
già su la verde piagia a le vïole.

Né fiore è in terra, in mar pesce, in ciel stella
né in tutto quel che 'l mondo immenso cinge
è cosa che non senta del mio ardore;

e questa crëatura umana e bella
no il sente lei, o non sentir s'infinge;
sola no il sente, e tu il consenti, Amore?

130

Se passati a quel ponte, alme gentile,
che in bianco marmo varca la rivera,
fiorir vedreti eternamente aprile,
e una aura sospirar dolce e ligera.

Ben vi scorgo sinor che v'è una fiera
che abate e lega ogni pensier virile,
e qualunque alma è più superba e altiera,
perso la libertà, ritorna umile.

Ite, s'el v'è in piacer, là dove odeti
cantar li augei ne l'aria più serena,
tra ombrosi mirti e pini e fagi e abeti.

Ite là voi, che io son fugito apena,
libero non, ché pur, come vedeti,
porto con meco ancora la catena.

129. Sonnet 108

My misfortune grieves me, and grieves me so
my pen cannot reveal to what degree.
Indeed I do reveal it, and would more
if she who does not listen only would.

I made my sorrow known to the Sun above,
for the dolphins out at sea I played the fool,
and then complained as well of my poor luck
to the violets upon the verdant shore.

There is no flower on earth, no fish at sea,
no star, nor, in all that this vast world includes,
one thing that has not heard of my obsession;

And yet this beautiful and gentle creature
does not hear of it, or so pretends;
is she alone, Love, deaf with your consent?

130. Sonnet 109

If you, O gentle souls, but cross that bridge
that spans the river with its marbled white,
you'll find eternal April flowering,
and a gentle breeze that seems to sweetly sigh.

But let me warn you of a beast that's there
that downs and binds the thoughts of every man;
and the soul that is most proud, that is most vain,
losing its liberty, returns subdued.

Go there, if it pleases, where you hear
the birds all singing in that stiller air
mid shady myrtles, beeches, pines and firs.

Go to the place from which I've just now fled,
no, not free, for as you well can see,
I carry with me still my chains from there.

---

that bridge: metaphorical passageway to the world of love.

131

Come puote esser che da quella giaza
venga la fiama che me incende il core?
come puote esser che cotanto ardore
non struga il gielo e il corpo mio disfaza?

Vogliàn noi creder che Natura faza
da tanto fredo uscir tanto calore?
on ver che la possanza sii d'Amore
che l'amplo mondo e la Natura abraza?

D'Amor procede, che forzò Natura
a far quel monstro de atomi diversi,
che il cor ha giaza e li ochi foco ardente.

Li ochi di foco e il cor di giaza dura
fiè concrear Amor, per più potersi
mostrar excelso intra le umane gente.

132

1. *Novo diletto a ragionar me invita*
de quello ardor che più se fa vivace,
e la mia vita dolcemente ariva.
Ma nanti che da me facia partita
l'alma che a poco a poco se disface,
nanti che al tutto de spirar sia priva,
agia il cor lasso tanta tregua o pace
da il dolce fiamegiar che intro lo impiglia
che mostrar possa altrui per maraviglia
quanto a se stesso nel suo fin compiace;
perché, come sovente se asumiglia
a ogni animal che di suo voler more,
così contento è lui morir de amore.

2. *Novo piacere e disusata voglia*
che il cor mio prende de il suo dolce male
nel viso altiero e de mercé ribello!
Così par che non senta morte o doglia
tra gli Indi più deserti uno animale,
che un corno ha in fronte e tien nome da quello.

131. Sonnet 110

How can it be that from that frozen ice
there comes a flame that puts my heart on fire?
How can it be that such intensity
does not destroy the ice or my own flesh?

Do we really think that Nature can
emit from so much cold such burning heat?
Or is it not instead the power of Love
embracing all the world, and Nature too?

The source is Love, that forced on Nature to create
from diverse particles so strange a thing,
with heart of ice and eyes of burning fire.

Love let those eyes of fire, that frozen heart
of ice be formed together just to show
himself supreme among our human kind.

132. Canzone 8 [9]

1. A new delight invites me now to speak
about that passion which grows more intense,
and moves my life so sweetly to Death's shore.
Before my soul, which slowly wastes away,
takes leave entirely and parts from me,
before it is deprived of every breath,
may my tired heart have peace or truce enough
from the sweetly burning flames consuming him
to show to all the world as though a wonder
the pleasure he derives from his demise;
for, since he often bears a close resemblance
to every beast that dies of its own will,
my Heart is likewise glad to die for love.

2. What strange pleasure and unknown desire
for his own sweet torment grasps my heart
in that proud face that is opposed to mercy!
So too, it seems, remotest India has
a beast that senses neither death nor pain,
with a one-horned brow from which it gets its name.

Forzia né inzegno a sua presa non vale,
fuor che da il grembo virginile accolto,
ove ogni ardir, ogni poter gli è tolto,
e lui si sta, né di morir gli 'n cale.
Ed io, per mia cagion, me sono avolto
in tanto lieta e dilettosa sorte
che partir non me scio da la mia morte.

3. *Dove la forcia più del sol se aduna,*
sotto il cerchio più largo al nostro polo,
ne la terra odoriffera e felice,
vive uno augello, in quella gente bruna,
che sempre al mondo se ritrova solo
sancia altro paro, ed ha nome Fenice.
Quando da li anni sente tardo il volo,
cinamo incenso cassia e mira prende,
e bate l'ale se che il sol lo 'ncende;
arde se stesso, e manca sancia dolo.
Così la fiamma mia lieto me rende,
e dami foco tanto dilettoso
che arder mi sento e di partir non oso.

4. *Sotto la tramontana al breve giorno,*
ove l'onda marina in giel se indura,
un picolo animal tra' monti nasce,
bianco di pelo e di facione adorno
e sì nemico al tutto di lordura
che sol di neve candida si pasce.
Tanto gentile il fece la Natura
che se, forsi cacciato, il luto vede,
sostien da quello il delicato pede
e più belleza che la vita cura.
Ben fa maravigliar, ma chi no il crede
venga a veder un uom che muor tra noi
non per la sua beltà, ma per l'altrui.

5. *Canta uno augello in voce sì süave,*
ove Meandro il vado obliquo agira,
che la sua morte prende con diletto.
Lassar le usate ripe non gli è grave,
ma con dolce armonia l'anima spira,
né voce cangia al fin né muta aspetto.

Not force nor wit can serve to capture it,
save when it rests upon a virgin's lap,
where it loses all its drive and all its strength,
and there it stays, and shows no fear of dying.
And I, for my own reasons, cloaked myself
in such a happy and delightful fate
I don't know how to keep me from my death.

3. Where the power of the sun is most intense,
beneath the widest circle of our pole,
in a land of fragrance and felicity
there lives a bird among the dark-skinned people,
alone among the creatures of the world
with no equal, and its name is Phoenix.
When it feels its flight slowed down by years,
it gathers incense, cinnamon, cassia and myrrh,
and beats its wings to help the Sun ignite them;
it burns itself, and feels no pain in death.
So, too, does my flame bring me happiness,
and so delightful is the fire it gives
I feel the burning yet dare not to flee.

4. Beneath the north wind, where the days are short,
where ocean waves are hardened into ice,
a little creature's born amid the hills,
adorned with pure-white fur and the finest form
and such an enemy of unclean things
it only feeds upon the cleanest snow.
And Nature made it so genteel, that if,
when being hunted, it should see some mud
it keeps its dainty paw from touching it,
caring more for beauty than for life.
It makes one wonder; yet whoever doubts it
may come to see a man die in our midst
for another's beauty rather than his own.

5. A bird sings, where Maeander makes its way
upon its twisting bed, with a voice so sweet
it takes its death as though it were a pleasure.
To leave its usual shores is not a burden,
for its soul expires with sweet harmony,
nor does it change its voice or look in dying.

L'unda de il fiume il novo canto ammira,
e lui fra l'erbe fresche a la rivera,
perché nel suo zoir doglia non spera,
segue cantando ove Natura il tira.
Così me tragge questa bella fiera
a volontaria morte e dolce tanto
che per lei moro, e pur morendo canto.

Dunque tra li animali il quinto sono,
ché a morte de mia voglia me destino;
ma siano Amore, e quel viso divino
che ora me occide, e il Sol che io abandono,
sian testimoni al spirto peregrino
che altro remedio al suo lungo martìre
trovar non puote che amando morire.

133

Or che sotto il Leon più boglie il celo,
aridi e' fiumi e rasciuta è ogni vena,
l'umor ne l'erbe se mantien apena,
sanza neve son l'alpe e sanza gelo.

Ed io di più fervor il cor me invelo,
che già mi dete ascoso occulta pena;
or l'ho scoperto per fiaccata lena
e pòrtol ne la fronte sanza velo.

Adesso che il ciel arde e il mondo avampa,
sotto il sol vado, torrido e affanato,
dove alta voglia e gran desir me chiama.

Felice chi da' laci d'Amor campa,
ma felice vie più, vie più beato
chi amato è parimente quanto egli ama.

The river's waters welcome its new song,
and on the fresh, young grass along the bank
it goes on singing still where Nature leads,
for it expects no sorrow with such joy.
So does this lovely savage beast drag me
to such a sweet and voluntary death
I die for her, still singing as I die.

I am, therefore, the fifth among those creatures,
for I willingly submit myself to death;
may Love, and that divinely fashioned face
that kills me now, and the Sun I leave behind,
bear witness that my wandering spirit
can find no other remedy for this
long martyrdom except to die while loving.

The four animals to which the poet compares himself (unicorn, phoenix, ermine, and swan) all voluntarily sought their own deaths, according to the medieval tradition of the bestiaries (Benvenuti, 583). The ermine would rather die than be sullied.

Phoenix: passage derived from Ovid's *Metamorphoses* 15, 392–400 (*LBL* 280).

5.1, *Maeander*: a river of Asia Minor that flows by a tortuous course into the Aegean; now called Menderes.

133. Sonnet 111

Now that the heavens boil beneath the Lion,
and every river and every spring is dry,
the grass has hardly any moisture left,
the mountains are without their snow and ice.

And I conceal my heart in greater fervor,
which, hidden, gave me so much secret pain:
but now I'm forced by weakness to expose it,
and bear it on my brow without a veil.

Now that the heavens burn and the world's ablaze,
I walk beneath the sun, distressed and scorched,
to where great passion and desire call.

Happy is the one who flees Love's bonds,
but happier by far and far more blessed
is he who's loved as much as he does love.

134

Il sol pur va veloce, se ben guardo,
e il tempo che se aspetta mai non vene;
ben par che il gran desir nanti me mene,
ma il corpo resta adietro ignavo e tardo.

Il sol di fuor me scalda, ed io dentro ardo;
il mio cor falso m'ha lasciato in pene:
esso è veloce e nulla cosa il tene,
ma passa avanti più legier che pardo.

Egli è davanti già del suo bel lume,
dove Amor lo rinfresca a la dolce ombra
e tienlo ascoso sotto a le sue piume;

ed io pur mo' son gionto a picol fiume
che rotto ha il varco e il mio passar ingombra,
acciò che lunga indugia me consume.

135

Qual sopra Garamante on sopra Gange
se aduce il cervo paventoso e stanco,
batendo per lo affanno il sciuto fianco,
quando fatica e caldo inseme lo ange;

come l'onda corrente in prima tange
il spirto anello, il gran desir vien manco,
e il sangue torna sbigotito e bianco
per la fredura che il fervor afrange;

tal il mio cor, che di gran sete avampa,
nel suo bel fonte disïando more,
e piglia oltre al poter l'ampla dolceza:

the Lion: the constellation Leo, in antiquity, was always associated with the sun, which passed through it from mid-July to mid-August. Today the sun passes through Leo from mid-August to mid-September, the change being due to precession.

134. Sonnet 112

The sun moves rapidly, if I see well,
and yet the moment I await does not arrive:
it seems my great desire leads me forward,
but my body lags behind, in fear and sloth.

The sun beats down and, inwardly, I burn;
my own disloyal heart has left me grieving:
he is so nimble, nothing can detain him;
he moves ahead more swiftly than a leopard.

He has already reached his lovely light,
where Love, beneath sweet shades, refreshes him
and keeps him hid beneath his feathered wing;

and I've arrived just now at that small stream
which has a broken bridge to slow my way,
so that I am consumed by the long delay.

and I've arrived. . . : not clear where the poet has arrived.

135. Sonnet 113

As when the fearful and exhausted deer
arrives upon the Ganges or at Garamant
with thirsting flanks still heaving with distress
as heat and weariness combine to torture it;

When first the flowing water meets the heaving breath,
the great desire to drink is lessened some,
but the blood is quickly filled with icy fear
by the chill that shatters its first fervor.

So, too, my heart, which burns with such great thirst,
does die while gazing at her with desire,
drinking more pleasure than it can endure:

però che nel mirar questa vagheza
ha giunto tanto foco al primo ardore
che maraviglia n'ho se quindi campa.

136

Tu te ne vai e teco vene Amore,
e teco la mia vita e ogni mio bene,
ed io soletto resto in tante pene,
soleto, sancia spirto e sancia core.

Debb'io forsi soffrir questo dolore
che io non venga con teco? E chi me tene?
Ahi, lasso me, che con tante catene
me legò sempre e lega il nostro onore.

Oh, se io credesse pur che alcuna volta
di me te sovenisse, anima mia,
quanto minor sarebbe il mio martìre!

Ma quando io penso che me sarai tolta
oggi, e sì presso è la partita ria,
campar non posso, o di dolor morire.

137

Colui che il giorno porta è già ne l'onde,
on forsi oltre a Moroco splende ancora,
e fammi sovenir sempre quest'ora
de l'altro Sol che Crudeltà me asconde.

Donde procede il mio sperar, e donde
procede quel desir che me inamora,
se la fortuna mia pur vol che io mora
e tolto me è quel ben che me confonde?

Speranza vien dal Ciel, e il gran desire
vien dai begli ochi e da le chiome d'oro,
ed ambi dal pensier che perir vole.

for in contemplating so much loveliness,
it's added so much fire to its first passion
that I shall be amazed if it survives.

Garamant: see poem 23.

136. Sonnet 114

You're going away and Love is going with you,
and with you goes my life and all that I cherish;
and I remain alone with so much sorrow,
alone, without my spirit and my heart.

Must I, because I do not go with you,
endure this suffering? Who holds me back?
Alas, for I am bound by those same chains
with which our honor always held me fast.

Oh if I could believe, my dear, that you
upon occasion would remember me,
how much less pained would be my martyrdom!

But when I think that you'll be taken from me
today, and your cruel departure is so near,
I neither can endure, nor die of sorrow.

137. Sonnet 115

That one who brings the day is on the waves,
or is, perhaps, still shining past Morocco,
and always brings to mind at just this hour
that other Sun that Cruelty hides from me.

From where comes that desire, from where my hope
that causes me to fall in love with her,
if my own fortune wishes me to die
and lose that good that is destroying me?

Hope comes from Heaven, and my intense desire
comes from her lovely eyes and golden hair,
and both come from the thought that wants to perish.

Ora vegendo il giorno dipartire,
con lo emispero nostro me scoloro,
poiché me è tolto l'uno e l'altro Sole.

138

Ligiadro veroncello, ove è colei
che de sua luce aluminar te sòle?
Ben vedo che il tuo danno a te non dole,
ma quanto meco lamentar te dèi!

Ché sanza sua vagheza nulla sei,
deserti e' fiori e seche le vïole:
al veder nostro il giorno non ha sole,
la notte non ha stelle senza lei.

Pur me rimembra che io te vidi adorno,
tra' bianchi marmi e il colorito fiore,
de una fiorita e candida persona.

A' toi balconi alor si stava Amore,
che or te soletto e misero abandona,
perché a quella gentil dimora intorno.

139

Io sento ancor nel spirto il dolce tono
de l'angelica voce, e le parole
formate dentro al cor ancor mi sono.

Questo fra tanta zoglia sol mi dole,
che tolto m'ha Fortuna il rivederle.
Quando vedrò più mai nel dolce dire
da quelle rose discoprir le perle?

Quando vedrò più mai lo avorio e l'ostro
nel süave silenzio ricoprire
ligiadre parolete? Il tacer vostro
contro a mia voglia a lamentar me invita.

Ancor sarà che io senta il gentil sono,
e questa spene sol me tene in vita,
per questa il mondo ancor non abandono.

Now seeing that the day is on the wane,
I too grow darker with our hemisphere,
since each of my two Suns is taken from me.

138. Sonnet 116

O happy, little balcony, where is
that lady that often lights you with her glow?
I see that you do not lament your loss;
but, oh, how much you ought to cry with me!

For you are naught without her loveliness,
and the blossoms droop, and the violets are dead:
to these eyes of ours the day is without sun,
the night, without her, has no other stars.

Yet I remember that you were adorned,
amid the colored flowers and white marble,
by a person with fair skin and florid hue.

Back then, there stood on you the God of Love,
who has abandoned you, alone and sad,
because he now dwells near that noble one.

139. Ballata 11 (Ballata Mezzana)

I hear still in my soul the dulcet tones
of that angelic voice, and the words are still
now being formed down deep within my heart.

Just this, amid such joy, does cause me pain:
that Fortune keeps me now from hearing them again.
When will I ever see in such sweet speech
the pearls revealed again beneath those roses?

When will I ever see again that red
and ivory covering such graceful words
with gentle silence? Silence that is yours
invites me to lament against my will.

It well may be that I shall hear again
that gentle sound, this hope keeps me alive;
that's why I've not abandoned yet this world.

140

Nel mar Tireno, encontro a la Gorgona,
dove il bel fiume de Arno apre la foce,
uno aspro scoglio ha il nome che me coce
e che me agela, e che me afrena e sprona.

A la cima superba il vento intona,
e l'onda intorno il bate in trista voce,
ma lui si sta sicuro, e non gli noce
il vento altiero e il mar che il circumsona.

Questo altro scoglio mio tanto è più duro
quanto è più bello, e tanta è sua belleza
quanta Natura ne può dare e Jove.

Lui dal vento de Amor si sta sicuro
e l'onde sue focose in tutto speza;
speza sua forza, che può tanto altrove.

141

Questa legiadra e fugitiva fera,
per la cui vista ne le selve io moro,
ha candida la pele e chiome d'oro,
vista caprina, mobile e legiera.

De un corno armata è la sua fronte altera,
che ognor che al cor mi rede, me scoloro,
e l'ochi söi quai nell'alto coro
splendono e' ragi de la terza spèra.

Lei sdegna in tutto ogni conspetto umano
e ne li alti deserti sta solinga,
sì che a' nostri ochi è tropo rara in vista.

E pur la segue ancor il desir vano
e nel seguirla se stesso alosinga,
dicendo: il tempo al fine il tutto aquista.

140. Sonnet 117

In the Tyrrhenian Sea not far from Gorgon's isle,
where the lovely river Arno has its mouth,
there is a rough-hewn rock whose name both burns
and freezes me, and reins and spurs me on.

The wind intones upon its haughty peak,
and the waves beat with a melancholy voice;
but it stands firm, uninjured by the wind,
indifferent to the sea that wails there around.

Just as it is more beautiful, so is
this other crag of mine more harsh; her beauty
is as great as Jove and Nature can bestow.

It stands unmenaced by the winds of Love,
and dashes all his burning waves to pieces;
it shatters the power that elsewhere does so much.

Tyrrhenian Sea: the portion of the Mediterranean that is bounded by Corsica, Sardinia, Sicily, and the western shore of Italy.

Gorgon's Isle . . . a rough hewn rock: Gorgona and Capraia, two small, rather desolate islands near the northern tip of Corsica in the Tuscan archipelago. Cf. Dante, *Inferno*, 33.82. Capraia, of course, reminds him of Antonia Caprara.

141. Sonnet 118

This graceful, fleeting, untamed beast,
for the sight of which on wooded lands I die,
has snow-white skin and golden locks of hair,
and a swift and light and nimble caprine air.

Her forehead, proud, is armed with but one horn,
and I grow pale each time she fills my heart,
and her eyes shine just as brightly as the rays
of the sphere that holds third place in Heaven's choir.

She scorns entirely all human warmth,
and stays alone in far, deserted heights,
making the sight of her rare to our eyes.

And yet a vain desire still follows her,
and while pursuing her cajoles itself
and says: time will in the end subdue all things.

142

—Fior scoloriti e palide vïole,
che sì süavemente il vento move,
vostra Madona dove è gita? e dove
è gito il Sol che aluminar vi sòle?—

—Nostra Madona se ne gì co il sole
che ognor ce apriva di belleze nove,
e poiché tanto bene è gito altrove,
mostramo aperto quanto ce ne dole.—

—Fior sfortunati e vïole infelice,
abandonati dal divino ardore
che vi infondeva vista sì serena!—

—Tu dici il vero, e nui ne le radice
sentiamo el danno, e tu senti nel core
la perdita che nosco al fin te mena.—

143

Sperando, amando, in un sol giorno ariva
la nostra etade a l'ultima vechieza;
quella speranza che sì ben fioriva
come caduta è mo' di tanta alteza!

Come fa mal colei che me ne priva!
Ché il nostro amore e l'alta sua belleza
farebbe odire in voce tanto viva
che se apririan le pietre per dolceza.

Sperai con tal desir, e fui sì presso
al fin del mio sperar, che io vuò morire,
pensando ora che fui, che sono adesso.

Copri dentro, dolor, non mi far dire;
ma pur questo dirò: non rivien spesso
sì bella préssa a chi non scia tenire.

caprine air: playing on the name Caprara.
the sphere that holds third place: again, the planet Venus.

142. Sonnet 119

"You fading blossoms and pale violets
that the wind so gently moves in its embrace,
where has your lady gone? And where has gone
the Sun that used to bathe you in its light?"

"Our lady has departed with the warmth
that always opened us to show more beauty;
and since so fine a thing has gone away,
we let show openly how much we grieve."

"Unlucky blossoms and sad violets,
you are abandoned by that heavenly flame
that once infused you with serenity."

"You speak the truth: we feel within our roots
the harm that's done; and you feel in your heart
the loss that leads you to life's end with us."

143. Sonnet 120

Hoping, loving, in a single day
we are borne unto the final stage of life;
how low that hope which blossomed once so well
has fallen from what were such lofty heights!

How wrong is she who now deprives me of it!
For I would sing our love and her great beauty
in a voice so full of life for all to hear
the stones would split asunder in delight.

I hoped with such desire, and was so near
to having hopes fulfilled, that I want to die
now thinking what I was and have become.

Stay hidden, grief, let me not speak of it.
Yet I'll say this: that such a lovely prize
does not return to the one who cannot keep it.

144

Io son tornato a la mia vita antica,
a piagner notte e giorno, a sospirare,
dove già non credea più ritornare,
ché pur sperava alfin Pietade amica.

Ahi, lasso, che io non scio quel che io me dica,
tanto mia doglia me fa vanegiare;
non spero, e non potei giamai sperare
in questa fera di mercé nemica.

Ben fu tradito il misero mio core,
che un poco il viso li mostrò Ventura,
perché sua doglia poi fosse maggiore.

Sempre la bianca sorte con la scura
di tempo in tempo va cangiando Amore,
ma l'una poco, e l'altra molto dura.

145

1. *Nel doloroso cor dolce rivene*
la rimembranza del tempo felice,
quando mia sorte più me téne in cima.
Quella antica memoria ancor elice
li usati accenti e la voce mantene
al süave cantar come di prima.
Ligiadri versi e graziösa rima
che usar solea nel mio novello amore,
a che non travi fore,
se da quella crudiel non son udito?
Così cantando aquetaremo il core
che tacito non trova alcuna pace,
il cor che se disface
pensando a quel piacer dove è partito.
Ahi, lasso, ove è fugito,
ove ènne il tempo fugitivo andato,
nel qual sopra ogni amante fui beato?

2. *Era in quela stagione il ciel dipinto*
nel clima occidental di quelle stelle
che del pigro animale il fanno adorno:

144. Sonnet 121

I've turned again to my former way of life,
to crying night and day, to wishful sighs,
to where I never thought to turn again,
for at last I hoped to have a friend in Pity.

Alas, I know no longer what I say,
since suffering now makes me rave so much;
I do not put my trust, nor ever have,
in this fierce beast, compassion's enemy.

My wretched heart was certainly betrayed,
as Fortune briefly cast his gaze on him
so that his sorrow then would be increased.

Love always alternates good luck with bad
with unexpected turns; but the one endures
so brief a time, and the other so much more.

145. Canzone 9 [10]

1. To a dolorous heart so sweetly comes again
the memory of happy, by-gone days
when my good fortune kept me riding high.
That ancient memory now still evokes
the notes heard long ago, and prompts my voice
to singing just as sweetly as before.
You elegant and graceful Verse and Rhymes
that I engaged when love for me was new,
why not now draw you out,
yes, even though that cruel one hears me not?
Thus shall we, singing, pacify the heart
that finds no peace at all in being still;
that heart that is consumed
by thinking of that joy and where it's gone.
Alas! where has it fled,
where has that transient moment gone when I,
among all other lovers, was most blessed?

2. The western reaches of the sky that season
were painted with the stars that there adorn it
with the figure of the lazy beast,

per che di chiare e splendide fiamelle
nel liquido sereno avea distinto
la fronte al Tauro e tutto il dextro corno.
Girava il sole al cerchio equale intorno,
e da l'artica parte e da l'australe
l'uno e l'altro animale
che lo amoroso Jove in piume ascose,
quel che cantando sotto a le bianche ale
a la fresca rivera Leda accolse,
e quel che de Ida tolse
il biondo Ganimede e in celo il pose.
Or stelle aspre e noiose
de lo Angue e del Delfin disperse in celo
stringon la terra e l'onde in tristo zielo.

3. *Era la terra verde e colorita*
di celeste color, di color d'oro,
di perso e flavo e candido e vermiglio.
Apria Natura ogni suo bel lavoro,
la palida vïola era fiorita
e la sanguigna rosa e il bianco ziglio.
Li amorosi augelleti el lor conciglio
facian cantando in sì dolce concento
che potean far contento
qualunque più di noglia il cor se grava.
Ogni arborsel di nova veste incento
o fronde o fiori in quella stagion ave,
e l'aura più süave
tra le verde fogliette sospirava.
Ed or la stagion prava
li arbori e l'erbe di belleza spoglia,
e' fiumi de unda, e me colma di doglia.

4. *Piovea da tutti e' celi amore in terra*
e ralegrava l'anime gentili,
spirando in ogni parte dolce foco;
e i giovanetti arditi e i cor virili
sanza alcun sdegno e sanza alcuna guerra
armegiar si vedean per ogni loco;
le donne in festa, in alegreza, in gioco,
in danze perregrine, in dolci canti;
per tutto leti amanti,
zente lezadre e festegiar giocondo.

so that the heavens' clear, resplendent flames
distinguished Taurus' brow and his right horn
in the heavens' liquid-like serenity.
The sun turned equal circles in its course
and on the arctic and the austral side
soared those two creatures
that concealed in feathered garb the amorous Jove,
the one who, singing, had, beneath white wings,
embraced Queen Leda by the cool stream's edge,
the one who stole fair Ganymede
from Ida's peak and placed him in the sky.
But now the troubling stars
of the Serpent and the Dolphin spread above
hold earth and sea in a cold and bitter grip.

3. Back then the earth was green and painted
with celestial color, and the color of gold,
and with vermillion, yellow, white and perse.
And Nature opened up her lovely works:
the violet, so pale, was then in bloom,
as were the blood-red rose and snow-white lily.
The love-birds gathered as a council then
by singing in such perfect harmony
that they could fill with cheer
whoever had a heart weighed down by woe.
It was the season when each little tree
was dressed in newest garb of flower or frond.
and the gentlest little breeze
passed like a sigh through verdant little leaves.
And now corruption's season
robs the trees and grass of beauty, and rivers
of their flow, and fills me full of sorrow.

4. Love rained upon the earth from every heaven
and brought its joy to every noble soul
by kindling its sweet fire all about.
Young men of passion with courageous hearts
were seen to arm themselves throughout the land
without the threat of war and without anger;
And ladies took to festiveness and gaiety,
and games, and novel dances, and sweet song;
happy lovers everywhere,
and cheerful folks and gay festivity.

Non sarà più, che io creda, e non fu avanti
fiorita tanto questa alma cittade
di onor e di beltade
e di tanto piacer guarnita a tondo.
Bandite or son dal mondo,
non pur da noi, Bontade e Cortesia,
in questa etade dispetosa e ria.

5. *Colei che alor mi prese ed or mi scaccia,*
che il spirto mio manten da me diviso,
tal che di vita privo incendo ed ardo,
mi se mostrò con sì benegno viso
che ancor par che membrando me disfaccia
l'ato süave di quel dolce guardo.
Girava il viso vergognoso e tardo
vèr me talor di foco in vista accesa,
come fosse discesa
Pietà dal cielo a farla di sua schiera.
Indi fu l'alma simpliceta apresa,
il senso venenato, il cor traffitto
da li ochi, ove era scritto:
—Fole è chi aiuto d'altra donna spera—.
Or più non è quel che era,
ma spietata sdegnosa altera e dura,
stassi superba, e del mio mal non cura.

Canzon, da primavera
cangiata è la stagione e il mio zoire
in nubiloso verno e in rio martìre.

This lovely city will not be again,
I think, nor ever was before, so decked
with honor and with beauty,
and filled in every way with so much pleasure.
Now banished from the world,
though not by us, are Courtesy and Goodness,
in this spiteful, wicked age of ours.

5. She who welcomed me but does no more,
who holds my spirit captive out of me
so that I burn although deprived of life,
approached me with sure kindness in her eyes,
that only thinking back on it, her sweet
and gentle look seems to consume me still.
With modesty she slowly turned her face
toward me with eyes that were at times on fire,
as though Compassion had
come down from heaven to call her to its band.
Then was my foolish soul inflamed by Love,
my senses poisoned and my heart transfixed
by eyes wherein was writ:
"A fool alone awaits another's aid."
She is no more what she
once was, but, spiteful, scornful, proud and cruel,
she stands off caring not about my pain.

My song, the season's changed
from spring to cloudy winter, and my joy
has turned into a painful martyrdom.

---

the lazy beast: Aristotle (*Historia Animalium*, 600a–b) and a strong tradition ("Of considerable persistence is the association of the bear with laziness, an association which perhaps stems from the bear's habit of hibernating" [Rowland, 34–35]), would support the commentators who have consistently seen this as a reference to Ursa Major, the Great Bear, even though it never approaches the western horizon, and is, in fact, closest to the zenith in spring. At the time of the vernal equinox, it is not possible to have Ursa Major in the western quadrant with Taurus visible. The dilemma is most easily resolved if we understand *nel clima occidental* ("the western reaches of the sky") to refer to the "western world" rather than to the western portion of the sky.

two creatures that concealed the amorous Jove: travelling with the sun are Cygnus (the Swan) and Aquila (the Eagle), Zeus/Jove's two avian personae.

Queen Leda: object of Zeus' passion when he took the form of a beautiful white swan.

Ganymede: Zeus snatched him from Mount Ida and carried him off to Mount Olympus.

the Serpent and the Dolphin: constellations of winter.

146

A che te me nascondi, e vòi che io mora,
crudiele? E che farai poi che io sia morto?
che farai poi, crudiel, se occidi a torto
un che te ama cotanto e che te adora?

Io sarò di tormento e pena fora,
dapoi che mia fortuna vol tal porto;
or sia così, che pur me riconforto,
se tanto mal se sgombra a l'ultima ora.

Non voglio vita, non, sancia tua pace,
né cosa vòlsi mai con tuo dispetto;
e così me morò, se pur te piace.

Ma tu dimi in tua fede: e che diletto,
che zoglia hai de un meschin che se disface
per star bandito dal tuo dolce aspetto?

147

Ben fu mal'ora e maledetto punto,
disventurata festa e infausto gioco,
tempo infelice e sfortunato loco,
dove e quando ad amar prima fu' giunto.

Da indi ogni piacer mi fu disgiunto:
ardo nel giazo ed agiazo nel foco,
e in doglia mi consuma a poco a poco
il venenoso stral che il cor m'ha punto.

Ahi, despietate stelle e crudel celo,
se da voi forsi vien nostro destino
e vostra forza noi qua giù governa!

Tante volte cangiasti il caldo al gelo,
la rosa al pruno; ed io, sempre meschino,
mai non fui scoso da la doglia eterna.

146. Sonnet 122

Why do you hide from me and wish my death,
cruel lady? What will you do when I am dead?
What will you do, cruel lady, if wrongfully
you kill the one who loves and worships you?

My pain and torment will have ended then,
since destiny has willed that port as mine;
so let it be, it even comforts me,
if finally such hurt can be undone.

I want no life, no, not without your peace,
nor did I ever want what you would scorn;
and so I'll even die, if you'll be pleased.

But tell me truthfully: what joy is there,
what pleasure's gained for one poor wretch who dies
when banished from the sweetness of your sight?

147. Sonnet 123

It was a cursèd time and cursèd place,
a sorry celebration and a wretched game,
a too unhappy time, unlucky place
there where and when I first began to love.

From that time on I lost all sense of pleasure,
I burn in ice and freeze within a fire;
the poisoned dart that has transfixed my heart
destroys me slowly with relentless pain.

O wicked heavens and unlucky stars,
if destiny descends to us from you,
and if your power governs us below!

So often did you turn the heat to ice,
the rose to thorn, while I, forever wretched,
was never freed of my eternal grief.

148

Solea cantar nei mei versi di prima
quel crespo lacio d'or che il cor mi prese,
e quel guardo süave che me incese
già da le piante extreme a l'alta cima.

Or Tema e Spene in combatuta rima
de amore e de dureza fan contese,
e son le sue ragion sì adentro intese
che per se stesso il cor se rode e lima.

Fermo è de amar colei che Amor disvia,
e così a mal suo grado vol seguire
con novi passi per l'antiqua via.

Forsi tacendo ancor farò sentire
che io son mutato e son quel che io solia
a la mia vita che mi fa morire.

wretched game: while *gioco* usually means "joy" in the *Amorum Libri*, I agree with (*SC*) that here it may refer literally to a social game, an occasion which would have allowed the poet the opportunity to express his affection to his lady. Such a game is described in *Orlando Innamorato*, I.12.7–8.

148. Sonnet 124

In early verses I would often sing
of the curly, golden snare that seized my heart,
and the gentle gaze that set me all aflame,
consuming me from lowly soles to crown.

Now Fear and Hope debate in warring verses
that speak of love and then of cruelty,
and the arguments are so well put by both
my heart consumes himself in indecision.

He firmly loves the one that side-steps Love,
and so to his own detriment would go
with freshened steps upon the ancient way.

Perhaps in silence I will still reveal
that I am changed, and yet just as I was,
to the one who gives me life and makes me die.

---

my heart consumes himself: the personification demands the masculine form of the reflexive pronoun. The consumption expressed by the verbs *rodere* and *limare* is both an "eating away" and a "wearing down." *Limare* may also suggest the polishing of verses, as in the opening octave of the *Orlando Furioso*, where the poet's wits are "limed" away by his lady as he "limes" his verses.

149

Rine(ro) Gualando

Letto ho, Rinieri, il tuo pianto süave,
che vivo vivo par che arda e sospiri;
misero me, con quanta arte me tiri
a ramentarme del mio stato grave!

O del mio cor serrato unica chiave,
che a mio diletto tanto me martìri,
perché non sei presente? E ché non miri
come un'alma gentil dolce se agrave?

Acciò che quello altero e crudo core,
che a sì gran torto mia mercé mi niega,
odendo tal pietà se fèsse umano.

Rinier mio dolce, ben fun teco Amore,
anzi è ancor teco, e le tue rime spiega
e scrive e' versi toi con la sua mano.

150

Non credeti riposo aver giamai,
spirti infelici che seguìti Amore,
ché morte non vi dà quel rio Signore,
ma pena più che morte grave assai.

Odito aveva, e poi istesso il provai,
che non occide l'omo il gran dolore:
se l'occidesse, io già di vita fore
sarebbe, onde mi trovo in pianti e guai.

Né sua alegreza ancora al fin vi mena,
che fuge come nimbo avanti al vento,
e in tanta fuga se cognosce apena.

Così fra breve zoglia e lungo stento
e fra mille ore fosce e una serena,
amante in terra mai non fia contento.

149. Sonnet 125

Rine(ro) Gualando

I've read, Rinier, your sweetly-worded plaint,
which vividly portrays your sighs and passion;
poor me, with what great skill you badger me
to recollect the depth of my sad state!

O single key that can unlock my heart,
and torture and delight me in one stroke,
why aren't you here? why aren't you watching how
a sweet and gentle soul aggrieves itself?

So that that proud and unjust heart of hers,
which wrongfully denies me my reward,
in hearing of such grief, would be made kinder.

Dear Rinier, friend, Love truly was with you,
indeed still is, and he inspires your verse
and writes your poetry with his own hand.

The dedication is to a friend of the poet as yet unidentified.

150. Sonnet 126

Unhappy spirits, don't think that you'll find rest
as long as you go chasing after Love,
for that cruel Lord does not deliver death,
but suffering far greater than death's pain.

I'd heard, and then discovered for myself,
that great affliction does not kill a man:
for if it killed, I'd long have left this life;
instead I find myself in tears and woe.

Nor does Love's joy pursue you to the end,
but rather flees like clouds before the wind,
and in that flight is hardly recognized.

And so, between brief joy and lengthy trial,
a thousand cloudy hours and one serene,
a lover'll never be content on earth.

151

Dialogus Cantu Isdem Desinentiis Respondente
Versibus Rithimis Conversis

1. *—Chi te contrista ne la età fiorita,*
o misero mio core?
Dove è quel dolce ardore,
e la assüeta zoglia ove è fugita?
Come succisa rosa e colto fiore
è languida toa vita;
quella beltà che te arse dentro e fore
come è da te bandita?—
—Così m'ha cuncio Amore,
e la speranza al gran desir fallita
ha di tal foco incesa mia ferita
che ogni pena è minore;
ma nanti che partita
facia da te con tanto mio dolore,
per mia voce fia odita
la crudiel tirannia di quel Signore.—

2. *—Forsi per altrui colpa il tuo disdegno*
a lamentar te tira,
e forsi oltraggio ed ira
te fan nemico a l'amoroso regno;
ma se ben dritto il tuo iudizio amira,
Amore è in sé benegno,
e con virtute sempre a l'alma aspira
bontade e pensier degno.—
—Deh, se ciò credi, agira
li ochi al mio stato, che de Amor è un segno,
e potrai divisar nel mio contegno
se 'l tuo pensier delira.
Vedi il Signor malegno
quanto lontano al ciel or me ritira;
onde io di duol son pregno,
mirando quanto indarno se sospira.—

151. Canzone 10 [11]

A Song in the Form of a Dialogue between the Poet's Soul and Heart

1. "Who, in your youthful bloom, so troubles you,
O wretched Heart of mine?
Where is that gentle passion,
where has our customary joy now fled?
Just like a severed rose or fresh-picked bloom,
your life is languishing;
how is the beauty that engulfed you once
with flames now banished from you?"
"It's Love that's fixed me so,
and the failure of my hope in its desire
has kindled since such burning in my wound
no other pain compares;
but yet before I take
my leave of you in so much agony,
that Lord's cruel tyranny
will be revealed to all by my own voice."

2. "Perhaps another causes you your wrath
that leads you to complain;
perhaps abuse and ire
make you an enemy of Love's sweet realm,
but if your judgement is well aimed you'll find
that Love himself is kind,
and in his virtue always fills the soul
with goodness and fine thoughts."
"Indeed, if that's your view,
look now upon my state, a sign of Love,
and you may judge by how you see me act
if you are raving madly.
Just look and see how far
that evil Lord has pulled me back from heaven;
hence I am filled with grief
in knowing that my sighs are all in vain."

3. *—Non sei tu per Amor quel che tu sei,*
se in te vien Legiadria,
se Onor e Cortesia?
Ah, pensa pria se lamentar te dèi!
Lamentar di colui che l'armonia
infonde ai vagi occei!
che infonde a' tigri umana mente e pia,
e fa li omini Dei!—
—Non son quel che io solia,
ma son ben stato, più che io non vorei,
suggeto a quel crudel ed a colei
che la mia fede oblia.
Mai non puòte per lei
aver riposo ne la vita mia,
e così me disfei
con spene incerta e certa gelosia.—

4. *—Se quella che de amor prima te incese*
a te forsi non rede
quella usata mercede
che al tuo desir già per bon tempo rese,
perché da l'altre il tuo voler recede
se una sola te offese?
Né per unico exemplo se concede
che tutte sien scortese.—
—Crede a me—dico,—crede,
che il mar levato e l'alpe fien distese,
la terra ignota e il ciel ne fia palese,
quando in donna fia fede.
Se questa che mi prese,
che è il fior di quelle che il ciel nostro vede,
suo detto non atese,
che faran l'altre che li son soppede?—

5. *—Or questo adunque è quel che te sospende?*
Questo geloso vento
lo usato foco ha spento,
se spento se può dir quel che te incende?
O che nel duol vanegi, o l'argumento
per me ben non se intende:
ché, se da lei sei libero e discento,
Amor de che te offende?—

3. “Are you not what you are because of Love,
if you know Happiness
or Courtesy and Honor?
Ah, think first if you really should complain!
Complain about the one who fills the birds
with harmony of song!
who gives to tigers human, pious thoughts,
and turns men into gods.”
“I'm not what I once was,
instead I've been subjected, more than I
would want, to that cruel Lord and her who is
forgetful of my faithfulness.
Because of her, my life
can never find repose,
and I give up my faith
in doubtful hope and certain jealousy.”

4. “If she who first inflamed your heart with love
no longer grants to you
the customary favor
she once exchanged with you for your desire,
why does your will recede before all others
if only one offended you?
One cannot from a single case conclude
that all lack courtesy.”
“Believe me when I say
the sea will rise, the alps will be spread flat,
the earth unknown and heaven manifest
when trust is placed in woman.
If she who captured me,
the flower of those that dwell beneath our sky,
did not maintain her faith,
what will those others do that are her foot-stool?”

5. “Is that then what has filled you with such doubt?
Has jealousy's cold wind
extinguished that old flame,
if one can say ‘extinguished’ for what burns you?
You either rave with pain or what you say
makes little sense to me:
for, if you're free of her and of your bonds,
just how does Love offend you?”

—Vie più cresce il tormento,
quando altri meco del mio mal contende,
e lui, che quel non sente, me riprende
se a ragion me lamento.
Dal colo ancor mi pende
gran parte di quel laccio onde era avento,
e sì nei piè discende,
che al dipartir de Amor son grave e lento.—

Canzone, il cor, già guasto
da lo amoroso foco, ancor fa guerra
a quel che regna in celo e regna in terra
e regna nel mar vasto;
e l'alma pur se afferra
già per antica usanza a far contrasto,
e tal ragion disserra,
che io per me stesso a iudicar non basto.

152

Ecco la pastorela mena al piano
la bianca torma che è sotto sua guarda,
vegendo il sol calare e l'ora tarda,
e fumar l'alte vile di luntano.

Erto se leva lo arratore insano
e il giorno fugitivo intorno guarda
e soglie il iugo a' bovi, che non tarda,
per gire al suo riposo a mano a mano.

Ed io soletto, sanza alcun sogiorno,
de mei pensier co il sol sosta non ave,
e con le stelle a sospirar ritorno.

Dolce affanno d'amor, quanto èi süave!
Ché io non pòsso alla notte e non al giorno,
e la fatica eterna non me è grave.

"Far greater is my torment
when others would debate my plight with me,
and they, who do not share that plight, reproach me
even when I'm right to grieve.
There hangs yet from my neck,
the greater portion of that snare that bound me,
and falls about my feet,
in a way that makes me slow to flee from Love."

O song, my heart, laid waste
by flames of love, still wages war against
the one who rules in heaven and on earth
and rules across vast seas;
and my soul as well holds fast,
opposing him as is her ancient way,
and makes such arguments
that I alone cannot be the judge of them.

---

the one who rules in heaven and on earth: Love.

152. Sonnet 127

See there, the shepherdess leads down to the plain
the snowy flock that is her constant care,
seeing the sun sink low and the hour grow late,
and smoke from far-off chimneys start to rise.

The bent and weary plowman stands up straight
and looks around to glimpse the fleeing light,
then quickly frees his oxen from their yoke
so that he too in turn may find repose.

And only I have found no respite yet
from thoughts which rest not with the setting sun,
and so return to sighing with the stars.

Love's woe so sweet, how comforting you are!
For though no night or day can bring me peace,
the endless toil of love for me is light.

153

Cruciatus

Né il sol, che ce raporta il novo giorno,
che sì jocundo in vista or s'è levato,
né de la luna l'uno e l'altro corno
che ancora splende in mezo al ciel stellato,

né l'unda chiara a questo prato intorno,
né questa erbetta sopra al verde prato,
né questo arbor gentil di fiori adorno
che intorno ha scritto il nome tanto amato,

né quel bel augelleto e vago tanto,
che meco giorna a la fiorita spina
e i miei lamenti adegua co il suo canto,

né il dolce vento e l'aura matutina,
che sì süave me rasuga il pianto,
me dan conforto in tanta mia roina.

154

Il terzo libro è già di mei sospiri,
e il sole e l'anno ancor non è il secondo;
tanto di pianti e di lamenti abondo
che il tempo han trapassato e' mei martìri.

Among the sources of inspiration for this poem one can cite Virgil: *Eclogues*, I.83; *Aeneid*, IV. 522ff.; Dante's Canzone "Io son venuto al punto de la rota"; (Contini 43) *Inferno*, II. 1–6; Petrarch 22 and 50. The possible allusion to the fourth book of the Aeneid would be especially ironic, for the reference there is to Dido's acutely unbearable burden of love.

153. Sonnet 128

Crossed

No, not the Sun, that with a cheerful face
has risen now to bring to us new day ,
nor either of the horns there of the Moon
which still gleams bright against the starry sky,

nor the limpid waters that surround this field,
nor this young grass that lies upon it green,
nor this so noble tree adorned with blooms
that bears her cherished name etched on its bark,

nor even that fine bird so fair that starts
the day with me before the flowered thorn
and equals my lament with its own song,

nor that sweet wind and early morning breeze
that gently dry away my tears each day,
can comfort me in such deep desolation.

For the title, see poem 22.

name etched on its bark: "It was surely a primitive instinct that, long before its recording in literature, impelled young men to write or carve the names of their mistresses on trees or inscribe them on walls." (Renssaeler W. Lee, 9) Cf. 2.104, where the poet addresses the tree upon which he has inscribed his memories.

154. Sonnet 129

This is already my third book of sighs,
and yet it has not even been two years;
I am so filled with tears and with complaints
my suffering has sped ahead of time.

Insensato voler, dove me tiri,
a lamentar del mio stato giocondo?
Qual più diletto me paregia il mondo.
se avien che gli occhi nel bel viso agiri?

Ben muta ancor dureza questa voglia,
a cui non basta che una volta pèra,
ma vol che io consumi in foco e in zielo.

Qual fia quella pietà che mi disoglia
e doni l'ale a l'anima ligera,
che quindi si svoluppi e voli al celo?

155

Chorus Simplex Cantu Tetrastico

Tornato è meco Amore,
anci vi è sempre e mai non se partio,
ma il mio dolce disio
per sua nova pietà fatto è magiore.

Chi segue e dura un tempo, vince alfine:
non è cor sì feroce
che amando e lamentando non se pieghi.

Sparsi ho tanti sospiri e tante voce,
e sparsi ho tanti prieghi
che mitigate ho mie pene meschine;

e le luce divine
lassan l'orgoglio dispetoso e rio,
e con sembiante pio
rendon speranza al mio timido core.

Where, foolish passion, are you taking me,
to grieve about the happy state I'm in?
What greater pleasure can the world provide
than setting eyes upon that lovely face?

Well does her cruelty alter my desire,
for she's not pleased to see me perish once,
but rather be consumed in fire and ice.

Where is that pity that will set me free
by putting wings upon my weightless soul,
which then, unbound, can soar to the skies above?

155. Ballata 12

Ballata Grande

Love has returned to me,
indeed has always been with me, not gone,
but my desire so sweet
has been increased by her renewed compassion.

Who perseveres will, in the end, win out:
There is no heart so fierce
that love and lamentation cannot bend it.

I've spewed so many sighs, so many words,
I've spewed so many prayers,
that I have eased somewhat my wretched pain;

and her heavenly eyes
cast off the wicked, spiteful gaze of pride,
and with a pious look
restore hope's glimmer to my timid heart.

The full meaning of the title of this poem is obscure.

156

Ben dissi io già più volte, e dissi il vero,
che una süave e angelica figura
esser non puote dispietata e dura,
né viso umano asegna core altero.

Mai puòte dimostrare un bene intero
sanza summa beltade la Natura;
e chi forsi no 'l crede, ponga cura
a quella Diva in cui sperava e spero.

Ché la dolce aparenza e il dolce guardo
sua dolce voglia non lasciò mentire,
se ben già dimostrò quel che non era.

Essa m'ha tratto adesso dal morire,
che se creata il Ciel l'avesse altera,
ogni altro aiuto al mio scampo era tardo.

157

Il cielo ed io cangiato abiàn sembianti,
io tutto leto e lui di nimbi pieno;
dove io fui tristo e lui tutto sereno,
lacrima or esso ed io lassiato ho i pianti.

Quel vivo Sol che se ascondea davanti,
fatto ha la luce a l'altro venir meno;
e' vagi lumi del celeste seno
son nel bel viso accolti tutti quanti.

E l'altro sol vedémo, invidïoso
de' capei d'oro e del vermiglio volto,
mostrassi in vista scuro e nubiloso.

E poi che al tristo parangon fu colto,
più non se mostra e tien il viso ascoso,
però che il pregio di beltà gli è tolto.

156. Sonnet 130

I've often said before, and it is true,
that one who has a kind, angelic look
can't also be unmerciful and cruel,
nor can a gentle face conceal a haughty heart.

And Nature cannot show us perfect good
unless it is by means of perfect grace.
Who thinks this not the truth should contemplate
the Goddess who both was and is my hope.

For her gentle nature did not falsify
her sweet appearance and her kindly gaze,
and show therein a nonexistent good.

She now has saved me from the grasp of death,
for if she had been made by Heaven proud,
no other aid would have delivered me.

I've often said: a variation on the Aristotelian/stilnovistic doctrine that states that each "form" must be embodied in a particular kind of matter, and that each emotion requires a particular and suitable physiology; thus, love can only reside in a gentle heart.

157. Sonnet 131

The sky above and I have traded looks,
for I am filled with cheer and he with clouds;
whereas I once was sad and he serene,
now he is shedding tears while I have ceased.

That living Sun that used to hide from me
by contrast has decreased the other's light;
the finest lights of our celestial vault
have all been gathered in her lovely face.

We see the other sun, so envious
of her golden hair and of her crimson blush,
present himself with a dark and clouded face.

And caught in that unfair comparison,
he hides his face and does not show himself,
because he has been robbed of beauty's prize.

158

Né viso virginil de zigli ornato,
né fresche rose a bei crin de auro intorno,
né tronco vedrò mai de edere adorno,
né de vïole e fiori adorno un prato,

che io non abia ne l'alma e in cor segnato
ciò che già mi mostrava un lieto giorno;
di lui cantando a ragionar ritorno
(dolce memoria!) e il tempo bene andato.

Le rose me son foco, e' zigli un giazo,
e l'edere sì forte m'hano avento
che io non fia sciolto mai dal suo bel lazo.

Così di fiori e de vïole cento
a mio diletto mi consumo e sfazo,
e voglio in tal pensier morir contento.

159

Cum Ro(mam) Foret Eundum

Chi piagnerà con teco il tuo dolore,
amante sventurato, e le tue pene,
poiché lasciar t'è forza ogni tuo bene
(dispietata Fortuna!) e il tuo Signore?

Partir conventi e qui lasciare il core,
lasciare il core e partir te convene!
Miser chi signoria de altri sostene,
ma più chi serve altrui servendo Amore!

Ahimè dolente, ahimè, de che ragiono?
Pur scio che certo me convien partire,
e la vita crudiel non abandono?

Ben credo a quel che ho già sentito dire
ed a mio grave costo certo sono,
che doglia immensa non ce fa morire.

158. Sonnet 132

No maiden's face by lilies all adorned,
nor dewy roses laced through golden hair,
nor ivy-covered tree will I behold,
nor field of green bedecked with violets,

without recalling in my heart and soul
all that a happy day once showed to me;
I turn again in song to speak of it
(sweet memory!) and of that happy past.

The roses are a fire, the lilies ice,
the ivy's vine a bond that holds me so
that I shall never flee her splendid trap.

Girded by violets and other blooms,
to my delight I lead myself to ruin,
and with such thoughts I wish to die content.

Cf. Petrarch 312.

159. Sonnet 133

On Having To Go To Rome

Who, wretched lover, will shed tears with you
because of all your suffering and pain,
now that you're forced to leave behind (cruel fate!)
all that you treasure, and your Lord as well.

You must depart and leave your heart behind;
you are obliged to leave your heart and go!
A wretch is he who bears another's rule,
but more the one who serves by serving Love.

Unhappy me! Alas, what do I say?
Indeed, I know that I must soon depart,
and yet I do not leave this cruel world?

Well do I now believe what I've heard said,
and to my own dismay I know it's true,
that endless anguish does not bring us death.

160

Chorus Simplex Rithmo Interciso

Io me vo piagnendo,
e partomi da te contro a mia voglia,
con tanta doglia   che al morir contendo.

Come viver potrò da te lontano,
gentil mio viso umano
che solo eri cagion de la mia vita?
Or sbigotita   a te se aresta in mano:

teco rimansi e l'alma, che n'è gita,
il cor dolente invita
a starsi teco, onde io son fatto insano,
cercando invano   e non trovando aita.

Ma se non è partita
pietà da te più come esser si soglia,
ancor gran zoglia   al mio ritorno attendo.

Io: read as two syllables.

161

—Qual anima divina o cor presago
ridir mi può che fa la luce mia?—
—Stassi soletta, e con malinconia
piagnendo, ha fatto de' begli ochi un lago.—

—Quel viso adunque e la puerile imago,
misero me, più mai qual fu non fia?—
—Non dir così, ché qualle esser solia
farasse al tuo ritorno, e ancor più vago.—

—Viso gentil, che ne gli ochi mi stai,
ne li ochi, ne la mente e in mezo il core,
quando sarà che io te rivegia mai?

On Having To Go To Rome: For the occasion of the coronation of Borso d'Este as duke of Ferrara and Cavaliere of St. Peter by Pope Paul II (Easter Sunday, 14 April 1471), Boiardo travelled to Rome with the lords of Correggio, Carpi, and Mirandola at the head of an entourage of 500 gentlemen dressed, for the most part, in gold and silver brocade (see *Z* and Gundersheimer [156–58]). The journey lasted from March 14 to May 18. *ST*, *SC* and *U* state, incorrectly, that the pope was Sixtus IV.

160. Ballata 13

Ballata Mezzana with Internal Rhyme

I go away lamenting,
and take my leave of you against my will
with so much grief I'm in a war with death.

How shall I live so far away from you,
my kind and noble face
that were the only reason for my living?
Now filled with fear, my life is in your hands:

It stays with you; and my doleful heart invites
my soul, which has departed,
to stay with you; and I am driven mad,
searching in vain for help and finding none.

But if pity has not left you
anymore than it has left you in the past,
great joy awaits me still at my return.

161. Sonnet 134

"What knowing heart or what divining soul
can tell me what my light is doing now?"
"She is alone and, sadly shedding tears,
she's turned her lovely eyes into a lake."

"That visage and that youthful person, then,
alas, will be no longer as before?"
"Not true, for it will be when you return
just as it was before and fairer still."

"O noble face that lingers in my eyes,
there in my eyes, and in my mind and heart,
when will I ever look at you again?

Temo, né sanza causa è il mio timore:
ché per cagioni e per ragione assai
in terra è mal sicuro un sì bel fiore.—

162

De' leti giorni e del tempo migliore,
doppo la dura e cruda dipartanza,
sol di tanto mio ben questo me avanza,
che de dolce penser notrisco il core.

E meco nel camin sen viene Amore,
ragionando di fede e di leanza;
fugio la tema e prendo la speranza,
e me contento del mio stesso errore.

Così davanti a me la mi confingo
che de essermi lontana si sospira
e del mio mal pietosa se condole.

Ben vede l'alma mia che io la losingo
in vanitade, e meco se ne adira,
né in cosa falsa dilettar se vole.

163

Da' più belli ochi e dal più dolce riso,
da la più dolce vista e meno oscura
che in terra dimostrasse mai Natura,
né imaginasse Altrui nel paradiso;

da' crin che mostrar d'auro e da un tal viso
che rose se mostrava e neve pura,
da una celeste e angelica figura
che avrebbe un tronco, un marmo, un fer conquiso,

partir, lasso me, puòte? ed ancor vivo
sanza quelle parole e quella voce
che me fèr già di sé don sì giolivo?

Ahi, come alto diletto spesso noce!
Ché, se per caso averso om ne vien privo,
quanto il danno è magior tanto più coce.

I am afraid; my fear is not unjustified:
for there are many reasons why on earth
so fair a flower's place is so unsure."

162. Sonnet 135

From happy, bygone days and better times,
after the bitterness of leaving her,
just this remains of all the joy I knew,
that I can feed my heart on memories.

And Love is my companion on the way,
discussing faithfulness and loyalty;
I flee from fear and grasp at hopefulness,
and am content to let myself be fooled.

So I forge here an image of her sighing
because she is so far away from me,
and piteously bemoaning my sad state.

My soul knows well that my vain images
deceive her, and she grows irate with me,
not wanting to delight in what is false.

163. Sonnet 136

The loveliest eyes of all and sweetest smile,
the gentlest and by far the fairest sight
that Nature has revealed upon the earth,
or God imagined in His paradise;

And hair that seemed of gold, a face that seemed
composed of roses and of pure white snow,
a figure so celestial and angelic
it could have vanquished wood or marble or iron,

could I, alas, have left all these behind?
Do I live without those words, without that voice
that made themselves so glad a gift to me?

How often great delights can also harm!
For if, by chance, one is deprived of them,
the greater is the loss, the more the sting.

164

Mentre che io parlo e penso il tempo passa
e fassi antiquo nel mio petto amore,
anzi se aviva il tramortito ardore
e se rinova, e me più vechio lassa.

L'alma mia, del suo ben privata e cassa,
poi che è partita a forza del suo core,
conta e' giorni passati e conta l'ore,
e per longo dolor la facia abassa.

Longo dolor, che fai de l'ora uno anno,
del giorno fai più lustri e tempo eterno,
come hai de la mia etade il fior batuto!

Acciò che io riconosca con mio danno
che non sol lunga state e lungo verno,
ma lunga doglia può far l'om canuto.

165

Cruciatus

Dolce sostegno de la vita mia
che sì lontana ancora me conforti,
e quel che il mio cor lasso più disia
nel dolce sogno dolcemente aporti,

deh, qual tanta pietade a me te invia,
qual celeste bontà tuo' passi ha scorti?
Ché per tua vista l'alma, che moria,
ratene e' spirti sbigotiti e morti.

Non mi lassare, o sogno fugitivo,
ché io me contento de inganar me stesso
godendomi quel ben de che io son privo.

E se più meco star non pòi adesso,
sembianza de colei che me tien vivo,
ritorna almanco a rivedermi spesso.

164. Sonnet 137

While I converse and ponder, time moves on
and love grows old residing in my breast;
rather, that failing passion is revived
and is renewed, and leaves me older still.

My soul, deprived and cheated of its prize,
which has been lifted from its heart by force,
counts all the bygone days and all the hours,
and bows its head because of long-felt pain.

O long-felt pain, that make each hour a year,
and make each day an endless span of years,
oh how you've crushed the flower of my youth!

So that I see at last to my dismay
that not just passing seasons make man old
but long-felt sorrow also turns him gray.

165. Sonnet 138

Crossed

O you sweet staff of life that comfort me
even though you are so far away,
and bring to me so sweetly in sweet dreams
just what my weary heart desires most,

what boundless mercy, pray, sends you to me,
and what celestial goodness guides your steps?
For by the sight of you my soul, near death,
restores its dying and despondent spirits.

O fleeting dream, do not abandon me,
for I am now content to fool myself
enjoying that of which I am deprived.

And if you cannot linger here with me,
O vision of the one who gives me life,
at least come frequently to visit me.

Crossed: see poem 22.

166

Quanta aria me diparte dal bel volto
che mai non fia partito dal mio core;
quanti giorni son già, quante son l'ore
che io fui dal gentil viso a forza tolto!

Quante volte la facia e il pensier volto
dove lasciai tra l'erbe il mio bel fiore;
quante volte se cangia il mio colore,
temendo che d'altrui non sia ricolto!

Quanti monti son già, quante alpe e fiumi
che vargan questi membri afflitti e stanchi,
lasciando il spirto fugitivo adetro!

Quando fia adunque mai che il mio duol manchi?
Qual doglia sarà più che me consumi,
se in tanta pena morte non impetro?

167

Io vidi quel bel viso impalidire
per la crudiel partita, come sòle
da sera on da matino avanti al sole
la luce un nuvoletto ricoprire;

vidi il color di rose rivenire
de bianchi zigli e palide vïole,
e vidi (e quel veder mi giova e dole)
cristallo e perle da quilli occhi uscire.

Dolce parole e dolce lacrimare,
che dolcemente me adolcite il core
e di dolcezza il fàtti lamentare,

con voi piangendo sospirava Amore,
tanto süave che nel ramentare
non mi par doglia ancora il mio dolore.

166. Sonnet 139

How distant am I from the lovely face
that never shall be absent from my heart!
How many days have passed, how many hours
since I was forced far from her gentle gaze!

How many times have I turned my face and thoughts
to where I left my flower on the green!
How many times have I changed in color since,
for fear it would be picked by someone else!

How many hills and craggy peaks and streams
these worn and weary limbs have crossed,
leaving behind a spirit bent on flight!

When will my pain, if ever, be assuaged?
What grief might yet exist that can consume me,
if I've not found death in so much hurt?

How distant am I: literally, how much air separates me. . . . Cf. Petrarch 129.60.
changed in color: the colors of fear, anger, jealousy, etc.

167. Sonnet 140

I saw that lovely face of hers grow pale
because she found departure to be harsh,
just as a little cloud will cast its shadow
on the light in evening or in early morn.

I saw the color of the rose transformed
into white lilies and pale violets;
I saw, too, (and that sight gave pain and joy),
how pearls and crystal poured forth from those eyes.

Sweet sounding words and sweetly falling tears
that gently bring sweet comfort to my heart,
and cause it to lament with such delight,

while shedding tears with you Love also sighed
so sweetly that, as I remember it,
my pain does not yet seem to me like grief.

168

Cantus Trimeter

1. *Apri le candide ale e vieni in terra*
a piagner meco, Amore,
che nel mio sommo ben meco cantavi.
Non può sanza tua aita aprire il core
sue pene tanto gravi,
ché un tropo alto dolor la voce serra.
Ben ho da lamentarmi in tanta guerra
che il Ciel me face a torto,
e la sventura mia
tenendomi lontano al mio conforto:
perduto ho lei di cui viver solia,
e non me occide la fortuna ria?

2. *Dapoi che me partio da quel bel volto,*
non ebi ora serena,
né spero aver più mai se io non ritorno.
Sempre in sospiri e lamentando in pena
mi sto la notte e il giorno,
né altro che doglia nel mio petto ascolto.
Fiorito viso mio, chi te m'ha tolto?
Chi m'ha da te partito,
perché vivendo io mora,
come uom di venenato stral ferito,
che de morire aspetti de ora in ora,
vie più che morte lo aspettar lo accora?

3. *Io mi credea con tempo e con fatica*
spiccar dal cor insano
il gran dolor che io presi al dipartire;
or vedo quel sperar falace e vano,
ché io non posso fugire
il dol che meco vene e il cor me intrica.
Lui per l'alpe deserte se nutrica
del mio crudiel affanno,
né per tempo se abassa,
ché, se me stesso forsi non inganno,
oggi compitamente il mese passa
che io me partivo, e il mio dol non mi lassa.

168. Canzone 11 [12]

A Song in Tercets

1. Spread out your pure white wings and come to earth
to cry with me, O Love,
as in my greatest joy you sang with me.
Without your help my heart cannot give vent
to pain as deep as this,
because too great a sorrow seals his voice.
I have good cause to grieve in a war so fierce,
unjustly waged by Heaven,
to grieve of my misfortune
that keeps me far away from my sole comfort:
have I lost the one for whom I lived
without this cruel misfortune killing me?

2. Since being distanced from that lovely face
I've had no peace of mind,
nor do I hope to have till I return.
Both day and night I am immersed in sighs
and in the wails brought on by pain,
and I hear but grief resounding in my breast.
My flowered face, who'se taken you from me?
Who'se drawn me away from you
so that I die while living,
like a man struck by a poisoned dart who waits,
expecting with each passing hour to die,
tormented more by waiting than by death?

3. I thought that with some time and with some toil
I'd wrest from my ailing heart
the suffering that my leaving left with me;
I see now that such hope is false and vain,
for I cannot escape
the pain that follows me and foils my heart.
It wanders through the craggy wilds and feeds
upon my bitter troubles
not lessening with time,
for, if I do not deceive myself in this,
today marks one full month that has gone by
since I left her, yet grief has not left me.

4. *Non mi lassa il dolor, ma più se accende*
qualor più se aluntana
a la cagion che rimembrando il move:
ché or de' begli ochi, or de la facia umana,
or d'altre viste nove
il dolce imaginar spesso me offende;
e l'alma adolorata non intende
quanto il pensier süave
che seco è in ogni loco
facia la pena più molesta e grave,
come l'unda la febre aquetta un poco
e in picol tempo rende magior foco.

5. *Ma se io dovesse ben morir pensando*
di voi, donna gentile,
non fia chi tal pensier mi traga mai.
Ben fòra d'alma timideta e vile,
se la vita con guai
cercasse e dolce morte avesse in bando.
Di voi non pensaragio alora quando
serò sottera in polve,
né vi porrò in oblio,
se un'altra morte l'anima non solve;
ma se disolta puote aver disio,
eterno fia con vosco il pensier mio.

Felice mia canzon, tu che gir pòi
là dove il Ciel mi vieta,
al mio paese divo,
quanto gir debi graziosa e lieta!
Vanne dicendo:—Io lasciai un che è privo
de ogni suo spirto, e sospirando è vivo.—

4. My anguish does not leave me, but intensifies
whenever it is distanced more
from the source that with remembrance gives it life:
for now with her lovely eyes or gentle face
then with some newer sights
my sweet imagination injures me;
and my anguished soul does not well understand
just how that tender thought
that's with it everywhere
can make the pain more troublesome and deep,
like the water that will bring a fever down
and in no time at all will raise its flame again.

5. But if I were to die from thinking of you,
my dear and noble lady,
no one could ever drive that thought from me.
Well would I be of weak and timid heart
if I sought a life of woe
and chose then to forsake so sweet a death.
I'll not be thinking of you when I have turned
to dust beneath the ground,
nor will I soon forget you,
if another death does not undo my soul;
but if it can, undone, still have desires,
my thoughts will be with you eternally.

My happy song, you that are free to go
where Heaven forbids me be,
there in my precious land,
how thankfully and joyfully you'll go!
Go there and say: "I've left a man deprived
of all his spirit, who only lives by sighing."

---

the craggy wilds: the poet crossed the Apennines on the journey to Rome with Borso's entourage.

169

In Prospectu Romae

Ecco l'alma città che fu regina
da l'unde caspe a la terra sabea,
la trïonfal città che impero avea
dove il sol se alza insin là dove inchina.

Or levo fàtto e sentenzia divina
sì l'han mutata a quel che esser solea
che, dove quasi al ciel equal surgea,
sua grande alteza copre ogni ruina.

Quando fia adunque più cosa terrena
stabile e ferma, poiché tanta altura
il Tempo e la Fortuna a terra mena?

Come posso io sperar giamai sicura
la mia promessa? Ché io non credo apena
che un giorno intiero amore in donna dura.

170

Ex Urbe Ad Dominam

Sapi, unico mio ben, che ancora io vivo
e maraviglia del mio viver prendo,
ché, secondo natura, io non intendo
come io mi campi di mia vita privo.

Ogni cosa mortal sempre ebi a scivo
fuor che te sola, da cui vivo e pendo;
or tu me èi tolta, ed io co il Ciel contendo,
ché sanza spirto a morte non arivo.

Io vivo pur ancor, ma in tanta pena
meno la trista vita e in tanti guai
che di portar me stesso non ho lena.

Sì son mutato a quel che me mostrai
che, se forse ventura a te mi mena,
a gran fatica me cognoscerai.

169. Sonnet 141

In Sight of Rome

Behold that famous city that was queen
from the Caspian waters to the Sabaean shores,
triumphal city that held reign from where
the sun is seen to rise to where it sets.

But now misfortune and divine decree
have changed her so from what she was before
that where she once rose up to match the heavens,
all kinds of ruins cover her past glory.

Whenever will there be an earthly thing
that is firm and fixed, if greatness such as this
is beaten to the ground by Time and Fortune?

How can I ever hope to have her promise
kept to me? For I hardly can believe
that love endures a day in womankind.

Caspian waters . . . Sabaean shores: from the Caspian Sea to the southern end of Arabia, land of the people called Saba' (Yemeni).

170. Sonnet 142

From the City to my Lady

Do know, my one true love, that I still live,
and that I marvel at my being alive,
because, by nature's law, I do not see
how I survive deprived of my true life.

I've always loathed all mortal things except
for you, the one through whom I live and thrive;
you're absent now, and I object to Heaven,
because I cannot die without my spirit.

I go on living, but I live my life
in so much pain and in such misery
I lack the strength I need just to endure.

I am so different now from what I was
that, if my destiny leads me to you,
it will be hard for you to know it's me.

171

Baptista mio gentil, se tempo o loco
me potesser cangiar da quel che io era,
forsi che e' laci de la bella fera
Roma avria scossi o ralentati un poco.

Ma né festa regal né molto ioco
né del mio Duca la benegna cera
né in tanti giorni questa terra altera
m'hano ancor tratto de l'usato foco.

Così luntano ancor me avampa il core
la testa bionda e l'angelico viso
che avanti a gli occhi mi presenta Amore.

Questi non sarà mai da me diviso
mentre che io viva, e poi, di vita fore,
meco me 'l portarò nel paradiso.

172

Il Tempo, Amor, Fortuna e Zelosia
per sé ciascuno e insieme mi fan guerra;
l'ultima, più crudiel, me chiude e serra
ogni ritorno a la speranza mia.

Indi Fortuna dispetosa e ria
me tien tanto lontano a la mia terra,
e il dispietato Amore il cor me afferra
con più furore assai che non solia.

Fra questo il Tempo fuge, e de mia etade
seco fugendo se ne porta il fiore,
disutilmente perso in vanitade.

Ciò che esser deve, ben presage il core,
però che al mondo fòr le volte rade
che lunga vita avesse un gran dolore.

171. Sonnet 143

My dear Battista, if both time and place
could change me from the person that I was,
perhaps then Rome would have jostled loose the bonds
in which that lovely untamed creature holds me.

But neither royal pleasures, nor good sport,
nor even that kind face of my dear Duke,
nor this great city in so many days
have rescued me from my habitual fire.

My heart is set aflame from far away
by that blond head and that angelic face
that Love presents to me before my eyes.

These visions will not leave me while I live,
and after I've abandoned life on Earth
I'll take them with me into Paradise.

Battista: this person has not been identified.

my dear Duke: Borso d'Este, lord of Ferrara, and duke of Modena and Reggio since 1452, now made duke of Ferrara by Pope Paul II (see poem 159).

172. Sonnet 144

Time, Fortune, Love, and Jealousy wage war
on me by taking turns or by uniting.
The last of these, most cruel, cuts off and bars
each pathway of return to my one hope.

Then Fortune, wicked, spiteful as she is,
keeps me at distance from my native land,
and Love, unmerciful, assails my heart
with greater fury than is usual.

During this battle Time takes flight and steals,
as it escapes, the flower of my youth,
lost uselessly because of vain pursuits.

My heart already knows what is to be,
since in this world it has been rare to see
great suffering that had a lengthy life.

173

Quanto fuòr dolce l'ultime parole,
misero me, che ténero il mio core,
quando lassarlo a lei, che il trasse fore,
tanto me dolse che oggi ancor mi dole!

Ciò che se scrive e ciò che dir si suole
süavemente a un dipartir de amore,
sarebbe un rivo aposto al mar magiore
una piccola stella appresso al sole.

Quei begli ochi eran fisi in tanto affetto
che sembrava indi una altra voce uscire
dicente:—Ora m'è tolto ogni diletto.—

Deh, perché alora non pòte io morire,
tanto contento in quello ultimo aspetto
che dal quel viso al ciel potea salire?

174

Chorus Simplex

In quel fiorito e vago paradiso,
là dove regna Amore,
lasciai piagnendo a la mia donna il core,
e vivo pur ancor da lui diviso.

In un sol punto mi fu tolta alora
ogni mia cara cosa e precïosa:
restò la vita, che ebbi sempre a vile.

Doe cose fòr mia spene, e sono ancora:
Ercule l'una, il mio Signor zentile,
l'altra il bel volto ove anco il cor se posa.

E questa e quella a un tempo m'è nascosa,
né me occide il dolore!
che forsi torneria, di vita fore,
al mio caro Signor ed al bel viso.

173. Sonnet 145

How sweet they were to me, her parting words,
that seized upon my heart, oh wretched me,
when leaving it to her who drew it out
so grieved me that it grieves me still today!

What usually is written or is said
so tenderly when lovers separate,
would be a rivulet beside the sea,
a little star placed very near the sun.

Those lovely eyes were set with so much love
it seemed another voice came forth from them
to say: "All pleasure now is taken from me."

Alas! Why could I not have died right then,
so happy with that final look at her face
I could have risen from her face to Heaven.

174. Ballata 14

Ballata Grande

In that fair and gracious paradise,
there, where Love holds reign,
I left my heart to her with tearful eyes,
and still today I live apart from it.

In one brief moment every precious thing
held dear was taken from me on that day:
and life alone, which I despised, remained.

Two things gave hope to me, as they still do:
The one was Ercole, my gentle Lord,
the other was the face that won my heart.

But both are hidden from me at one time,
and sorrow does not slay me!
And even after death I might return
to my dear Lord and to her lovely face.

Ercole: brother of Borso d'Este; became duke upon his brother's death in 1471.

175

Ove son gitti e' mei dolci pensieri
che nel bon tempo me tenean gioioso?
Dove è la Stella, dove è il Sole ascoso
che me scorgeva a sì lieti sentieri?

Piacer mondani, instabili e legieri,
fole è chi per vui crede aver riposo;
rèndene exemplo il mio stato amoroso
tornato a casi dispietati e feri.

Ché cangiata ho mia zoglia in tanti mali,
e presa ho vita sì diversa e nova
che apena quel che io fui de esser consento.

A me credeti, miseri mortali,
credete a me, che ne ho verace prova,
che ogni vostro diletto è fumo al vento.

176

Cruciatus

Doe volte è già tornato il sole al segno
che porta intro a le corna Amore acceso,
poi che il mio cor, di libertade indegno,
fu tra le rose dolcemente preso.

Né li veduti exempli, né lo inzegno
che natura mi dede, m'han diffeso,
anzi son stato a me tanto malegno
che gionto ho sempre carco al mio gran peso.

Or che io non posso, on che poter non voglio,
tento la fuga e indarno me lamento
e sto ne l'alto error pur come io soglio.

Qual fia la fine a sì lungo tormento?
Ché io cognosco il mio mal e no il disoglio,
né solver lo potrò se io non mi pento.

175. Sonnet 146

Where have they gone, all those sweet thoughts of mine,
that kept me full of cheer in happy times?
Where is that Star, where hides that other Sun
that guided me along such joyful paths?

Inconstant and uncertain worldly pleasures,
a fool is he who thinks to find his peace in you;
a fair example is my amorous state
that's turned into a cruel and savage thing.

Because I've turned my joy into so many ills,
and taken up a life so strange and new,
I hardly know myself as the man I was.

Believe me, wretched mortals one and all,
believe me, for I have a certain proof,
your pleasures are but smoke upon the wind.

176. Sonnet 147

Crossed

The sun has twice returned now to the sign
that carries Love aflame between its horns
since my heart, not worthy of being free,
was gently taken prisoner amid the roses.

Not past examples nor the cleverness
that Nature gave to me protected me;
but rather to myself I was so cruel
I added further burdens to my heavy load.

Now that I've lost the power or the will,
I try to flee and hopelessly lament
and stay as always fixed in my deep error.

What ending will there be to such long torment?
I know my ailment yet I can't escape it,
nor shall I loose its grip without repenting.

Crossed: see poem 22.

the sign that carries Love: the constellation Aries. In antiquity Aries contained the vernal equinox, the point at which the sun crosses the celestial equator so that spring begins in the northern hemisphere. The poet fell in love under its sign (see poems 71 and 116).

177

Il ciel veloce ne ragira intorno
e menaci volando a morte oscura;
misero, lasso, a che nostra natura
leva a la fronte sì superbo il corno?

Ecco io che mo' surmonto al tempo adorno
e de mia etade tengo la verdura;
ov'è la fede che me rassicura,
che la mia vita duri ancor un giorno?

E pur ne le terrene cose e frale,
ove a mia voglia me stesso legai,
ancor me assido debole e confuso.

Lèvame tu, mio Dio, da tanto male,
rompe lo arbitrio che donato m'hai,
poiché a mio danno per sciocheza lo uso.

178

Spesso mi doglio e meco mi lamento
(ché altri che me non ho che il mio mal pesi)
de' giorni che de amore ardendo spesi,
che dovea più per tempo essere ispento;

e quanto più vi penso, più mi pento:
misero me, perché me stesso offesi?
Deh, perché prima ben non me diffesi
da' laci ove or me spicco lento lento?

Ché se il tardo pentir ben salva l'alma,
il lungo star nel mal pur la tormenta
ne la sua vita e ne la nostra ancora.

Quando porrò mai giù la grave salma?
che me assicura il tempo che io mi penta?
Ché io non scio di mia morte il giorno o l'ora.

177. Sonnet 148

The heavens swiftly fly about their course
and lead us, flying, to an unknown death;
oh wretched me, alas, why does our nature
raise so proud a horn upon its brow?

Behold how I now pass beyond my youth
and seize upon the fullness of my years;
where is the faith that gives me some assurance
that my life will last another day?

And yet, though weak and vanquished, I remain
sitting among the frail and earthly things
to which I bound myself by my own will.

Deliver me, my God, from so much grief,
and crush the will that you have given me,
since I am using it to harm myself.

178. Sonnet 149

I often grieve and cry in solitude
(for I alone am burdened by my pain)
about the days I spent burning in love,
a love that long before should have expired;

The more I think of it, the more do I
repent. Poor me, why did I harm myself?
Alas, why did I not defend myself
against the bonds I now am slow to break?

For if late repentance truly saves a soul,
its lingering in evil will torment it
here on earth and in eternity.

When will I put this heavy burden down?
What will assure me I'll repent in time?
For I do not know my day or hour of death.

179

Moralis Alegoria Cantu Tetrametro

1. *Zefiro torna, che de amore aspira*
naturalmente desïoso instinto,
e la sua moglie co il viso dipinto
piglia qualunque e' soi bei fiori amira.
Ma chi riguarda al ciel che sopra agira
non teme e' laci de la falsa amante,
e la sua rete che a morte ne tira
lo ochio sol prende cupido e vagante.
Ecco l'aria roseggia al sol levante:
driciamo il viso a la chiara lumera,
che la anima non pèra
per volger li ochi al loco de le piante.

2. *Che riguardati, o spirti perregrini?*
Il color vago de la bella rosa?
Fugeti via, fugeti, ché nascosa
è la loncia crudiel ne' verdi spini.
Non aspettati che la luce inchini
verso lo occaso, ché la fera alora
esce sicura ne' campi vicini
e li dormenti ne l'ombra divora.
Per Dio, non aspettati a l'ultim'ora!
Credeti a me che giacque sopra al prato,
e benché io sia campato,
mercé n'ha il Ciel, che vol che io viva ancora.

3. *Se ve colcati ne' süavi odori*
che surgon quinci a la terra fiorita,
in brieve giorno avreti dolce vita,
in lunga notte morte con dolori.
Uno angue ascoso sta tra l'erbe e' fiori,
che il verde dosso al prato rassumiglia;
nulla se vede, sì poco par fòri,
né pria si sente, se non morde o piglia.
Forsi il mio dir torreti a maraviglia,
ma salir vi convien quel col fronzuto;
né si trova altro aiuto:
chi provato ha ogni scermo vi consiglia.

179. Canzone 12 [13]

An Allegorical Song in Quatrains

1. The Zephyr, that arouses passion's instinct
naturally with love, is now returning,
and his wife with painted face will seize
all who admire her attractive blooms.
But he who looks to heaven overhead
fears not the snares laid by a faithless lover,
for her net, that draws the trapped to death,
falls only on the wandering, lustful eye.
See how the air turns red with the rising Sun:
let's raise our eyes to meet the shining light,
so that the soul won't die
by turning her eyes to the realm of plants.

2. What is it that you stare at, wandering spirits?
The subtle color of the lovely rose?
Be off with you! Go hide yourselves! For there
amid green thorns the cruel leopard hides.
Don't linger here until the light descends
into the western sky, for then the beast
comes safely out into the nearby fields
and in the shade devours those who sleep.
For God's sake, don't wait till the final hour!
Believe the one who lay upon the green
and though I did survive,
it's Heaven's mercy that wants me alive.

3. If you recline amid the sweet perfumes
that issue from the flowered land here 'round,
for one short day you'll have a sweet, sweet life,
for one long night a death in agony.
A serpent hides amid the grass and flowers
that has a back as green as these green fields;
it can't be seen, so well is it concealed,
nor is it heard until it strikes and bites.
Perhaps you'll be surprised by what I say,
but you must leave by climbing that green hill;
nor is there other aid:
one who has tried all tricks advises you.

4. *Quel dolce mormorar de le chiare onde,*
ove Amor nudo a la ripa se posa,
là giuso ad immo tien la morte ascosa,
ché una sirena dentro vi nasconde
con li ochi arguti e con le chiome bionde,
co il bianco petto e con lo adorno volto;
canta sì dolce che il spirto confonde,
e poi lo occide che a dormir l'ha colto.
Fugeti mentre il senso non vi è tolto,
ché il partir doppo il canto è grave affanno;
ed io, che scio lo inganno,
quasi contro a mia voglia ancor l'ascolto.

5. *Non vi spechiati a questa fonte il viso,*
ché morte occulta vi darà di piglio:
in quel fioreto candido e vermiglio
sol per mirarsi se cangiò Narciso.
Legette il verso a lettre d'oro inciso
nel verde marmo di sua sepultura,
che dice:—Lasso chi è di sé confiso,
ché mortal cosa picol tempo dura.—
Lassati adunque al basso ogni vil cura,
driciati ad erto la animosa fronte;
avanti aveti il monte
che ne la cima tien vita secura.

Canzon, se alcun te lege e non intende
dentro a la scorza, di' lui chiaro e piano
che in tutto è pazo e vano
qualunque aver diletto in terra attende.

4. That gentle murmuring of limpid waters,
where Love reclines unclothed upon the shore,
hides death below the surface in their depths,
for there within the waters hides a siren
with sparkling eyes and flaxen colored hair
and with white breasts and with a lovely face;
she sings so sweetly she confounds the soul,
and, having caught it sleeping, she then kills it.
Escape while you have not yet lost your senses,
for fleeing after hearing will be hard;
yet I, who know the trick,
still listen, though, it seems, against my will.

5. Don't gaze at your reflection in this fount,
for here a lurking death will pounce on you:
Narcissus, merely looking at himself,
was turned into a white and crimson bloom.
Read the verse engraved in golden letters
upon the green-hued marble of his tomb,
that says: "Woe to the overconfident,
for mortal things endure so brief a time."
Leave all your base concerns, then, down below,
raise up your valiant brow to face the heights;
you have ahead the mount
that holds a surer life upon its peak.

My song, if someone reads and does not grasp
what lies beneath your skin, be clear and plain
and say that vain and mad
is he who hopes for pleasures here on Earth.

Zephyr: Zephyrus, the god of the West Wind.

his wife: Iris, the goddess of the rainbow. "According to Alcaeus . . . she is the mother by Zephyrus of Eros, a conceit which means no more than that in moist spring weather men feel amorous." (*OCD*, 551) All other commentators see this as a direct reference to spring.

180

Ne la proterva età lubrica e frale
de amor cantava, anci piagnea più spesso,
per altrui sospirando; or per me stesso
tardi sospiro e piango del mio male.

Re de le stelle eterno ed immortale,
soccori me, ché io son di colpe oppresso,
e cognosco il mio fallo e a te il confesso,
ma sancia tua mercé nulla mi vale.

L'alma corrotta da' peccati e guasta
se è nel fangoso error versata tanto
che breve tempo a lei purgar non basta.

Signor, che la copristi de quel manto
che a ritornar al ciel pugna e contrasta,
tempra il iudizio con pietate alquanto.

Finis

180. Sonnet 150

Back in my wanton, vain, and fragile youth,
I sang of love, or rather I more often cried,
while sighing for another; now I sigh
and weep for me because of my affliction.

Eternal and immortal King of the stars,
please help me, for I am oppressed by sins,
and recognize my fault and do confess it,
but to no end unless you show me mercy.

My soul, corrupted and despoiled by sin,
has steeped so long in error's filthy mire
a brief purgation cannot serve to cleanse it.

O Lord, who cloaked it in that very mantle
that resists its own return to Heaven,
temper some your judgement with compassion.

The final poem echoes the conclusion of Petrarch's *Rime sparse*; cf. esp., Petrarch 364, 365. It is the traditional recantation of courtly poets.

End

INDEX
AND
BIBLIOGRAPHY

First Line Index

Poem No.

Selected Bibliography

Bibliographies (Chronological)

Medici, Domenico. "La Critica Boiardesca dal 1800 al 1976: Bibliografia Ragionata." *Bollettino Storico Reggiano* 10, no. 34 (July, 1977): 5–125.

Bregoli-Russo, Mauda. "Rassegna della Critica Boiardesca: 1972–1983." *Annali d'Italianistica* 1 (1983): 159–73.

Molinaro, Julius A. *Matteo Maria Boiardo: A Bibliography of Works and Criticism from 1487–1980.* Toronto: Canadian Federation for the Humanities/Fédération Canadienne des Etudes Humaines, 1984.

Principle Editions of the *Amorum Libri* (Chronological)

Sonetti e Canzone [sic] del Poeta Clarissimo Matheomaria Boiardo Cõte di Scandiano. Reggio: Francesco Mazalo, 1499.

Sonetti e Cãzone [sic] del Poeta Carissimo [sic] Matheo Maria Boiardo Conte di Scandiano. Venice: Giovan Battista Sessa, 1501.

Sonetti e Canzone [sic] del Poeta Clarissimo Matteo Maria Boiardo Conte di Scandiano. Ed. Antonio Panizzi. London: W. Whittingham, 1835. Rare edition of 50 copies. Exact reproduction by Società Tipografica dei Classici Italiani, Milan, 1845.

Le Poesie Volgari e Latine di Matteo Maria Boiardo, Riscontrate sui Codici e sulle Stampe. Ed. Angelo Solerti. Bologna: Romagnoli-Dall'Acqua, 1894.

Il Canzoniere (Amorum Libri). Ed. Carlo Steiner. Turin: UTET, 1927.

Tutte Le Opere di Matteo M. Boiardo. 2 vols. Ed. Angelandrea Zottoli. Milan: Mondadori, 1936–37.

Orlando Innamorato, Sonetti e Canzoni di Matteo Maria Boiardo. 2 vols. Ed. Aldo Scaglione. Turin: UTET, 1951.

Opere Volgari: Amorum Libri-Pastorale-Lettere. Ed. Pier Vincenzo Mengalo. Bari: Laterza, 1962.

Opere di Matteo Maria Boiardo. Ed. Ferruccio Ulivi. Milan: Mursia, 1986.

English Translations from the *Amorum Libri*

An Anthology of Italian Lyrics From the Thirteenth Century to the Present Day. Ed. and tr. Romilda Rendel. New York: Frank-Maurice, Inc., 1926. 42–43.

Clerke, E[llen] M[ary]. *Fable and Song in Italy.* London: Grant Richards, 1899. 139–52.

Italian Poets of the Renaissance. Ed. and trans. Joseph Tusiani. Long Island, N.Y.: Baroque Press, Inc., 1971. 56–62.

Lyric Poetry of the Italian Renaissance: An Anthology with Verse Translations. Ed. L. R. Lind. New Haven: Yale Univ. Press, 1954. 214–21.

The Penguin Book of Italian Verse with Plain Prose Translations of Each Poem. Ed. George Kay. Baltimore: Penguin Books, 1958. 138–40.

Boiardo Criticism

Alexandre-Gras, Denise. *Le Canzoniere de Boiardo: Du Pétrarchisme à l'Inspiration Personelle.* Saint-Etienne: Publications del l'Université de Saint-Etienne, 1980.

Altucci, Carlo. "Boiardo Lirico." *Giornale Storico della Letteratura Italiana* 106 (1935): 39–80.

Anceschi, Giuseppe, ed. *Il Boiardo e La Critica Contemporanea: Atti del Convegno su Matteo Maria Boiardo, Scandiano-Reggio Emilia 25–27 Aprile 1969.* Florence: Leo S. Olschki, 1970.

Benvenuti, Antonia Tissoni. "Matteo Maria Boiardo." In *La Letteratura Italiana: Storia e Testi.* Vol. 3, tome II: *Il Quattrocento: L'Età dell'Umanesimo.* 10 vols. Bari: Laterza, 1972. 293–364. Author may appear as: Benvenuti or Tissoni Benvenuti or Tissoni-Benvenuti.

———. "Rimatori Estensi di Epoca Boiardesca." In *Il Boiardo e la Critica Contemporanea: Atti del Convegno di Studi su Matteo Maria Boiardo, Scandiano-Reggio Emilia, 25–27 Aprile 1969.* Florence: Leo S. Olschki, 1970. 503–10.

———. "Tradizioni Letterarie e Gusto Tardogotico nel Canzoniere di M. M. Boiardo." *Giornale Storico della Letteratura Italiana* 137 (1960): 533–92.

Bertoni, Giulio. *Nuovi Studi su Matteo Maria Boiardo.* Bologna: Zanichelli, 1904.

Bregoli-Russo, Mauda. *Boiardo Lirico.* Potomac, Md.: José Porrúa Turanzas [Studia Humanitatis], 1979.

———. "Uno Strumento Interpretativo degli *Amores* di Boiardo." *Critica Letteraria* 32 (1981): 519–26.

Contini, Gianfranco. "Breve Allegato al Canzoniere del Boiardo." *Ezercizi di Lettura.* Florence: Le Monnier, 1947. 291–307.

Giamatti, A. Bartlett. "Headlong Horses, Headless Horsemen: An Essay on the Chivalric Epics of Pulci, Boiardo and Ariosto." In *Italian Literature: Roots and Branches. Essays in Honor of Thomas Goddard Bergin.* Eds. Giose Rimanelli and Kenneth John Atchity. New Haven: Yale Univ. Press, 1976. 265–307.

Mengaldo, Pier Vincenzo. *La Lingua del Boiardo Lirico.* Florence: Leo S. Olschki, 1963.

Molinaro, Julius. "Boiardo as Lyric Poet: Considerations Old and New." *Forum Italicum* 7 (1973): 98–106.

Panizzi, Antonio. *Orlando Innamorato di Bojardo: Orlando Furioso di Ariosto: With an Essay on the Romantic Narrative Poetry of the Italians.* 9 vols. London: William Pickering, 1830.

Pernicone, Vincenzo. "Il Quattrocento." Antologia della Letteratura *Italiani.* 5 vols. Milan: Rizzoli, 1966. 2: 5–876.

Piemontese, Filippo. *La Formazione del Canzoniere Boiardesco.* Milan: Carlo Marzorati, 1953.

Ponte, Giovanni. *La Personalità e l'Opera del Boiardo.* Genoa: Tilgher, 1972.

Reichenbach, Giulio. *Matteo Maria Boiardo.* Bologna, Zanichelli, 1929.

Saccone, Eduardo. *Il "Soggetto" del* Furioso *e Altri Saggi tra Quattro e Cinquecento.* Naples: Liquori, 1974

Scaglione, Aldo. "Contributo alla Questione del 'Rodundelus' del Boiardo." *Giornale Storico della Lettertura Italiana* 128 (1951): 313–16.

———. "Matteo Maria Boiardo." *Grande Dizionario Enciclopedico.* 20 vols. Turin: UTET, 1954. 3: 231–34.

Zitarosa, G. R. "Il Boiardo." *Aspetti Letterari* 5 (1965): 1–21.

Zottoli, Angelandrea. *Dal Boiardo all'Ariosto.* Milan: Carabba, 1934.

———. *Di Matteo Maria Boiardo, Discorso.* Florence: Sansoni, 1937.

General Sources

Bertoni, Giulio. *La Biblioteca Estense e la Cultura Ferrarese ai Tempi del Duca Ercole I (1471–1505).* Turin: Loescher, 1903.

———. *L'*Orlando Furioso *e la Rinascenza a Ferrara.* Modena: Umberto Orlandini, 1919.

Calgrosso, Gianotto. *Nicolosa Bella: Prose e Versi d'Amore del Sec. XV, Inediti.* Eds. F. Gaeta and R. Spongano. Bologna: Commissione per i Testi di Lingua, 1959.

Ciavolella, Massimo. *La 'Malattia d'Amore' dall'Antichità al Medioevo.* Rome: Bulzoni, 1976.

Culler, Jonathan. "Apostrophe." In *The Pursuit of Signs: Semiotics, Literature, Deconstruction.* Ithaca: Cornell Univ. Press, 1981. 135–54.

Alighieri, Dante. *Rime.* Ed. Gianfranco Contini. Turin: Einaudi, 1946.

da Tempo, Antonio. *Delle Rime Volgari*. Ed. G. Grion. Bologna: G. Romagnoli, 1869.

De' Conti, Giusto. *Il Canzoniere: Prima Edizione Completa* [*La Bella Mano* and *Rime Sparse*]. Ed. Leonardo Vitetti. Lanciano: R. Carabba, 1918.

de Man, Paul. "Anthropomorphism and Trope in the Lyric." *The Rhetoric of Romanticism*. New York: Columbia Univ. Press, 1984. 239–62.

De Robertis, Domenico. "L'Esperienza Poetica del Quattrocento." *Storia della Letteratura Italiana*. Vol. 3. Milan: Garzanti, 1965.

di Tommaso, Andrea. "Insania and Furor: A Diagnostic Note on Orlando's Malady." *Romance Notes* 14, no. 3 (1973): 583–88.

Durling, Robert M., trans. and ed. *Petrarch's Lyric Poems: The Rime Sparse and Other Lyrics*. Cambridge, Mass.: Harvard Univ. Press, 1976.

———. "Petrarch's 'Giovene Donna Sotto un Verde Lauro.'" *MLN* 86 (1981): 1–20.

Elisatti, Massimo. *Storia di Ferrara*. Milan: Camunia, 1986.

Fava, Domenico. *La Cultura e la Stampa Italiana nel Quattrocento*. Vol. 1, *Modena-Reggio Emilia-Scandiano*. Modena: Dante Cavallotti, 1943.

Foster, Kenelm. *Petrarch: Poet and Humanist*. Writers of Italy Series. Edinburgh: Edinburgh Univ. Press, 1984.

Foucault, Michel. *Scritti Letterari*. Ed. Cesare Milanesi. Milan: Feltrinelli, 1971.

Freccero, John. "The Fig-Tree and the Laurel: Petrarch's Poetics." *Diacritics* 5 (Spring, 1975): 35–41.

Garin, Eugenio. "Motivi della Cultura Filosofica Ferrarese nel Rinascimento." *La Cultura del Rinascimento Italiano*. Florence: G. C. Sansoni, 1961. 402–31.

Gundersheimer, Werner L. *Ferrara: The Style of a Renaissance Despotism*. Princeton, N.J.: Princeton Univ. Press, 1973.

Hošek, Chaviva, and Patricia Parker, eds. *Lyric Poetry: Beyond New Criticism*. Ithaca, N.Y.: Cornell Univ. Press, 1985.

Longhi, Roberto. *Officina Ferrarese*. Florence: Sansoni, 1956.

Mazzacurati, Giancarlo. *Il Problema Storico del Petrarchismo Italiano (dal Boiardo a Lorenzo)*. Naples: Liguori, 1963.

Marsh, David. *The Quattrocento Dialogue: Classical Tradition and Humanist Innovation*. Cambridge, Mass.: Harvard Univ. Press, 1980.

Minns, Ellis H. *Sythians and Greeks: A Survey of Ancient History and Archeology on the North Coast of the Euxine from the Danube to the Caucasus*. 2 vols. New York: Biblo and Tannen, 1965.

Pernicone, Vincenzo. "Il Quattrocento." *Antologia della Letteratura Italiana*. Vol. 2. Milan: Rizzoli, 1966.

Reese, Gustav. *Music in the Renaissance*. New York: W. W. Norton, 1954.

Rowland, Beryl. *Animals with Human Faces*. Knoxville: Univ. of Tennessee Press, 1973.

Solerti, Angelo. *Ferrara e la Corte Estense*. Città di Castello: Lapi, 1891.

Spongano, Raffaele. *Gianotto Calagrosso: Nicolosa Bella: Prose e Versi del Secolo XV*. Bologna: Commissione per i Testi di Lingua, 1959.

———. *Nozioni ed Esempi di Metrica Italiana*. Bologna: Riccardo Pàtron, 1966.

Weiss, Georg. "Elementi Tardogotici nella Letteratura Italiana del Quattrocento." *Rivista di Letterature Moderne e Comparate* 10 (1957): 101–30. 11 (1958): 184–99.

———. "Il Termine di Tardo-gotico nell'Arte Settentrionale." *Paragone* 31 (1952): 24–34.

Wimsatt, W. K. *Versification: Major Language Types*. New York: New York Univ. Press [Modern Language Association], 1972.

On Translation

Benjamin, Walter. "The Task of the Translator: An Introduction to the Translation of Baudelaire's *Tableaux Parisiens*." *Illuminations*. Trans. Harry Zohn. New York: Harcourt, Brace & World, 1968. 69–82.

de Man, Paul. " 'Conclusions' Walter Benjamin's 'The Task of the Translator' Messenger Lecture, Cornell Univ., March 4, 1983." *Yale French Studies* 69 (1985): 25–46.

Frawley, William, ed. *Translation*. Newark, Del.: Univ. of Delaware Press, 1984.

Graham, Joseph F., ed. *Difference in Translation*. Ithaca, N.Y.: Cornell Univ. Press, 1985.

Sayers, Dorothy L. *The Poetry of Search and the Poetry of Statement*. London: Victor Gollancz Ltd., 1963.

Reference Works Cited

Encyclopaedia Brittanica. 11th ed. 29 vols. New York: The Encyclopaedia Brittanica Company, 1910.

Encyclopedia of Poetry and Poetics. Ed. Alex Preminger. Princeton, N.J.: Princeton Univ. Press, 1965.

The New Century Classical Handbook. Ed. Catherine B. Avery. New York: Appleton-Century-Crofts, Inc., 1962.

The New Grove Dictionary of Music and Musicians. Ed. Stanley Sadie. 20 vols. London: Macmillan, 1980.

The Oxford Classical Dictionary. 2d ed., ed. N. G. L. Hammond and H. H. Scullard. Oxford: Clarendon Press, 1970.

Atlas

Grosser Historischer Weltatlas. Vol. 1, *Vorgeschichte und Altertum*. Munich: Beyerischer Schulbuch-Verlag, 1972.

Though best known for his unfinished epic poem, *Orlando Innamorato*, Boiardo was also an unusually fine lyric poet. The fame of the epic has long overshadowed his *Amorum libri*, which has often and deservedly been called the most important verse collection of the Italian quattrocento and the single best example of Italian lyric poetry in the Renaissance.

This is the first English translation, based on Pier Vincenzo Mengaldo's critical edition (Bari, 1964); Mengaldo's text, revised, is printed on facing pages. Besides text and translation, Di Tommaso also provides a critical introduction which discusses the character of Boiardo's work, his place in European lyric traditions, and the Petrarchan tradition. The volume also contains explanatory notes, a selected bibliography, and an index of first lines.

Andrea di Tommaso, Associate Professor of Italian and department Chair at Wayne State University, is the author of *Structure and Ideology in Boiardo's* Orlando Innamorato (Chapel Hill, 1972). He has received a Fulbright Fellowship to Italy (1964–65) and a translation grant from the National Endowment for the Humanities (1983–84). His article, "Boiardo/Ariosto: Textual Relations and Poetic Integrity," in the *Stanford Italian Review* won the President's Award of the American Association for Italian Studies.

mrts

medieval & renaissance texts & studies
is the publishing program of the
Center for Medieval and Early Renaissance Studies
at the State University of New York at Binghamton.

mrts emphasizes books that are needed —
texts, translations, and major research tools.

mrts aims to publish the highest quality scholarship
in attractive and durable format at modest cost.